T0320161

SOUTH KOREANS in the DEBT CRISIS

ASIA-PACIFIC
Culture, Politics,
and Society

Editors: Rey Chow,
H. D. Harootunian,
and Masao Miyoshi

SOUTH KOREANS in the DEBT CRISIS

THE CREATION OF A NEOLIBERAL WELFARE SOCIETY

Jesook Song

Duke University Press
Durham and London
2009

Printed in the United States of America on acid-free
paper ∞

Designed by Heather Hensley

Typeset in Quadraat by Tseng Information Systems, Inc.

Library of Congress Cataloging-in-Publication Data
appear on the last printed page of this book.

Duke University Press gratefully acknowledges the
support of the University of Toronto, which provided
funds toward the production of this book.

To my interlocutors

CONTENTS

South Koreans will long remember November 21, 1997, the day when South Korea accepted the terms of an International Monetary Fund (IMF) bailout precipitated by a lack of dollars with which to repay debts to foreign financial institutions. Major newspapers heralded the day as Korea's "second national day of humiliation," the first being the Japanese colonization of Korea on August 22, 1910. It was the beginning of the Asian Debt Crisis, or "IMF crisis," in South Korea, which officially took place in that country from December 1997 to July 2001 and which resulted in unprecedented mass layoffs and socioeconomic chaos.[1]

South Korean people who lived through the Asian Debt Crisis (the crisis) became familiar with new idioms such as "IMF homeless," "new intellectuals," "family breakdown," "unemployed person with higher education," and "venture capital." These phrases represent the frantic and fragmented social response to the crisis. "IMF homeless" (*aiemep'ŭ silchik nosukcha*) spoke to escalating homelessness during the crisis; "new intellectuals" (*sin chisigin*) stood for a new generation of workers with high-tech information skills who had become redundant in the job market but had the potential to lead a transformed, postcrisis South Korea; "family breakdown" (*kajŏng haech'e* or *kajok haech'e*)—ubiquitous in the media, academy, and government—indexed a widespread sense of moral deterioration; "unemployed person with higher education" (*kohangnyŏk sirŏpcha*) labeled candidates applying to a specialized public works program (*konggong kŭllo saŏp*) for well-educated jobless people; and "venture capital," "venture industry," and "venture business" (*bench'yŏ k'aepital, bench'yŏ ŏpkye, bench'yŏ saŏp*) promised new, high-risk, high-return investment and business methods. For many South Koreans these were not meaningless abstractions, but the terms through which they came to think about their familial, social, and economic predicament.

The crisis resulted in much writing and reflection on political change (such as the election of the renowned democratic movement leader Kim Dae Jung as president in 1998), economic restructuring, the increasing unemployment rate, "faltering" family values, and new investment methods for individuals and companies. Rare, however, are studies that scrutinize the way in which these new idioms—veritable popular discourse—operated as a crucial governing technology of South Korean society. This book recognizes that these idioms and images are critical to the new democratic and neoliberal regime that was consolidated during the crisis. In it, neoliberalism is defined as an advanced liberal mode of social governing that idealizes efficiency and productivity by promoting people's free will and self-sufficiency. Thus, both liberalism and neoliberalism do not just refer to political economic principles but to social ethos. I use *(neo)liberalism* to refer to both classical and emergent forms of liberalism. The major difference between neoliberalism and liberalism is the ascendance of finance capital over assembly-line industrial capital and the seeming withdrawal of the state (which is instead working through quasi- or nonstate agencies).[2] This book illustrates how this constellation of idioms operated together in the course of a coordinated response to the crisis and a shift to neoliberalism. It offers a portrait of this response, and as such an analysis of contemporary South Korean society and (neo)liberal governing.

This book provides a comprehensive picture of developments in South Korean welfare society during the crisis. *Welfare society* refers to the pannational efforts of the state and civilians to regulate social insecurity, instability, and inequality by providing assistance programs to deprived populations. At the heart of this book are two types of citizen that were deemed worthy of state welfare in popular discourse and produced during the crisis: the "IMF homeless" and the "new intellectuals."[3]

To outline the developments of the crisis, I gather and contextualize narratives from formal interviews with un(der)employed young adults working in public works programs, government officials working on homelessness and youth unemployment policies, and social reform activists working in homeless shelters. I also draw on informal conversations with academic and government experts, police officers, a taxi driver, and homeless women. I analyze visual texts (film and TV dramas); spatial texts (the Seoul Train Station Square and Pangnim textile factory); novels and mass-media reports; and public events (symposiums, seminars, and demonstrations). These methodologies present a comprehensive picture of the multiple ways in which neoliberal society was coordinated and engineered.[4]

The book is the culmination of twenty-nine months of field research (from May 1998 to July 2000, March 2001, and October 2001) and two years of follow-up research (2003–2005). The major location of the field research was Seoul, where I worked as a leader of a public works program, the Youth and Women Unemployment Monitoring Team (Ch'ôngnyôn Yôsông Sirôp Taech'aek Monit'ôring T'im, hereafter the team). The team was created to assist the Seoul City Committee for Unemployment Policy (SCCUP, Sôul-si Sirôp Taech'aek Wiwônhoe), which was appointed during the crisis. Although SCCUP and the team were not formally a part of the city administration, our assignment afforded me privileged access to both governmental and quasi- and nongovernmental spaces and actors involved in issues such as homelessness and youth unemployment.

My research subjects include city officials, un(der)employed young adults (some of whom were members of the team), and experts or so-called "intellectuals"[5] (chisigin), including government or academic experts, semi- or nongovernmental organization (NGO) members, and social reform activists. I consider these diverse groups of people to be social engineers and crisis knowledge brokers who together defined, delimited, and determined social policy on homelessness and youth unemployment, using the discourse of the crisis as a pretext for promoting these norms and policies (Shin 2000). They each contributed in different ways and to varying degrees to the production of "governable subjects," namely, citizens worthy of welfare subsidies.

This book demonstrates that South Korean neoliberal social management not only prioritized particular populations (the homeless and underemployed youth) in order to control labor and sociopolitical insecurity, but also promoted governable subjects within these prioritized populations by discriminating between "deserving" welfare citizens and the "undeserving." In the case of homeless policy, for example, "the IMF homeless" (aiemep'û silchik nosukcha), or short-term street people considered employable, were rendered "proper" homeless people, while long-term street people— "the rootless" (purangin)—were designated as undeserving of support.

Similarly, in the case of the policy on un(der)employed youth, "new intellectuals" (*sin chisigin*), or "creative" contributors to the information and service industries, were designated as promising, while "good-for-nothings" (*paeksu*), who did not make use of their education in flexible labor markets, were disparaged. A range of social engineers contributed to defining the governable subjects of a neoliberal welfare state. All of these social engineers were privileged "employable" and "self-sufficient" subjects who could manage themselves without depending on the state.

This book is an ethnography of social governing, not of state bureaucracy. *Governing* (or *governmentality*, as Foucauldians say) refers to liberal political reasoning and technologies that are suffused throughout society by various social actors and spheres, such as NGOs, businesses, residential communities, families, schools, and individuals as well as state administrative institutes (Barry, Osborne, and Rose 1996; Dean 1999; Foucault 1991).[6] I use the term *governing* in order to avoid confusion between government as state machinery and government as a way in which power is exercised over populations and individuals at the same time (Foucault 1991, 2003; Lemke 2002; Guala 2006). The Foucauldian notion of governmentality is an alternative that helps avoid the confusion, but I limit the usage of it in this book to only theoretical moments. I refer to the broader context of managing society in general as *governing* and the state machinery, administration, or bureaucracy as *government*. I decided not to use *governance* to avoid a disciplinary confusion (scholars of policy and planning studies commonly use the term when evaluating the effectiveness of policies, which is far from my focus on the epistemological meaning and operation of the policies in connection to public discourse).[7] I think *governing*, particularly *social governing*, is a useful and accessible term to remind readers that this book is neither about state bureaucracy nor policy- and planning-centered.

While bureaucracy focuses on the institutional operation of the state and is predicated on a rigid binary between the state and the society, the concept of social governing allows for a much broader analysis of various social domains and actors implicated in the control of populations. The bureaucracy is a legitimate unit of analysis and a productive site for the anthropological study of the state,[8] but a limited study of state bureaucracy cannot encompass South Korea's IMF response. Because my research focused on the process of knowledge production in response to the crisis, I necessarily had to look beyond the bureaucracy to the diverse people and events that comprised the response. I refer to social governing because governmental, quasi-governmental, and nongovernmental agents all operated as social engineers who together fashioned the meaning of what has become contemporary South Korea's neoliberal welfare citizenship.

In addition to city officials, the team, and experts and social reform activists, I consider journalists, writers, and directors of the mass media (film, fiction, nonfiction, TV drama) to be crucial social engineers and crisis knowledge brokers. Although I did not interview them, their works and representations of homelessness, unemployment, family breakdown, and emerging new industries played a critical role in the amplification of neoliberal social governing in South Korea. While homeless people are not central ethnographic figures in this work, unemployed youth are featured prominently, because my focus is on social engineers themselves rather than on the objects of their governing; while underemployed youth were active participants in the construction of public discourses and policy ideas, homeless people were not agents in the making of neoliberal subjectification. I am aware of what it means not to portray their agency, but I do not include them as social engineers to make the point that homeless people did not participate in the social governing of homelessness.[9]

Echoing the experience of many ethnographers, when I embarked on my field research I did not set out to research (neo)liberalism and welfare issues. I arrived in Seoul in May 1998, ready to conduct research on the transformation of Korean sociopolitical movements in the aftermath of the emergence of sexuality politics (sôngjôngch'i) in the early 1990s (Seo 1996). I hypothesized that in South Korea the democratization movement and the emergence of sexuality politics signaled a significant change in the alignment of collective consciousness and individual desire. Sexuality politics refers to political movements mobilized around nonheteronormative sexuality and gender; these political movements involved college and university student activists and other social activists who challenged social norms of institutional marriage, the gendered division of labor, gender and sex identities, sexual orientation, and sexual partnership. This work drew on my interests throughout my college years in Seoul, where I was active in various political movements, including the politically radical religious movement, the student political movement (opposing class disparities and the military dictatorship), and women's movements.

My original research interest in how the individual identity–based desire for social change distinguishes itself from national identity–based political goals remains at the heart of this book. When this book asks how social engineers, many of whom were progressive actors, became agents of neoliberal welfare society, it takes on the porous boundary between the state and (civil) society. This question also allows us to think of the democratized period before the crisis (1987–1997) as a time when individuals celebrated liberal freedoms, including the freedom to explore the endless commodification of their bodies, desires, and skills. The process of liberal subjectification in the democratized era in itself is not the focus of this book. However, the crisis knowledge brokers in this book—many of whom cultivated liberal selfhood in the democratization process—reveal how they unwittingly became the rank-and-file engineers of an intensifying neoliberalism during the crisis.

When I arrived in the field, the consequences of the crisis had just begun to become apparent and many people, including those who had been laid off, envisioned a prompt return to their workplaces. I had no idea how critical the crisis situation would become, and I was unable to sympathize with the mass-media depictions of the crisis as the "second war" (the "first" being the Korean War).

Eventually it became clear that I had to refocus my study because of the impact of the crisis on my original research population. Many of my subjects were young women and men in their twenties and thirties actively involved in small guerilla groups for sexuality and gender movements in and beyond the campus.[10] These individuals varied in their education level, family background, and attitudes toward gender roles. But overall, their sources of income were unstable and irregular even before the crisis. Most were involved in part-time, day-labor, freelance, contract-job (kyeyakchik), and subcontract (p'agyônjik) work. Thus, in 1997, when the crisis began, causing a dramatic increase in the unemployment rate (2.5 percent before the crisis; 7.5 percent from 1998 through 2000), people in the marginal labor market could not sustain their jobs and their sociopolitical activities. Every time I met with them, a major topic of discussion was how to survive by patching together part-time jobs (arûbait'û)[11] and how to retain economic independence and preserve identity in the face of new economic insecurities. The insecurity came from the awareness that increased gender discrimination and homophobia in the workplace were leading to job loss. It is not an exaggeration to say that many group members failed to participate in political and social meetings because they could not afford the public transportation fees in Seoul and its suburbs. The loss of jobs also often meant the loss of independent living places and gathering spaces for organizations, as well as, in the case of women, an increase in familial pressure to marry.

I myself had a hard time finding employment, in spite of my status as an advanced doctoral student from a U.S. university, a credential that in the past had considerable currency in the South Korean job market. I tried to make a living through freelance translation while conducting my research. But the translation industry was also experiencing dire times, so it was not unusual for me to wait for more than five months to get paid and to put in extra unpaid hours in order to receive payment.

Despite these circumstances, over the course of the first year of the crisis, the mass media, including progressive newspapers and governmental offices concerned with unemployment policies, rarely showed concern for marginalized populations, among them women in need of employment. Government policies, large civic organizations, and the mass media all spotlighted the layoffs of middle-aged male breadwinners, while remaining silent about the fact that women were the first to be laid off and perpetuating the assumption that women were not a major source of household income. Many young women college graduates were not given a chance to apply for jobs in big companies during their hiring season, whereas young men were prioritized.

This kind of gender discrimination was not immediately recognized and amended by the government. Although Kim Dae Jung's administration had the reputation of being the first with an appreciation of gender equality, it defended prioritizing men's employment as compensation for obligatory military service. When a feminist campaign protested the inequality and demanded the removal of the promotion credit given to men for military service (kun'gasanjômje p'yeji undong), a conservative backlash led to phone and online harassment of women's organizations and women's studies departments (including death threats and the hacking and shutting down of Web sites).

Although I tried to protect my research from being overwhelmed by the crisis, I could not resist the growing concern of women's and other groups marginalized in the labor market; I was compelled to look at unemployment policies.[12] In the first six months after my arrival in Seoul, I became active not only in organizing feminist and sexuality networks and support groups but in searching for channels to communicate with government policy makers who controlled the allotment of unemployment relief funds. Feminist networks offered a means of intervention; an academic expert consultant to the SCCUP arranged a meeting for me with city officials in the Labor Policy Division (Koyong Anjông Taech'aek-kwa) and another feminist academic expert connected me to the Presidential Commission for Women's Affairs. I found myself chastised for questioning governmental policies on women. I was up against the rhetoric that proclaimed the crisis as a calamity affecting the nation *as a whole*, leaving no room for other concerns. As one bureaucrat put it, "Even male breadwinners have lost their jobs, why bother with the question of women, who depend upon men or families?" In a similar vein, as I was one of the highly educated (*kohangnyôk*) underemployed young women panelists at a city office unemployment workshop, the head of the Labor Policy Division asked me if I was married or living with my family. When I answered no to both questions, he shook his head and said, "Can't you solve your [employment] problem by getting married?"

Rather than continuing my research on a population involved in sexuality politics, I slowly began to focus on those who were selected as "deserving" in the new welfare system launched during the crisis. In particular, because unemployed men with breadwinning capacity emerged as a priority for welfare while unemployed women were reprimanded and ignored as undeserving, I began to question the systemization of neoliberal welfare society that normalized a gendered division of labor.

After contacting the Seoul City Labor Policy Division and the Presidential Commission for Women's Affairs, I decided to focus on working in and with the Seoul city office. This was in part because the commission was somewhat unstable (it was new, temporary, and the directorship had already turned over several times). But more importantly, there was more progressive civilian support in the city through the structure of the SCCUP. I knew some SCCUP members through academic and feminist networks in South Korea and had heard of others who were considered to be reliable experts. City officials' statements of the insignificance of women's unemployment also motivated me to try to change perceptions in the city administration.

In addition, there were rumors that the city administration wanted to set up a think tank to address unemployment issues.[13] Seoul, the capital city and the biggest metropolitan center, held one-quarter of the country's total population of over 40 million. The city administration was stunned by the sudden economic disaster after three decades of stable prosperity. The need for a think tank was especially true following the election of Kim Dae Jung as president and the appointment of Kim's party member, Ko Kôn, as the new mayor of Seoul in 1998. (Ko Kôn initiated the restructuring and downsizing of the city government in response to the crisis.)

It was in this political context that I proposed the establishment of a qualitative research team as part of a think tank supervised by SCCUP to assist the Seoul city administration in policy making. My idea was well received, although the city administration was reluctant to designate a permanent research team. There was resistance from city officials toward nonbureaucrats such as me. This intensified during the crisis because government officials were under threat of losing their jobs in the first downsizing of the Korean bureaucracy since the Korean War. At that time, the IMF required the South Korean government to perform "structural adjustment" (kujojojông) in systems of government, finance, and in corporations; many long-term city officials and senior officials were pressured into "voluntary" early retirement (myôngyet'oejik), causing them enormous anxiety. Even if they managed to keep their jobs, city officials faced reduced wages (70 percent of their precrisis wages) and the elimination of group benefits such as meals (hoesik) or sport contests (ch'eyuk taehoe). Officials also faced mandatory job changes. For example, one mid-level official I knew, consenting to suggestions by higher authorities, changed positions three times in a year (1998–1999); and a high-level official position in the Women's Affairs Division went through four replacements in a year and a half (1999–2000).

The anxiety of the city officials—provoked by fears of discharge, displacement, and reduced salary—provides a partial explanation for the ill-feeling and awkward communication between them and public works program members. As a city official explicitly stated (see chapter 4), many could not handle encountering inexperienced "youngsters" in their daily workplace just when their own decades-long sweat in the state machinery

was being depreciated. Many middle-aged officials who dealt with homelessness and unemployment policies had a personal investment in those
policies, in that they saw themselves as potential laid-off workers or even
homeless men. (Homeless people were predominantly seen as middle-
aged men on the streets after suddenly losing their stable white-collar
employment.) Further, city officials' inability to cope with the information era was unfavorably compared with that of the tech-savvy "new intellectuals" epitomized by the young public-works program members, such
as the Unemployment Monitoring Team members. City officials dealing
with homeless issues were particularly resentful and hostile toward me

xviii

and other team members who asked about the existence of homeless
women. Although there were friendly officials, who even invited the team
to socialize after work, they were not able to protect the team from hostile
officials who reflected the prevailing conservatism about women's claim
to equal attention during the crisis.

This problem of conservative gender perceptions in the Korean state
administration was better addressed by the Roh Moo Hyun government
(2003–2008), which, under the advice of feminists and women administrators, established the Ministry of Gender Equality and Family in 2005.
Feminist organizations in the government administration have insisted
on improved gender-sensitivity training (Korean Women Link 2005).
However, during the crisis, conservative gender perceptions were dominant and went unchallenged in practice. As a result of this conservative
climate, most of the narratives expressed by city officials were either quite
blunt or antagonistic, as I will address in detail.

Therefore, after four months (September to December 1998) of negotiations for funding and a home office, the qualitative research team was
created as a public works program, rather than from regular positions
for specialists in the government (pyŏljjŏngjik), with the condition that
researchers came from the ranks of the unemployed. In order to lead
the team, I had to register as an unemployed person in my parents' ward
office under a new category—"unemployed person with higher education"
(kohangnyŏk sirŏpcha). This is the group I designate as un(der)employed
youth who were involved in engineering social governing not only of
homelessness but of their own unemployment.[14]

The team started work in January 1999 and lasted until June 2001 (I officially left in December 1999, but remained involved until July 2000). The

team members (three to twelve researchers over the period) were actively connected to young feminist NGO and nonprofit organization (NPO) networks outside the city office, and voiced the issues of the marginalized labor market—the unemployed in general and women in particular. I recruited them through feminist and sexuality politics networks, such as FReE-WAR, women's studies programs, and a network of women with disabilities. I knew some of them before they joined the team as they were my original research project informants, but many others I came to know through the team.

Many young feminist activists in the team had attended college in the late 1980s and early 1990s, and had therefore experienced, directly or indirectly, students' antistate political activism. The military dictatorship officially ended in 1987, but the first civilian president was former military coup leader Roh Tae Woo, and oppressive political measures continued during his presidency. College feminist activists blossomed in the early and mid-1990s, and joined the pan-democratization movement in South Korea, urging reform of the corrupt and ineffective governmental bureaucracy. Some of the team members organized workshops and street rallies to protest women college graduates' weak job prospects and to urge government intervention in hiring processes and illegal layoffs of women employees.[15]

The team drafted numerous reports on the unemployment of people with disabilities, women, and youth to attract the attention of policy makers. Team members monitored the situation of homeless women's shelters and the referral and shelter system for women in need of special protection. They also addressed the lack of government support for women's small businesses and Internet resources for unemployed women, and developed creative ideas for businesses for underemployed youth.

The irony of the team's position is that it epitomized prevailing (neo)liberal social governing. The team was a space for many members to learn how to regulate themselves and others in the name of efficiency and productivity, through their free will and ability for self-improvement— the ideological engine of (neo)liberal subject production. Michel Foucault would call this the logic of (neo)liberal governmentality, and Karl Marx would see it as the capitalist appropriation and exploitation of labor power for maximizing production through free individuals choosing to work for a wage. All members received the same workfare subsidy as an affiliate of a public works program, based on a daily wage system (what would now be $25 per day and $500–700 per month).[16]

We were state-sponsored temporary researchers, gathering information about marginalized people and unemployment-related social policies. The team members and I were both state agents and state subjects, a unique position that offers a useful lens to see how the neoliberal state promotes an efficient welfare society. This position complicated and disrupted the city officials' deliberate efforts to distinguish "civil" from "governmental" in constructing state knowledge.[17] At the same time, it was not always easy to govern the team, in part because team members were spatially and organizationally separated from the city administration and experts. Although many of us were skilled at guerilla group activities that were spontaneous, creative, and relatively unstructured, we had little experience working in an institutional context that involved structured working hours, formalistic report systems, and formal communication in general. Therefore, team members, including myself, learned how to efficiently manage a group of free individuals—sometimes through disciplinary regulations, in the case of frequent lateness and delayed assignments, and other times through "democratic" ways of taking responsibility based upon "free will," becoming a miniature of liberal governmentality.

I was one of the few members who worked on the team for a full year. The temporary positions rarely lasted any longer because of a labor law that forced employers to pay health insurance and pension benefits after a year. Most team members resigned because of the workfare system or because of frustration with city officials. The team's contract, like those of other public works programs, expired every three months, meaning we had to regularly re-register as unemployed and substantiate our efforts to find jobs elsewhere in order to renew our contract. We provided a crystal-clear example of means-tested workfare (needing proof of zero income and of attempted but failed job searches). This temporary employment format meant that none of the team members were constant players in the construction of homeless and unemployment policies. Even so, the team's reports to the city of Seoul regarding the homeless women's shelter system and unemployed youth are critical texts for this book.

This book is interested in the field research that comprised the team's reports; it is also interested in the process of knowledge creation within and outside the reports. In this sense it represents the meta-ethnography of what was itself an ethnographic process. It traces and contextualizes the process and background of making the reports, and analyzes the categories and concepts used in the process of designing and implementing policies that the reports could not afford to problematize. For example, to support the need of homeless women's shelters for more workers, the team suggested providing more public works program workers to the shelters, even though we knew that this type of assistance would not satisfy the shelters' need for reliable people with stable employment. There was no room to discuss the problem that homeless women were invisible and could only be dealt with as charity objects while homeless men were seen as structurally unemployed within the system. This was especially true because there was no long-term research on homeless people in general or on homeless women in particular in South Korea. In my capacity as a temporary government researcher, I even used the tactic of naturalizing women's physical weakness—a view that I reject in my theoretical work— to highlight the necessity of providing assistance to homeless women's shelters. If these were the strategic decisions I made as an activist at work in the government, this book is the choice I made as a reflective scholar— to problematize the very process of constructing the "proper" welfare subject.

Like me and the other team members, many academic or government researchers (experts) and social reform activists were caught in the tension of both working for and critiquing the state administration. In this book, I tend to lump these groups together as intellectuals, or experts (Mitchell 2002). I met most of them at SCCUP meetings or in the course of researching homeless shelters. They were relatively well established in their socioeconomic positions and recognized as specialists in youth, women, urban housing, homeless people, and grassroots local movements. Most were over forty (at least a decade older than team members) and had gone through the intolerably suppressive dictatorship of the 1970s to 1980s, actively participating in the democratization movement. After the end of the dictatorship in 1987, many of them lost their militancy and oppositional stance. Some became civil society movement leaders or politicians, and others became ordinary businesspeople and housewives, appreciating the family, the power of the consumer, and the value of capital.

The crisis gave some members of this older generation of progressive intellectuals a nostalgic sense of having saved the society, of opening space for active participation to promote collective well-being, whether at the local level or at the level of the nation as a whole. Many of them were connected to NGOs and NPOs invited to partner with the government in implementing new social policies. Most of them were serving as consultants to committees or councils for the municipal, provincial, or federal governments. Their consultation and opinions, including criticism of the government, helped to engineer Korean society during the crisis, especially the policies concerning homelessness and underemployed youth.

Of the three major categories of social engineers in this book—city officials, underemployed youth, and experts—the last is the one with which I most identify. This is even more true now that I have a doctoral degree and a job as a professor. When I was in the field in my late twenties and early thirties, I was labeled by this group of experts and city officials as an underemployed youth and semiexpert. I had relatively good rapport with most of the senior experts; however, in the process of reflecting on the implications of our activities during the crisis, I found this expert group the hardest to contextualize because of my own sympathy for the dilemma of Korean experts who were trying to find an alternative to the neoliberalization of South Korea. Central to this book is the apparent paradox that former activist intellectuals became important agents of the government's (neo)liberal social governing. They were supportive of marginalized unemployed people, such as the team members, but at the same time they were producers or confirmers of government guidelines for "deserving" welfare citizenship. Even though they criticized government actions in relation to (neo)liberalism and capitalism, they maintained a respectful demeanor in government consultation and a relatively cooperative relationship with government personnel (see chapter 5). This book suggests that this dilemma is embedded in our daily lives, not only in South Korean (neo)liberal society but in every other (neo)liberal society around the globe.

ACKNOWLEDGMENTS

Many people and institutions have supported me during the research and writing of this book. Because I am unable to elaborate on my debt to each individual, I simply list here the people who helped me at each stage. I should note that despite all the valuable help I received, any mistakes or limitations are entirely mine.

For the period while I was conducting my doctoral field research in 1998–2000, I would like to thank Byun Do-yoon, Chang Phil-wha, Chang Yông-hûi, Cho(Han) Haejoang, Cho Oakla, Cho Soon-Kyung, Kim Chan-ho, Kim Eun-Shil, Kim Hyun Mee, Kim Su-hyun, and Lee Sanghwa. I am also indebted to a number of Seoul city officials, homeless women, under-employed young adults, shelter managers, and Youth and Women Unemployment Monitoring Team members, who will remain anonymous. My special thanks goes to my coworkers in the Youth and Women Unemployment Monitoring Team for carving out a social policy for marginalized welfare citizens and for encouraging me to conduct a long-term and in-depth analysis of these subjects.

When writing my dissertation at the University of Illinois, Urbana-Champaign, from 2000 to 2003, I received intellectually stimulating and wholehearted support from my patient advisor and mentor, Nancy Abelmann, and other dissertation committee members Matti Bunzl, Brenda M. Farnell, Michael Goldman, William F. Kelleher Jr., and Martin F. Manalansan IV. Thanks as well to Marsha J. Brofka-Berends, Jung-Ah Choi, Aya Ezawa, Zsuzsa Gille, David Hirsch, Motoni Fong Hodges, Theodore Hughes, Jinheon Jung, Hyunhee Kim, Soochul Kim, Soo-Jung Lee, Chris Lehman, Shenghwa Li, Alejandro Lugo, Curtis Marez, Noriko Muraki, Donald Nonini, Ramona Oswald, Pallassana R. Balgopal, So Jin Park, Sarah Philips, Jennifer Shaffer, Yoonjeong Shim, Akiko Takeyama, Michelle Wibbelsman, and Han-Sun Yang. I am especially grateful to Jennifer Shaffer, who took on the hard work of editing my dissertation.

I had rewarding and useful dialogues about my work at the Feminist Scholarship Forum, the Korea Workshop, the Korean Education Conference, the Socio-Cultural Anthropology Workshop, and the Transnational Studies Workshop at the University of Illinois, as well as at meetings of the American Ethnological Society/Canadian Anthropology Society. And thanks to the institutions that provided me with the following grants during the period: the Department of Anthropology Scholarship, the Dissertation Completion Fellowship, the Illinois Program for Research in the Humanities, and the Marianne A. Ferber Graduate Scholarship in Women's Studies. I was also awarded the Demitri Shimkin Award for the best thesis in anthropology at the University of Illinois and the Sylvia H. Forman Prize for the best graduate essay in feminist anthropology from the Association for Feminist Anthropology of the American Anthropological Association, for which I am grateful.

I began rewriting my dissertation as a book manuscript in 2003, when I began teaching at the University of Toronto. Chapter 1 was drafted for my presentation in "Contested Spaces: Critical Geographies in Korea" at the University of California (2004), and revised through its publication as "Historicization of Homeless Spaces: The Seoul Train Station Square and the House of Freedom" in *Anthropological Quarterly* 79, no. 2 (2006): 193–223, and as a chapter in *Sitings: Critical Approaches to Korean Geography*, University of Hawai'i Press (2008), 159–172. Chapter 2 is based on my piece "Family Breakdown and Invisible Homeless Women: Neoliberal Governance during the Asian Debt Crisis in South Korea, 1997–2001," *positions: east asia cultures critique* 14, no. 1 (2006): 37–65. Chapter 3 builds on "The Making of 'Undeserving' Homeless Women: A Gendered Analysis of Homeless Policy in South Korea from 1997 to 2001," *Feminist Review* 89 (2008): 87–101. A short form of chapter 4 is published as "'Venture Companies,' 'Flexible Labor,' and the 'New Intellectual': Neoliberal Construction of Underemployed Youth in South Korea" in *Journal of Youth Studies* 10, no. 3 (2007): 331–351. Chapter 5 was developed from presentations at the "Deconstructing Disciplinary Discourses of Development" seminar at the University of Toronto (2005); the "Nation, Culture, New Economy in East Asia" workshop at the University of Washington (2005); and the East Asian Studies Speakers' Series at McGill University (2006). I would like to thank workshop and conference participants who gave me feedback as well as organizers and editors, including Ann Anagnost, Andrea G. Arai, Tani E. Barlow, Peter Button, Linn Clark, Grace Fong, Andy Furlong, Roy Richard Grinker, Brian Hammer, Sharon Hayashi, Lisa Hoffman, Laurel Kendall, Namhee Lee, Anne McNight, Laura Nelson, Pun Ngai, Hai Ren, Timothy R. Tangherlini, Paul Willis, Hairong Yan, Robin Yates, and Sallie Yea.

The book writing was supported by the University of Toronto Connaught Grant (2003) and awarded by the Academy of Korean Studies Encouragement of Research for Excellent Journal Publication of Korean Studies in English (2007) for the *positions* article that became chapter 2.

I am also grateful for the support of seniors in my field, including Nancy Abelmann, Ann Anagnost, Tani E. Barlow, John Clarke, Harry Harootunian, Seung-Kyung Kim, Hagen Koo, and David Nugent. At the University of Toronto, I received splendid intellectual stimulation and institutional support. The East Asian Studies Department provided a generous subsidy for this book production as well as a collegial environment. My thanks go to consecutive chairs Richard Guisso, Andre Schmid, and Vincent Shen, as well as to other department members, including Juhn Ahn, Paul Chin, Norma Escobar, Hye-young Im, Yuki Johnson, Ikuko Komuro-Lee, Janet Poole, Atsuko Sakaki, Graham Sanders, Celia Sevilla, Lilah S. Vasquez, Curie Virag, and Meng Yue. I also received intellectual support from Joshua Barker, Ritu Birla, Alana Boland, Huikian Kwee, Tong Lam, Tania M. Li, Sanjukta Muterjee, Katharine N. Rankin, and Rachel Silvey from the Markets and Modernities project at the Asian Institute; from Jennifer Jihye Chun, Laam Hae, Ju Hui Judy Han, Hong Kal, Janice Kim, Jin-Ho Jang, Kang-Kook Lee, Hyun Ok Park, Soyang Park, Dong-Jin Seo, and Kwang-Yeong Shin from the Critical Korean Studies Workshop and Workshop on Neoliberalism in South Korea at the Centre for the Study of Korea; from Ping-Chun Hsuing, Linzi Manicom, and D. Alissa Trotz of the Transnational Feminist Studies group; from Bonnie S. McElhinny, Shiho Satsuka, Krystyna Z. Sieciechowicz, and Gavin Smith of the Anthropology Department; from the participants at the Dissertation Workshop on Markets and Modernities in Asia (2007); and from my students in Anthropology of Neoliberalism (Graduate course, 2005, 2007), Technology of Social Engineering (2006, 2007), and Post-War Korean Society and Culture (2003–2007). In particular, I appreciate various supports from graduate students, including Young-Hwa Hong, Merose Hwang, Sungjo Kim, Meaghan Marian, Erik Spigel, Jie Yang, Sunyoung Yang, and the research assistants Jiwon Bang, Lee Jinhwa, and Yoonhee Lee. Thanks also to Dean Pekka Sinervo of the Faculty of Arts and Science, Janice Boddy, Elspeth Brown, Michael Donnelly, Maria Ferramenta, Maureen FitzGerald, Richard Fung, Connie Guberman, Lynne Kutsukake, Eileen Lam, Marilyn Legge, Mei-Chu Lin, Hana Kim, Jeffrey Little, Hy Luong, Tim McCaskell, Carrie Meston, Ito Peng, David Rayside, Sarah Scott, Julia Sudbury, and Joseph Wong.

Regarding the final stages of this book's production, I would like to thank Molly Balikov, J. Reynolds Smith, and Sharon Torian at Duke University Press for their steadfast support. Jane Springer provided impeccable professional editorial help and valuable friendship.

Finally, I want to express my gratitude to friends, family, and people who have offered me generous emotional support and other kinds of care: Yongcho Chun, Haejin Grace Chung, Barry Gao, Han Sunjeong, Jin Yoo-Mi, Helen Kang, Jongbok Kim, Kim Myung Hee, Kim Pok Hee, Shiho Koshinaka, John Lehr, Dana Lerman, Hal and Karen Llowellyn, Barbara Lloyd, Chunha Park, Marion Pope, Sandra Rotholc, Song Seongsook, and, especially, Hon-Yee Choi.

Note on Translation and Naming

All translations of Korean words are mine unless otherwise noted. The English titles of Korean organizations that appear are the preferred translations of the organizations. Korean personal names, unless they appear in English publication, are transliterated by their pronunciation. A hyphen is inserted between the two sounds of first names, and the conventional order of Korean names (first name after last name with no interceding comma) is preserved. All research subjects quoted in this book are referred to by pseudonyms.

THE EMERGENCE OF THE NEOLIBERAL WELFARE STATE
IN SOUTH KOREA

Introduction   Theories of government and the traditional analyses of their mecha-
nisms certainly don't exhaust the field *where power is exercised and
where it functions*. The question of power remains a total enigma.
Who exercises power? And in what sphere? We now know with rea-
sonable certainty who exploits others, who receives the profits,
which people are involved, and we know how their funds are re-
invested. But as for power . . . We know that it is not in the hands
of those who govern. But, of course, the idea of the "ruling class"
has never received an adequate formulation, and neither have other
terms, such as "to dominate," "to rule," "to govern," etc.

MICHEL FOUCAULT, "INTELLECTUALS AND POWER" (EMPHASIS ADDED)

The crisis consists precisely in the fact that the old is dying and the
new cannot be born; in this interregnum a great variety of morbid
symptoms appear.

ANTONIO GRAMSCI, *SELECTIONS FROM THE PRISON NOTEBOOKS*

This book explores the South Korean neoliberal welfare state at the particular historical conjuncture of the Asian Debt Crisis (1997–2001) and
the political transition to the Kim Dae Jung presidency (1998–2003). It
focuses on concrete case studies to gauge the specificities and implications of the South Korean neoliberal welfare state and social governing.
In particular, unemployed youth and the homeless—both designated as
"deserving" neoliberal welfare recipients—became prominent targets of
social policy during the crisis.

Unique to South Korean social governing is that its neoliberal welfare regime was born in response to the crisis and appeared in the ab-

sence of a classical liberal welfare regime.[1] South Korea developed into a modern state through a process of capitalist modernization different from that implemented by the advanced nations that created the welfare state as a signature of distributive democracy early in the twentieth century. The first extensive welfare state in South Korean history, which is at the heart of this book, proclaimed that it would guarantee "a minimum standard of living for all national members," but focused its energies on neoliberal measures: employability, rehabilitation capacity, flexibility, self-sufficiency, and self-entrepreneurship (Presidential Secretary Planning Committee to Improve the Quality of Life 1999: 14–16). Neoliberal governing technologies during the crisis featured partnerships between governmental organizations (GOs) and nongovernmental organizations (NGOs) (minkwan hyômnyôk) to implement social policies, such as those to reduce homelessness and unemployment, and to reinforce family norms and a gendered division of labor. These technologies of governing garnered political legitimacy and, at the same time, mobilized new markets, industries, commodities, and labor populations suited to a post-Fordist global capitalism centered on the service and information industry.[2] In this way, the crisis response resulted in a neoliberalization that involved financial and conglomerate restructuring conducive to a free-market economy and to the emergence of a neoliberal welfare state.

This unique welfare state must be appreciated in its particular historical context, namely, at the conjuncture of the crisis and the presidential election of Kim Dae Jung.[3] The crisis was the nation's worst economic plummet since the Korean War (1950–1953), and the election of the respected former leader of the democratization movement (minjuhwa undong) was the most remarkable political event since the beginning of Park Chung Hee's military dictatorship in 1960. A timeline of Korean history highlights the significance: from 1960 to 1987, the country was a developmental state led by military dictatorships (in which the state planned the industrial structure so as to maximize economic development);[4] from 1988 to 1997 there were democratized civilian regimes, but with a state-planned economy in line with the military junta; from 1998 to 2003, there was a welfare state during the crisis (1997–2001) and Kim Dae Jung's presidency. I argue that the rationalization of neoliberal measures as the most advantageous for social governing during the crisis was not effected solely by the Kim Dae Jung administration. It was also taken up and orchestrated by civil leaders and organizations that wanted to enhance democratic society and quality of life. This involved making the state accountable to the dispossessed (as it had not been in the past) while at the same time promoting individuals' self-reliance and the ideal of liberal citizens free of subjection to and dependence on the state. This ideal was desired both by civilians who valued autonomy from the state as the primary measure of democracy and by state elites pushing neoliberal policies.

To make sense of this argument, two additional contexts are significant. One is that liberalization and democratization (1987 to the present) went hand in hand with fostering liberal citizens who could both vote to ensure political democracy and consume to safeguard economic prosperity. The second context was the necessity of establishing a capitalist state regime distinct from the authoritarian legacy of the developmental state. I will review the primary contexts (the crisis and the Kim Dae Jung presidency) and these two additional contexts to demonstrate the particular ways in which social policy and discourse on homelessness and youth underemployment were engineered in South Korea and how the Kim Dae Jung administration garnered the participation of multiple social engineers in the implementation of neoliberal social policies during the crisis.

The Asian Debt Crisis and the Kim Dae Jung Presidency

As the preface notes, the International Monetary Fund (IMF) bailout was a reminder of the past humiliation of losing the Korean nation to Japanese imperialism (1910–1945) and of the U.S. military occupation (Sonn 1999: 8). The national debt crisis has been interpreted as a sellout of the nation to foreign forces. This "humiliation" at the loss of sovereignty was readily connected to the need for nationwide cooperation to achieve economic independence, a cooperation that echoed the "repay debt movement" (kukch'ae posang undong) and the "Korean production movement" (Chosôn mulsan changnyô undong) instituted after Japan officially colonized Korea in 1910 (Eckert et al. 1990). At that time, Korean merchants and affluent nationalists created these campaigns to build the economic power necessary to support the nationalist independent movement.[5]

South Korea's national economy enjoyed market prosperity from 1960 to 1987 as a result of the developmental state's support of the big conglomerates (chaebôl) — to which bank loans were offered with few or no conditions—and people became accustomed to occupational stability in those large companies. Therefore, it was devastating when—after the signing of a standby agreement with the IMF on December 3, 1997— many workers faced layoffs as corporations downsized or collapsed. As a condition for receiving IMF bailout funds, the South Korean government agreed to restructure its industrial (big conglomerates), financial (banks), and government management systems along liberal free-market lines; these measures entailed the bankruptcy of many large conglomerates and banks and led to large-scale unemployment (Haggard, Pinkston, and Seo 1999; B. Kim 2000; Shin and Chang 2000).

The unemployment rate jumped from 2.5 percent before the crisis to 7–8 percent in 1998–1999. The figures for the high rate of unemployment during the crisis years excluded women at home and students who wanted and needed to work (Chang 1998; Chin 1998; Cho Soon-Kyung 1998, 1999; Haggard, Pinkston, and Seo 1999: 202; Kim Hyun Mee 2000; Park 1998).[6] The total population of South Korea is about 40 million, and the workforce population was about 10 million before the crisis; 1.5 million workers lost their jobs in 1998 (United Nations Development Program, UNDP 1999: 40). The percentage change in real gross domestic product (GDP) was 5.0 percent in 1997 and 5.8 percent in 1998. The percentage of the population in poverty was 8.5 percent in 1996 and 1997 and 12.0 percent in 1998. The percentage change in real wages between 1998 and 1999 was 10 percent (Shin and Chang 2000; UNDP 1999; World Bank 2000).

The crisis should be understood at the level of the regional Asian economy, as well as globally. The Asian Debt Crisis of 1997 began in Thailand on July 2, 1997, when foreign investors retreated from short-term and unhedged loans, fearing a currency hike after the collapse of "bubbles" in the stock and real estate markets. The fear—followed by a tendency to withdraw short-term investment—rapidly spread through other Asian countries, including Indonesia, Malaysia, the Philippines, and South Korea (Aslanbeigui and Summerfield 2000). In August 1997, the Kim Young Sam government, the regime prior to Kim Dae Jung's, perceived the impact of the Thailand crisis on South Korea and attempted to reform the financial system toward more transparency to attract foreign investors. However, the Ministry of Finance and Economy (MOFE), the Bank of Korea, and National Assembly members from both opposition and ruling parties objected to the financial reform (Haggard, Pinkston, and

Seo 1999: 206). By November of the same year, there were too few dollars left in the central bank to repay debts to international short-term lenders. When the Kim Young Sam administration sent economic distress signs to the governments of Japan and the United States, both referred him to the IMF for advice (B. Kim 2000).

Experts on international finance proposed two explanations for the crisis and the subsequent solutions. One ascribed the crisis to a lack of liberalization and democratic operation of financial and economic systems; this proposal suggested tighter monetary policies as the solution for the affected East and Southeast Asian countries. Particularly in the South Korean case, big conglomerates and their strong ties to government were criticized (despite their contribution to the country's rapid economic growth) for causing "illiberal" flow of money and goods and the resulting collapse of the national economy. The other explanation followed from post-Keynesian explanations and attributed the crisis to the indiscriminate pressure for liberalization put on Asian nations (as well as other non-Western nations) by the two major international financial institutions (IFIS)—the IMF and the World Bank. This view saw the Asian Debt Crisis as different from the Latin American economic recession of the 1980s (Aslanbeigui and Summerfield 2000; Chang 2002; Maurer 2002; Snyder 1999; Stiglitz 2000, 2002; Wade 1998). Tighter budget policies worked as a prescription for the Latin American economic crisis in the 1980s, because the Latin American nations did not have enough funds for promoting the national economy all the time. However, the post-Keynesian position held that East Asian nations already had tight budget policies due to the planned market economy of a developmental state. Therefore, in their eyes, the IMF's universal application of tighter budget policies could not but result in failure to overcome the crisis, particularly in Thailand, the nation most closely following the advice of the IMF (Stiglitz 2002: 126–127).[7]

Regardless of the origin of the crisis—an intra-nationally weak liberal economic structure or extranationally imposed liberal economic pressure—many Asian regimes decided to change the image and structural content of their protectionist economies to so-called liberal policies. In South Korea, there had been concern about slowing economic growth since the late 1980s. The threat of economic recession was frequently utilized by the military regimes to suppress labor during the international

5

oil shocks and devaluation of both the dollar and the yen. However, the crucial moment came after the end of the military regimes, when civilian regimes were under pressure from the United States, the IMF, and liberal economic experts to change the state-planned economy and open up to foreign markets. In addition, as labor unions gained greater bargaining power through democratization, labor power was no longer so easily exploited. The Asian Debt Crisis in South Korea resulted from a combination of the limits of state intervention in a liberalizing market and the unexpected mass withdrawal of foreign short-term hedge funds. Before the crisis, the South Korean state had made some efforts to avoid radical restructuring and sustain economic growth by promulgating "globalization" (segyehwa) (Samuel Kim 2000) and an "information society" campaign (Chông Yông-ho 1992). While the globalization campaign vanished during the crisis, the information society campaign was used to kill two birds with one stone. It responded to the unemployment crisis by connecting public works programs and supporting startup costs for innovative and risky small businesses (i.e., venture business). It also acted on the decade-long, futuristic vision of saturating the nation with new technology and new markets for postindustrial capitalist competition.

Eventually, it was the Kim Dae Jung government that administered the changes. During the crisis, it steered the South Korea state toward becoming a more flexible, capital-friendly postdevelopmental state. In December 1997, the month of the standby agreement with the IMF, Kim Dae Jung, a long-standing opposition leader, was elected president. The social need to improve quality of life had been building since 1988 and it exploded during the IMF crisis (Shin, Cho, and Yi 2003). It is possible that any candidate for the presidential election in 1997 would have had an opportunity to bring about widespread reform.[8] Yet Kim Dae Jung—as a participant in the democratic movement, with credentials from civil groups—was particularly well suited to implementing a social policy with "productive welfarism" that amplified South Korean social governing.

Kim Dae Jung, a Nobel Peace Prize winner during his presidency (in 2000), is a symbol of the matured democracy in South Korea. He endured previous military regimes' harsh persecution and repression of leftist and civil movements and was tortured as a communist sympathizer during a time of intraregional political conflicts between Kyôngsang Province in the southeast and Chôlla Province in the southwest. Kyôngsang Province had been politically, militaristically, and economically hegemonic in the previous four decades, and Chôlla Province became the target of political and economic ostracization and suppression.[9]

The fact that Kim Dae Jung was the first candidate from Chôlla Province to claim the presidential office was commemorated as a victory for democracy and the dispossessed. In this context, it was natural that he received wholehearted support from various dissident groups and individuals advancing democratization (chaeya seryôk) when he initiated a multifaceted response to the crisis. Kim Dae Jung's achievement can also be attributed to his effective deployment of policies in welfare, as well as renewed diplomacy with North Korea (S. Lee 2007).[10] As a prominent activist against the military dictatorship, he idealized liberal democracy, stressed social justice, and reduced state intervention in business and social affairs (Kim 1996, 1998).[11] During his exile in Britain before gaining the presidency, Kim Dae Jung developed a commitment to economic liberalization and governmental restructuring that limited business-government relations and corruption, a focus in line with the advice of international financial institutions.

Even before he was inaugurated in March 1998, Kim Dae Jung executed a series of plans for reform and restructuring. A crucial example was the establishment of the Tripartite Committee, which consisted of representatives from two labor union federations, the largest South Korean business association, and the state administration. This committee eventually made unprecedented decisions about workers' layoffs in South Korea. The establishment of the Tripartite Committee is one of the major markers of neoliberal technology introduced by the Kim Dae Jung government. Rather than regulating decisions solely through the state machinery, the Tripartite Committee attempted to resolve the precarious issue of unemployment by negotiating a consensus among different social forces. This shifted the South Korean state administration's method of operation from overt regulation to the mediation of diverse social and political forces to govern society.

The Growth of Civil Groups in (Neo)liberal Social Governing

Although the labor union representatives in the Tripartite Committee were harshly criticized by union members facing mass layoffs, Kim Dae Jung sustained dissenting groups' support because he had garnered respect from labor groups during the precrisis era. Further, it was the actual occurrence of the crisis and the escalating social anxiety following it that effectively pacified criticism and aided the restructuring of the postdevelopmental capitalist state (Shin 2000). Kim Dae Jung's expanded government funding of NGOs and nonprofit organizations elicited their participation in managing pivotal social assistance to the unemployed and homeless. In this context, Kim Dae Jung secured the support of many long-standing members of progressive civic groups by mobilizing partnerships between GOs and NGOs in response to the crisis. These partnerships were instrumental in implementing neoliberal social policies—such as those focused on homelessness and unemployment—in the name of the nation and democracy (Kwon 2003).

For instance, civil groups played major roles in promoting a "pan-national gold-collection campaign" (kûm moûgi undong) as a response to the crisis. During the campaign, the government asked ordinary citizens to contribute to repaying the national debt by donating their gold. This was reminiscent of the "repay debt movement" or the "Korean production movement" under Japanese colonial rule. Promising to save the nation from resurging disparity, the gold-collection campaign resulted in a significant collection of gold not only from middle-class citizens but from those with lower incomes. Public broadcast television stations heralded citizens who donated gold items (such as gold rings given to children for their first birthday celebrations, wedding jewelry, and family heirlooms) as a sign of patriotism. The campaign was handed over to respected delegates from the three most common religious groups (Buddhist, Catholic, and Protestant) to manage the collected funds and to distribute them to people in need, including those who had lost their jobs, the homeless, and women-headed households.[12]

The growth of civil groups during the crisis can be historically traced from the democratic era (1987 to present). The democratization movement (minjuhwa undong) targeted the ending of three decades (1960–1987) of military dictatorship in which the regime, in collaboration with big conglomerates, maximized economic development through the protectionist policies of a planned market economy. Maximization of economic development occurred at the expense of enhancing labor conditions and social policies. Dissident groups (chaeya seryôk) condemned capitalist industrialists' exploitation and the way the draconian state legitimized its regime through hatred of communism and North Korea. Dissident groups included intellectuals and activists in academia, the mass media, religious groups, the peasant movement, the labor movement, and colleges and universities. Social movements in the 1980s developed a common antidictatorship focus, although there were differences, depending on whether the ideological aim was nationalist (for unification) or leftist (for class liberation).[13] However, after democratization in 1987, civil society movements (*simin sahoe undong*) dominated the dissident groups–centered movements.

This change of focus in sociopolitical movements is related to liberalization; especially after attaining an officially civilian regime, democratization and liberalization went hand in hand. The democratization in 1987 followed historic mass protests calling for the end of the nearly thirty-year military dictatorship (Cho 2000a, 2000b, 2002). In the aftermath, South Korea experienced a growth of popular civil movements for women's rights, sexual identities, environmental issues, and economic justice (Moon 2002; Seo 1996). These movements were distinct from earlier ones and cultivated diverse types of civil activism, emphasized individualistic values and inclusive strategies, and targeted the middle class as a legitimate object of social activism. Examples are the People's Solidarity for Participatory Democracy (Ch'amyô Yôndae), Korean Federation for Environmental Movement (Hwan'gyông Yônhap), Citizens' Coalition for Economic Justice (Kyôngsillyôn), Korean Women Link (Yôsông Minuhoe), and Korean Women's Associations United (Yôyôn).

Hagen Koo (2001) and Doowon Suh (2003) interpret the legitimization of the middle class as a deserving object of social protection and activism as being a consequence of the white-collar workers who joined the 1987 democratization effort. Their participation was unprecedented and welcomed by blue-collar workers and student, civil, and political activists. In this context middle-class citizens came to be appreciated as the mainstay of these rising civil movements. Thus, civil society organizations emerged with a wider membership and flourished in the post-1987 era, becoming major social actors in the partnerships between GOs and NGOs encouraged by Kim Dae Jung. I consider this history as much an epistemological transition as an organizational change. Korean people who lived through the democratization movements strongly aspired to a liberal ideal of less state intervention and more individual freedom; thus the democratized

9

era provided an opportunity to explore such freedom both within and out-side social activism, as both consumers and entrepreneurs.

Enjoying the market and political freedom of their new liberal envi-ronment, the movements behind Korean democratization (including those of leftists) furthered liberal aspirations.[14] Yet these movements lost their ability to criticize the emergence of a (neo)liberal welfare state that minimized the explicit interference of state machinery.[15] Thus, while it was common for Kim Dae Jung to be criticized for betraying the spirit of Korean democratization because he promulgated a neoliberal welfare state, it was rare that dissident groups problematized their own liberal-ism. In other words, Kim Dae Jung's ideas were developed in the very matrix of nationalistic liberal activism in which many former leftist activ-ists participated. To understand the convergence of liberal forces with neoliberalization, it is useful to examine both historical and theoretical analyses of neoliberalism and its connection to liberalism, building on Foucauldian and Marxist perspectives.

Theorizing Neoliberalism: Marxist and Foucauldian Approaches

As noted in the preface, I consider neoliberalism to be a social ethos as much as a political-economic logic and a variant form of liberal social governing. It features new technologies and subjectivities corresponding to the evolvement of capitalist production with finance capital ascendant over industrial capital (Harvey 2005; Sunder Rajan 2006; Read 2002). But, like liberalism, neoliberalism builds on liberal democracy that garners governing power by assigning individual social members the freedom, re-sponsibility, and rationale to collectively choose an optimal form of social management in pursuit of the common good and economic prosperity. This does not mean that the neoliberal economy misuses the liberal politi-cal system. The assumption of liberalism as inherently more benign than neoliberalism is ahistorical. Liberal government and social governing have been just as heavily involved in capitalist and profit-centered calcu-lation as neoliberal governing, and both have used coercive power (and at the same time nurturing power) to make individuals "free" of the means of production—with the exception of the sale of labor power (Marx 1976; Perelmann 2000; Hindess 2004). Thus, neoliberalism can be understood as a post-Fordist liberal response to the achievement of a Fordist liberal mode of government (Hindess 1993).

But is it correct to use the notion of neoliberalism in the context of late industrialized countries and former socialist states? What about places such as South Korea and mainland China—where there was no clear establishment or historic presence of a liberal regime of government, but which exhibit neoliberal technologies and subjectivities parallel to and competing with societies that have a clear precedent of "old" liberalism? Simply put, yes, I think so. As with the discussion of modernities (Chow 1992; Hall et al. 1996; Ong 1996; Lofel 1999), I do not make the assumption that neoliberalism can occur or should be used only in places that have had classical liberalist economies and political regimes following the evolutionary model based on the Western European and North American experience.

First, the circulation of liberal ideas (although not consistently hegemonic) does not need the state to endorse liberal democracy. The definition of neoliberalism as "a liberal response to existing liberalism" (Hindess 1993) can consider liberal regimes more loosely. Korea's liberal regime was embedded and sedimented in the form of a democratization movement under the illiberal dictatorships of 1960–1987. It soon after experienced a civilian government with a partially liberal economy (1988–1997), then encountered another liberal regime that more systematically practiced a "liberal" economy and social governing.

Further, capital transactions—through investment, the search for cheaper labor, and communication technology—transgress not only the boundaries of nation-states but also the temporal regularity of capitalist evolvement in many late industrial countries (for example, Fordist production in liberal democracies to post-Fordist production under neoliberalism), because global sites were penetrated with similar languages to express what is needed and can be supplied. Language, such as that used to recognize laborers' qualities and qualifications as flexible, adaptable, and "self-governing," is crucial to the circulation of neoliberal commodities and technologies. Many scholars studying late-industrialized countries or post-socialist states use such language to describe a similar quality of workers in relation to capitalist market formations that arise in response to global market competition.[16]

With this understanding of neoliberalism as a variation of liberalism, what are the competing and complementing perspectives from Foucauldian and Marxist studies of (neo)liberalism? While the Foucauldian study of governmentality is helpful to explain the processes and technologies of (neo)liberal governing, the Marxist study of the capitalist state is useful to analyze the consequences of (neo)liberal governing in the capitalist labor market. According to Foucault, (neo)liberal governing of society operates through self-governing and self-governable agencies and actors: he uses the phrases "act upon others" or "conduct of conduct."[17] These agencies include quasi-governmental institutions, or NGOs, as well as GOs. Self-governable actors are individuals who embody the logic of self-sufficiency and self-enhancement as the measure of freedom and independence and actively participate in social engineering as reformers and volunteers. In other words, Foucault conceptualizes the way the liberal logic of governing controls populations or defends society not as a direct intervention, but inevitably involving multiple social engineers to produce self-responsible subjects (for instance, in this book, the employable homeless and entrepreneurial unemployed youth).

The Foucauldian literature demonstrates that liberal social governing entails the production and promotion of governable subjects—such as the "IMF homeless" or "new intellectual"—to optimize social control. Therefore, *governing the population* by promoting the "deserving" subject concurs with *regulation of the self* through creating a self-governable subject. Using this dual mechanism of producing governable subjects, (neo)liberal technologies operated across various levels and domains in Korean society: from government welfare policies to NGO actions to unemployed individuals' decisions about making a living. The ruling code of (neo)liberal government deviates from that of the absolute monarch in that it exercises control of the population by making the population live well, rather than through punitive exercises and suppression.

Michel Foucault coins the concept of biopower to explain the unique way the governing power and its techniques operate in modern liberal regimes. Biopower fosters population and enhances life ("make live or let die") as a way of controlling population. It is differentiated from the premodern monarch's threatening of life ("take life or let live") (Foucault 1990). This is related to Foucault's understanding of power that is neither solely possessed and exercised by a ruler (or a state machinery) nor necessarily intended to be oppressive or destructive (Foucault 1991, 1995).[18] In this way, Foucauldian scholars highlight the fact that social issues in modern liberal regimes are not inherently problems of state government but of the whole society, which challenges the presumption of a solid boundary between the state and the society. In brief, this is (neo)liberal governmentality, or (neo)liberal social governing. However, in Foucault's theory it is not clear how to locate different degrees and ways of exerting governing power among various social agencies and actors, in particular the state machinery. Thus, the impetus and consequence of state functionaries (such as the police and government officials) in making neoliberal welfare policies are not effectively analyzed. Karl Marx's study of the capitalist system is useful for understanding the significance of the welfare state's role in regulating labor (whether through encouragement or suppression).

Marx (1963) and Marxist scholars such as David Harvey (2005), Bob Jessop (1994, 2002), and Jamie Peck (2001) would not disagree with the way in which Foucault describes the (neo)liberal power operation as "acting upon others." However, they would express this as the "hollowed-out" or "rolled-back" state power. Different from the classic liberal states in eighteenth- and nineteenth-century Europe, the neoliberal state, in spite of a claim of reduced state interference, actually expanded its influence through partnerships with civil society. By outsourcing tasks to expert groups or entrepreneurs, or by taking a mediating role, the state machinery appeared neutral among stakeholders. The state machinery's function in a liberal political economy is concealed in a contradictory way. As Michael Perelman (2000) illuminates, the state has been involved in mobilizing a labor population for industrialization and capitalist production since the classical liberal regime was engineered by Adam Smith's theory of the "invisible hand." Although Smith advocated a small state government for a free market, he and other liberal thinkers were heavily invested in deploying the state as a medium to legalize land appropriation for transforming peasants into wage workers, as well as for primitive accumulation and achieving national wealth through colonization (Mehta 1992, 1999). Therefore, our very vision of a nonstate involved in a liberal political economy is historically inaccurate, and our differentiation of liberalism from neoliberalism is somewhat mythical. For example, the role of the Kim Dae Jung administration in the Tripartite Committee is an example of the neoliberal state's consistent but amplified concealment of a conciliatory technique.

In addition to the state's double play in liberal social governing, the

13

purpose and consequence of employing biopower is not as impartial as Foucault's theory might suggest. A Marxist understanding of biopower reveals that the technology of fostering (instead of threatening) is a way of making the labor population controllable for the benefit of capitalists. In particular, using biopower through the welfare state (that is, the [neo]liberal promotion of a "free individual citizen" or "employable and self-sufficient welfare citizen") implies the further complicity of the liberal political economy in the maintenance and advancement of capitalism. Welfare society is merely a tool for regulating the labor population through biopower (that is, elevating the quality of living for labor power). For example, the South Korean neoliberal welfare state continues to control the labor population. Implications of "free" are ambivalent in terms of citizens' position as free laborers. This "freedom" refers to the liberty of workers to sell their labor power to the owners of the means of production and implies the freedom of citizens to give their votes within democratic governance to endorse state administrators.

At the same time, "freedom" marks the abject situation of workers who do not have other means of maintaining their subsistence except by selling their labor power—the only commodity they can sell. Elucidating his theory of capital and labor, Marx succinctly sums up the twofold meaning of *free*: "free to sell labor power" and "free of means of subsistence and production" (1976). In that sense, since the emergence of the liberal state, the category of *citizen* has always been limited and applied only to the group of people who could work, buy commodities, and pay taxes, thus ultimately contributing to the maintenance of the capitalist liberal state along with its class structure (Clarke 2004; Hall et al. 1996).

Productive Welfarism: The South Korean Neoliberal Welfare State

Before the crisis, the major institutions in South Korea that had compensated for the lack of public provision through state-subsidized welfare programs were the family and big conglomerates (*chaebôl*). The ideology that families should tend to all familial and personal needs and be responsible for social and individual well-being has played an important role in social policies in South Korea (Kim, Hahm, and Yoon 1999; cf. Stevens 1997; Trifiletti 1999).[19] South Korea's successive military regimes helped reproduce a neo-Confucian paternalistic social order (Han and Ling 1998; Hort and Kuhnle 2000; Kwon 1999; Moon 2005; Tang 2000; Wong 2004).

The family was an object of moral policing even after the first welfare state was promulgated during the crisis (see chapter 2).

In parallel to this emphasis on the family, conglomerates supported a vast system of employee benefits in addition to a secure and relatively high wage structure (Janelli 1993; Kim 1992; Koo 2001). Family allowances for married employees, education allowances for children, housing allowances, and owner-driver car allowances covered many needs that might otherwise fall to the state. This shows how the South Korean developmental state not only incubated big conglomerates but also depended on them (E. Kim 1997, 1999; Sunhyuk Kim 2000; Yoon 1998).

A major factor in South Korea's economic fortunes, chaebôl in contemporary South Korea consist of various unrelated industries and businesses rather than a focused enterprise. Chaebôl have the following attributes: (1) founders' families have owned and managed the big businesses since the 1930s with a strong tendency toward Confucian patriarchy (e.g., Samsung); (2) they are composed of between 20 and 60 member companies whose products and services range across diverse industrial sectors, from light manufacturing to heavy industry;[20] and (3) capital, technology, and managers are mobile and interchangeable among member companies (E. Kim 1997). The average growth rate of the ten largest chaebôl during the 1970s, the peak time of export-oriented economic prosperity, was 27.7 percent—three and a half times greater than the entire South Korean economy. The national average itself was one of the highest rates in the world (E. Kim 1997; Woo-Cumings 1999). Chaebôl also employed a large proportion of the country's workers: the ten largest chaebôl employed almost 12 percent of all workers in manufacturing in 1987 and there were many more workers in numerous small and midsize companies that depended on subcontracts from chaebôl (B. Kim 2000). As a result, the restructuring of chaebôl during the crisis affected these small businesses, whose bankruptcies caused the unemployment of huge numbers of people. Even at the beginning of the crisis, in April 1998, the large groups had reduced their workforces by 12 to 28 percent (Haggard, Pinkston, and Seo 1999: 231). A leftist scholar notes that if Korean society ever had a welfare system, it was through rapid economic growth and stable employment (Sonn 1999: 175). The private sectors (industrial, market, and family) were already responsible for a social safety net before productive welfarism asserted the neoliberal ideology of self-reliability.

The heyday of chaebôl would not have been possible without the existence of the developmental state. The South Korean developmental state supported the conglomerates in several ways, including low-interest loans through the regularized bank system that helped light manufacturing in the 1960s and the heavy chemical industry in the 1970s to compete in the international market. Beginning with the Park Chung Hee administration (1960–1980)—the first military coup regime, which launched the first economic development plan in the 1960s—the state machinery gave exclusive support to chaebôl, while small enterprises and businesses were given only minimal encouragement. Meredith Woo-Cumings (1999: 1) defines the developmental state as "a shorthand for the seamless web of political, bureaucratic, and moneyed influences that structure economic life in capitalist Northeast Asia. The state form originated as the region's idiosyncratic response to a world dominated by the West, and despite many problems associated with it, such as corruption and inefficiency. Today state policies continue to be justified by the need to hone the nation's economic competitiveness and by a residual nationalism (even in the contemporary context of globalization)." Many citizens perceived the economy-oriented national project as inevitable, especially with the historical baggage of post–Korean War poverty and anticommunist sentiment. Thus, citizens participated in austerity to various degrees through movements such as the "new village movement" (*saemaûl undong*) and the "anti–excessive consumption movement" (*kwasobi ch'ubang undong*) in their domestic economics as well as in business and the national economy (Kwon 2000; Nelson 2000).

However, by planning markets and supporting chaebôl, the developmental state violently suppressed laborers through the surveillance of labor union movements and students' movements in support of workers' rights, associating them with communist sympathizers. Nevertheless, during neoliberalization (1997 onwards), the capitalist technology evolved to subsidize a particular group of laborers—the employable, short-term homeless (for example, the Pangnim textile factory, a prominent homeless site, which is discussed in chapter 1).

Under the protection of the developmental state, chaebôl had been the most desirable workplace for (elite) white-collar workers because of the family-oriented benefit system: children's tuition waivers until high school and low-interest college loans; additional salaries or subsidies for dependents including wives, patrilineal parents, and children; and accident and retirement allowances (Koo 1993; Lie 1998; Woo-Cumings 1999). One of the biggest dreams of blue-collar workers, including those working in the chaebôl, was to see their sons working in white-collar jobs in chaebôl after receiving a college education (see chapter 4). The street rallies and demonstrations of the 1987 democratization movement proved critical for chaebôl because the developmental state could not back chaebôl as much as it had previously. At the expense of maintaining global competitiveness through the use of cheap labor, chaebôl strategized to please their workers by expanding benefits and easing their position on wage negotiations with the labor unions. These strategies were crucial not only for their survival, but for maintaining workers' loyalty to the companies and, in the long run, weakening the labor unions' leadership (Koo 2001).

When the conglomerates were dismantled during the crisis, it did not just result in the economic instability of the white-collar middle class but affected the way in which youth and their parents planned for socio-economic security. The conglomerates were no longer the most desirable place to work, and government-supported venture businesses became a popular goal for young adults (see chapter 4). Accordingly, education with the aim of becoming independent, flexible workers—including English and computer classes—became popular (Park and Abelmann 2004). The opening up to finance capital and a flexible labor market went together with welfare state provisions to make youth deserving welfare citizens.

The South Korean government presented productive welfarism as the first extensive state welfare system to guarantee a "minimum standard of living" for its people. The 1999 government white paper on productive welfarism proclaimed that South Korean welfarism, by combining liberal and socialist systems, followed the "Third Way" (Presidential Secretary Planning Committee to Improve the Quality of Life 1999: 14–16). However, the "Third Way," as it was used originally by Tony Blair in Britain (with Anthony Giddens's theoretical support in 1998) and Kim Dae Jung in South Korea, is commonly evaluated as neoliberal, rather than a combination of a neoliberal and a social democratic system. The neoliberal emphasis on economic prosperity and the blueprint of productive welfarism are strikingly similar; the policies on productive welfarism buttress national economic prosperity and restrict the use of state funds.

THE EMERGENCE OF THE NEOLIBERAL WELFARE STATE

At first glance, the guaranteed minimum standard of living appears to contradict the economic imperative of productive welfarism. However, productive welfarism claims to epitomize an ideal form of governing society by establishing the welfare state at minimum cost.[21] Therefore this first welfare state in Korea was a logical next step in the formation of the South Korean capitalist state; it prioritized economic prosperity under the guise of social policy by referring to the cases of welfare failure in advanced capitalist societies and by appealing to the "wisdom" of workfare (K. Shin 2002; H. Song 2003). In workfare, the welfare cost is minimized through promotion of employability and flexibility of the labor population in addition to a pension plan and use of means tests.[22] Thus, "welfare" has been conceptualized as "workfare" or "postwelfare" in this initial stage of South Korea's first self-proclaimed welfare state. In other words, the idiosyncrasy of the South Korean welfare state is that it gives the appearance of a neoliberal welfare state but with the historic absence of classical liberal welfare.[23]

This absence is consistent with the prewelfare regime of the developmental state typical of late industrializing states in East Asia (Johnson 1982, Cumings 1999, Woo-Cumings 1999). These states upheld the capitalist logic of maximizing production and profit. After the Korean War, the developmental state was a governing tool of industrial capitalist hegemonic production through a planned market economy; it legitimized compressed industrialization and modernization to leap out of postwar poverty. Productive welfarism in the postdevelopmental state was a governing technology of finance capitalist production that reached the limit of profitability within Fordist production based on cheap labor. When the big conglomerates collapsed and the "venture" companies and finance capital arose, the South Korean transition was a process of searching for more efficient means of governing a labor population to enable it to adapt and succeed in the new capitalist market and infrastructure: the evolvement of capitalism from industrial capitalism (Fordism) to postindustrial and finance capitalism (post-Fordism) (Harvey 2005, Sunder Rajan 2006).[24]

The welfare state epitomizes liberal social governing in that it regulates the population through promoting a better quality of life (the well-being of the population), and appearing more democratic and generous than a despotic monarch or a military state. However, in terms of the goal of mobilizing the population for optimizing production and wealth under capitalism, the welfare state is as much a technology of labor population control as the developmental state. The launch of South Korea's first welfare state therefore exemplifies the interplay of (neo)liberal aspects within capitalism. Regardless of the lack of a classical welfare state, the South Korean neoliberal welfare state shows the raison d'être of welfare in a liberal government open to the market economy. In this context, homelessness and youth underemployment emerged as important matters of welfare society, with the aim of making them compatible with new capitalist production and labor power.

Homelessness and Youth Underemployment

Jean Comaroff and John Comaroff (2000) point out that youth have emerged as a "virtual citizenry" or precarious entrepreneurs of illegal and uncharted markets such as drug trafficking "along with other disenfranchised persons (notably the homeless and the unemployed)" in neoliberal capitalism (308). In the South Korean context, although youth were not aligned with illegal markets, it was not a coincidence that scenes and icons of homeless people and underemployed youth became simultaneous targets of media reports and welfare initiatives during the crisis. Both groups were recognized for the first time in South Korea's social policy history and thus celebrated as signs of a first welfare state that cared for every national member. The homeless population was the immediate and first object of attention of the Kim Dae Jung administration and the city of Seoul on the brink of the crisis. Underemployed youth gradually became a significant population to be rescued. My ethnographic chapters convey a sense that the whole society felt concerned about these particular populations. However, critical questions remain. Why were these youths and homeless people identified as crisis subjects if they had existed even before the crisis? Was it just a matter of increasing numbers? Further, how do we explain the fact that only certain segments of the homeless and young underemployed were recognized as appropriate recipients of public support if productive welfarism was intended to protect all citizens, especially unprotected and marginalized groups as a whole?

The homeless policy embodied the limitations of a neoliberal welfare state without a classical welfare regime. In the absence of a preexisting homeless policy, the first appearance of homeless policy conflated home-

lessness with unemployment. This linked only a specific group of homeless people as deserving of government support through public works
programs and homeless shelters. The deserving group consisted of men
who were living on the street for only a short term and were thus considered employable and capable of being "rehabilitated" into a heteronormative family. The national imperative of economic recovery justified
elevating this group to the status of the "IMF homeless" who deserved
support, while denouncing long-term street-living men and all homeless women as being unproductive (both men and women) or unethical
(women only).

20   Youth underemployment also symbolized the rise of a neoliberal welfare state without a preceding classical welfare regime. In the making of
a youth policy, underemployed youth were mobilized as those with information technology (IT) skills—namely, another surplus labor category
in the name of flexible labor and creativity. In making a distinction between "new intellectuals" (sin chisigin) and "good-for-nothings" (paeksu),[25]
labor was assumed as "productive" only if it had the ability to adapt to
information and communication technology and to commodify creative
ideas. Creative labor not capable of commodification was demarcated as
indolent. This (re)valuation of youth should be understood in the context of the South Korean state's role in promoting informationalization
and Internet technology in relation to venture capital and business in the
realm of welfare society. As chapter 4 details, good examples of the state
projects include the data digitalization project (chôngbohwa saôp), a mass-
scale public works program for making unemployed young adults into
appropriate welfare citizens, and the campaign for the "new intellectual"
for promoting innovative technology and ideas patentable and connected
to venture business and entrepreneurships.

The Korean case is somewhat similar to Tessa Morris-Suzuki's study
of Japan during the late 1960s through the 1980s (1988), when the state
took the initiative for technological innovation projects in the name of
the "information society" as a futurological preparation for information-
and communication-based postindustrial capitalism, mostly because of
the faltering economic boom and decreasing birth rate and labor population. Despite the similar role of the state in Japan and South Korea,
the temporal context of Japan does not show the full-fledged crisis of
unemployment and flexible labor markets as well as venture capital in

conjunction with ideological subjectification of self-sufficient individuals seen in South Korea during and after the Asian Debt Crisis. For example, the Japanese "knowledge economy" of the 1980s refers to the predominant computerization of office work as a continuum of stabilizing big conglomerate bureaucracy whereas the new millennium South Korean "knowledge economy" promotes self-enterprise through commodifiable "creative" ideas in the context of destabilizing big conglomerate-centered businesses in favor of more precarious venture businesses.

If homelessness was targeted to stabilize a surplus population of working poor and make them desire to be employed (to sell their labor power), youth underemployment was targeted to mobilize a different surplus population of young people who could create new commodities and new job markets—including their own jobs—to compete with global capitalism. Both "deserving" homeless people and underemployed youth received subsidies, mostly through public works programs set up by the Kim Dae Jung government. This policy was modeled after the New Deal that was implemented to counter the Great Depression in the United States in the 1930s (Chông Sông-jin 2006). However, while "deserving" homeless people were assigned to participate in low-wage public works programs, whether in construction or cleaning highways and natural environments, "deserving" underemployed youth, as upcoming middle-class people, were assigned to work in high-wage public works programs, such as the data digitalization project (chôngbohwa saôp) or programs for well-educated unemployed workers (kohangnyôk sirôp konggong kûllo saôp) that were mostly temporary research projects (including the work done by the Unemployment Monitoring Team).

The new state welfare system thus expanded to include the "middle class" (chungsanch'ûng or chung'gan kyegûp) as deserving welfare citizens in addition to the "working poor" (sômin). It was the first time in South Korea that the middle class was categorized as "deserving" of the state's attention and benefits. Inclusion of the middle class seemed absurd to many lower-level state administrators who were accustomed to the notion that a government with a tight budget could only afford to assist truly destitute people—a philosophy compatible with the principle of the developmental state, which operates through austere management of any issues but economic development. Civil activists or experts with activist backgrounds who expected Kim Dae Jung to realize more leftist ideals (for example, social democratic welfare) were also ambivalent about the inclusion of the "middle class" among people designated to receive welfare, despite the fact that they welcomed the middle class as a major target of civil society movements.

However, Kim Dae Jung's formation of the crisis-related welfare subjects through the orchestration of government officials, experts (including civil reformers), and the unemployed themselves—the three social engineers in this book—corresponded to the (neo)liberal account of deserving citizenship: individually employable and taxable citizens who do not depend on public provision but are self-sufficient and preferably responsible for other people, such as family and community. This formation of welfare subjects entails two ramifications of (neo)liberal social governing. It exemplifies the way in which (neo)liberal governing power operates simultaneously through the subjectification of individuals and the management of the population as a whole (that is, policy).

I began the preface by noting that this book traces the ways in which popular terms during the Asian Debt Crisis in South Korea, such as IMF *homeless, family breakdown, new intellectuals,* and *venture capital,* were actively used by multiple social actors, particularly social engineers and crisis knowledge brokers, in the course of discursively producing neoliberal welfare policies and subjects. These public discourses are central to the organization of this book, demonstrating how liberal social governing operated by producing self-enhancing subjects. Chapters 1 through 4 provide a background to each of the discourses, as well as highlight social engineers and their contribution to the neoliberalization of welfare society. Each chapter outlines a narrative strategy for locating the significance of these discourses in relation to homelessness and youth underemployment.

Chapter 1 features spatial signs observed during the crisis, guiding readers to two prominent sites of homelessness—the Seoul Train Station Square and the House of Freedom, the former Pangnim textile factory. Tracing the history of the developmental state to the neoliberal welfare state through its spatial history, this chapter outlines the construction of the homeless policy, fraught with the concerns of unemployment.

Chapter 2 demonstrates how nongovernmental actors—such as the mass media, popular culture, and intellectuals—represented particular images of homeless people. By contextualizing the urgency to talk about "family breakdown," this chapter leads readers to signs in the mass media, including popular films. It makes sense of the way in which the notion of family breakdown operated as a technique of crisis management, justifying the gendering of the homeless subject, and privileging the male breadwinner over the "irresponsible" female housewife.

Chapter 3 problematizes the ways in which homeless women became invisible to the public eye and to policy makers by eliciting personal narratives about homeless women from various social engineers who lived with or dealt with these women in the process of implementing policies on women's welfare. Two homeless women's personal backgrounds are followed by competing interpretations about homeless women's needs by city officials and homeless women's shelter managers.

Chapter 4 examines the situation of underemployed young adults — demonstrating that they were not only state subjects but state actors who actively participated in the process of promoting deserving youth welfare citizenship. Through the examples of a taxi driver's sons, and team members who were caught in the discursive and material realities of the "new intellectuals" and "venture capital," this chapter uncovers how youth emerged as IMF subjects. The welfare governing of youth also shows the way in which the (neo)liberal regime targeted labor control through welfare regulation. While homeless populations were means-tested with the criteria of employability and capacity for rehabilitation to be selected as "deserving" subjects, underemployed young adults were assessed and promoted as flexible and creative labor. The chapter demonstrates that in contrast to city officials' entrenched perceptions of homeless people, their understanding of underemployed youth was confused but undergoing dramatic shifts.

Chapter 5 prompts readers to interrogate a series of significant issues. Was there any resistance to neoliberalization? How is it possible that former student activists participated in neoliberal welfare society? If everybody is responsible for neoliberalization, what is the point of criticizing neoliberalism? Chapter 5 addresses these questions in the context of South Korean intellectual history.

The Coda outlines the book's broader implications by analyzing the specificities of South Korean neoliberalism in the local history of capitalist state evolvement. In doing so, it demonstrates the usefulness of combining approaches from Foucauldian studies of governmentality and Marxist studies of labor and state. The study of neoliberalism through the South Korean case not only reveals neoliberalism's connection to capitalism, but the fact that it is embedded in the daily lives of liberal democracy and the routine practices and thinking of liberal individuals.

THE SEOUL TRAIN STATION SQUARE AND
THE HOUSE OF FREEDOM

One

The spaces of cities are the spaces where the hegemonic struggles over liberalism are now being fought. Whose liberalism? Whose hegemony? The socially revisionist liberalism of "well-being" or the neo-liberal mantra of "international competitiveness"? There are clearly new alliances, new struggles, new forms of subject formation, new forms of consciousness, new narratives, and new and ongoing imperatives to rework the ever shifting articulations of state and nation, and nation and city.

KATHARYNE MITCHELL, *CROSSING THE NEOLIBERAL LINE: PACIFIC RIM MIGRATION AND THE METROPOLIS*

To attempt to make sense of South Korea's homeless policy during the Asian Debt Crisis, I examine the transformation of two symbolically charged physical spaces in Seoul: the Seoul Train Station Square (henceforth, the square) and the House of Freedom, the former Pangnim textile factory. The square and the House of Freedom are spatial foci for evolving homeless scenes and policy as well as sites of liberal and neoliberal historicity.

Building on the work of ethnographers on assemblages of governing technologies, I show urban space as a problematic and symptomatic location for such technologies (Anagnost 2004; Li 2007; Mitchell 2004; Ong and Collier 2005; Strathern 2000). In addition, I use ethnographic observations of changes in the spatial construction of the square and the House of Freedom to trace neoliberal welfare and labor discourses in relation to conceptions of homelessness and unemployment policies during the crisis. This chapter looks first at the square, where homelessness was most visible to the public during the crisis, then considers the development of the city's homeless policies and shelter system, and finally moves to the House of Freedom, the largest homeless shelter, which was created during the crisis for sorting homeless people, according to neoliberal principles, into the categories "deserving" and "undeserving."

The Transformation of the Square

The Seoul Train Station, renovated in 2004 into an ultramodern space comparable to an international airport (see figures 1 and 2), is one of the largest and oldest transit centers in Seoul (Kang Se-jun and Kim Kyông-ho 2004). It was built in 1925 by the Japanese colonial regime (1919–1945) as a hub for the numerous railroads connecting the Korean Peninsula to Manchuria, the route to the continent (Eckert et al. 1990: 269–273).

In spite of many repairs, the old buildings of the Seoul Train Station (figure 3) retain the typical architectural style of the colonial period, reminiscent of the European Renaissance (Cumings 1997: 148–154)—a style otherwise very rare due to efforts of the nationalist movement to eradicate colonial "shadows."[1] Even when bus and subway transport became more popular modes in South Korea, the Seoul Train Station remained one of the busiest locations in the city, as countless bus routes and two major subway lines meet in the station area. The square remains a place for all kinds of commuters, travelers, and people in general to pass time and meet other people.

Before the crisis, people in transit frequented the small businesses that catered to passing travelers. Mobile bars and restaurants (p'ojangmach'a) were set up near bus stops and waiting areas to sell alcoholic beverages and cheap food, such as noodles (kuksu and udong), fried vegetables and seafood (temppura), seaweed rolls (kimbap), and Korean sake (soju). Mini food stalls were situated near the bus stops, where bus tokens, gum, candy, and nonalcoholic beverages were sold (see figure 4). Fruit and rice-cake vendors set up their pushcarts and baskets at the entrance and on the stairs to the two subway stations, or walked among the people in the square, selling their goods.

Until the early 1990s, the square was also the site of mass demonstrations urging political action against various authoritarian regimes, including the April Revolution (Sa-Il-Gu Hyôngmyông) in 1960[2] and the April Demonstration Withdrawal (Sôul-yôk Hoegun) in 1980, the night before the Kwangju massacre.[3] Between 1998 and 2001—once the impact

Figure 1 The new Seoul Train Station building. PHOTOGRAPH BY JESOOK SONG

Figure 2 Inside the new Seoul Train Station building. PHOTOGRAPH BY JESOOK SONG

Figure 3 The old buildings of the Seoul Train Station, right next to the new building.
PHOTOGRAPH BY JESOOK SONG

Figure 4 Street vendors outside the Seoul Train Station. PHOTOGRAPH BY JESOOK SONG

Figure 5 Homeless people in the Seoul Train Station Square. PHOTOGRAPH BY JESOOK SONG

of the crisis really began to be felt—the square changed. During this time, the square became well known as a place where enormous numbers of homeless people resided. Those people were called the "IMF homeless," echoing the national resentment following the International Monetary Fund bailout. (As mentioned in the preface, the crisis itself was conventionally referred to as the IMF crisis.) When I visited Seoul in July 1998, rows of homeless people were lying on the ground in and around the square or in the station's underground tunnels. In August 1998, the city estimated that there were 2,000 homeless living in the square; in the winter the number increased to 4,000. It was hard to pass through some of the tunnels because so many homeless people used them as their shelters. Some used newspapers as layers against the cold, and many were surrounded by empty bottles of Korean sake (soju). The square had never been especially clean (sewage from mobile bars and restaurants as well as the "night soil" of drunken men were common) but during the crisis, city officials considered the square to be much filthier. In the early morning hours and at noon, long lines of homeless people waited for a free meal served by religious groups in several locations near the square (see figure 5). A quasi-governmental welfare agency and at least two nongovernmental organizations (NGOs) also provided support to the homeless at the square.

The quasi-governmental welfare agency was originally a civil group associated with the Anglican Church in Korea. The Anglican Church was a relatively small denomination compared to the Presbyterian, Baptist, and Methodist Churches; despite this, it was influential. For example, the Korean Anglican Church University is the only higher education institute in South Korea that offers an academic program specializing in the civil society movements. This NGO department (*aen chi o hakkwa*) is staffed by leading activist scholars such as Hee Yeon Cho, who has a background in labor and student activism (1980s) and the civil society movements (1990s). Lee Jae-Jung, an Anglican church minister who was president of the university and closely associated with Kim Dae Jung, was the first chair of the City Commission on Homeless Policy (Nosukcha Taech'aek Hyôbûihoe). He volunteered to run the agency for homeless people. During the crisis, the agency was used as a resource by the Seoul city government. As an example of outsourcing and privatization of state machinery and services, it demonstrates how a neoliberal regime uses what Foucauldian scholars have referred to as "governing at a distance" and "acting upon others," that is, outsourcing to nonstate agencies (Gordon 1991; Lemke 2001; Li 2007). The agency became known first as the Homeless Assistance Center (Nosukcha Chiwônsent'ô) in the winter of 1997, and in the spring of 1998 as the Homeless Rehabilitation Center (HRC, Nosukcha Tasisôgi Chiwônsent'ô). The addition of the word *rehabilitation* in the title is symbolic of the shift from a "poor relief" welfare regime to a neoliberal workfare regime.[4]

The center made homeless people register for a homeless identification card (*nosukcha k'adû*) in exchange for a free medical examination. Many homeless were either intentionally or inadvertently missing their resident registration cards (*chumin tûngnok chûng*), the most important identification document in South Korea. The homeless identification card functioned as a means of policing and surveillance: from it, the police could obtain information about the cardholders for the sake of security. The police sometimes used the homeless identification cards to investigate the background of the cardholder, and many street people resisted registering for the card. As Laura C. Nelson (2006) notes, credit card and private loan debt emerged as a salient phenomenon following the crisis, because credit cards were first introduced in South Korea during the crisis and people began using them as one of the only options for survival. There were reports that people in debt or in hiding blended into the crowd of street people. A TV drama series, *Bali esô saenggin il* (What happened in Bali) (Seoul Broadcasting System 2004), portrayed a male imposter who ran away with the savings of an "innocent" working-poor female protagonist. He hid and lived among homeless people in the hallway of a subway. In the 2002 *Lodû mubi* (Road movie), directed by Kim In-sik, a gay man, whose sexual orientation prompts him to leave his family, hides his identity by living among the anonymity of street people in the square.

Social workers who assisted street people in temporary homeless shelters told me that homeless people considered carrying a homeless identification card to be a risky and degrading experience. If shelter workers requested that they carry the card, it damaged their relationship with the homeless. It is at the heart of (neo)liberal governance that social security, in the protection of citizens' assets and lives (Gordon 1991: 35–41; Foucault 2003; O'Malley 1996, 1999), uses state machinery to exercise surveillance over its populations and markets. However, the free medical examinations and treatment often attracted the homeless because medical services were costly for anyone without health insurance.

The Humanitarian Practice Medical Doctors' Association (Indojuûi Silch'ôn Ûisa Hyôbûihoe) assessed the health condition of homeless people coming to the square (Pak Yong-hyôn 1999). A private welfare agency run by a renowned South Korean TV entertainer, the late Sim Chôl-ho, operated a bus with a hotline called the Telephone of Love (Sarang ûi Chônhwa) at the square and at a private homeless shelter, the Guest House (Gesûtû Hausû). The name *Telephone of Love* echoes other hotlines, such as the Telephone of Women (Yôsông ûi Chônhwa) for women suffering domestic violence and the Telephone of Hope (Huimang ûi Chônhwa) for people affected by a natural disaster. Telephone of Love workers served homeless people who were willing to complete a questionnaire about their family situation, hometown, employment history, and the length of time they had been living on the street. The answers were entered into a database of the homeless, run independently from the government. In return for this information, the agency provided clothing, toiletries, and nonperishable food.

During the day, as the square became busy with passengers, many homeless people would leave or were driven out by station guards. By

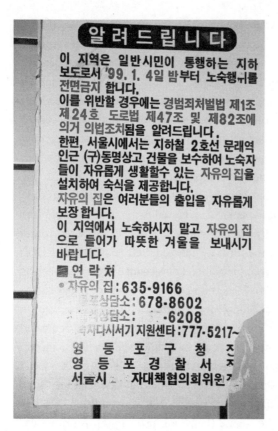

Figure 6 The prohibition against street living posted on the wall of a subway station.
PHOTOGRAPH BY JESOOK SONG

November 1998, the city made it illegal for street people to be in public places, so homeless people were not supposed to be in the square even at night (see figure 6). Instead, they were directed to a homeless shelter called the House of Freedom. However, there were still noticeable numbers of homeless staying in the square, accessing social services (supplied by both the HRC and Telephone of Love), and resisting the regulations and the environment of the homeless shelter system.

Politicians and high-ranking officials, accompanied by photographers, paid visits to homeless people to demonstrate that they were compassionate leaders. Although homeless people resided in many other public parks and subway stations, politicians and government officials targeted those staying in the square, which led to the square's homeless people becoming the tragic "face" of the crisis. For example, Ko Kôn, the mayor of Seoul at the time, visited the square on September 21, 1998 (Kwôn

Hyôk-ch'ôl 1998); Kim Mo-im, the minister of health and welfare, visited on June 2, 1998 (Ahn Ch'ang-hyôn 1998); and Ch'a Hûng-bong, the next minister of health and welfare, went on July 21, 1999 (Sôn Tae-in 1999). It is notable that homeless people in the square complained when reporters took pictures of them with Ko Kôn. The mass media (including newspapers, TV specials, soap operas, and novels) often dealt with the subject of the IMF homeless, frequently featuring dramatic scenes from the square.[5] The homeless became portrayed as the casualties of mass layoffs during the crisis, encouraging donations and funds for those on the edge of unemployment and homelessness.[6]

My visit in 2001 coincided with the time when the mass media and the government frequently reported that the crisis was over. The square had been rearranged into a huge, clean parking lot for the customers of the train station. I could not find any mobile bars or restaurants (p'ojangmach'a) within the barricades of the parking lot or in the nearby bus-stop area. There were only a few remaining fruit vendors with pushcarts or baskets.

The shifting policy on the street vendors is a good example of how surplus labor populations and marginal welfare citizens were inconsistently dealt with. Before the crisis, the government had attempted to eliminate mobile bars and street vendors in most of Seoul's public places with the intention of projecting the image of a clean metropolitan city—an image that would appeal to foreign travelers (Kim Su-hyun et al. 2001). However, during the crisis, there were several massive demonstrations and strong resistance from the owners of the mobile bars. They charged that the government was suffocating the poor working-class people who were managing to run marginally profitable businesses during such a terrible time. With increasing concern about social instability due to mass unemployment, the city reversed its order to remove the mobile bars. Initially, veterans of the Korean and Vietnam wars and their families, who were entitled to public assistance, were granted limited permission to run such businesses; however, these regulations changed as economic conditions fluctuated. During the crisis, it became common to see college students and unemployed people setting up mobile bars in residential areas.[7]

In 2001, once the crisis was officially over, street vending was again restricted. The change in policy seemed linked to the fact that South Korea and Japan were cohosting the FIFA World Cup in 2002. Situated prominently in the square and boasting huge glass windows on three sides, a large new gallery with a souvenir shop promoted the upcoming event through its panoramic glass storefront. The gallery shop took full advantage of the multimedia display of products with the 2002 World Cup logo and mascot: multiple TV monitors attached to the glass walls aired commercial advertisements and films specially produced by the South Korean government, while loudspeakers blasted out the 2002 World Cup theme song, which could be heard at the far edges of the huge square.

Kwangjang, a Novel

The square is also a politically charged trope for South Korean democracy and for liberal intellectuals torn between socialism and capitalist liberalism in the divided peninsula. The square has been one of the most popular public places to hold democratic rallies and demonstrations. The symbolic value of the square is magnified in a controversial intellectual novel, *Kwangjang* (The square) (1960), by Choi In-hoon. In the novel, the square, a metaphor for public space, contrasts with the figure of the cave, a metaphor for private space. The protagonist of the novel, Yi Myông-jun, contemplates going back and forth between the public space in need of democratization (the square) and the private space of the inner self seeking peace (a cave). Yi pursues ideological neutrality between fraudulent liberalism in South Korea and fascist communism in North Korea, ultimately committing suicide on the way to exile in a neutral nation. The historical significance of the novel is twofold. The novel's time frame encompasses the era that began with the end of Japanese colonialism (1930–1940s) and ended with the Korean War (1950–1953). It was written after the April Revolution (April 19, 1960), the first liberal uprising against the dictatorship in postwar Korea (and specifically against the regime of Syngman Rhee). One of the biggest street demonstrations of the revolution was held in the square. Although the novel does not mention the April Revolution, literary critics believe *Kwangjang* was inspired by the revolution's mass demonstrations in the streets and squares of Seoul, and they see the novelist's intention as urging intellectuals to pursue a democracy of their own (Hughes 2002).

Given this historical context and representation of the square as a revolutionary space used for rebellion by intellectuals and dissident groups, Seoul city officials were concerned that the homeless might start an uprising in the square during the crisis. However, leftist and liberal movement activists who had loudly protested against the draconian military state power failed to oppose the (neo)liberalization of the society in the name of the nation and democracy. In the same way as the protagonist in the novel, South Korean intellectuals during the crisis were torn between criticizing neoliberal state policies and participating in neoliberal technologies, such as promoting employable homeless in the square as deserving of welfare.

The neoliberal welfare policy on homelessness demarcated the new welfare subject as separate from both the "normal" citizen and the long-term homeless. At the outset of the crisis, three tiers of laid-off or unemployed people were established by the state and city administration in Seoul. In the first tier, workers who had been laid off with employment pensions by big conglomerates (*chaebŏl*) received unprecedented state benefits, including 70 percent to 80 percent of their previous salaries for extended periods; they were also granted free access to vocational education for reemployment. The second tier consisted of workers who were laid off without employment pensions but were registered as unemployed and could therefore work in public works programs (*konggong kŭllo saŏp*) or enroll in vocational schools that would train them with skills needed for low-income job markets. The third tier consisted of the IMF homeless (*aiemep'ŭ nosukcha*), people who were imagined as having become homeless during the IMF crisis–induced layoffs (see more below). Notably, the IMF homeless became the focus of government unemployment policies, making long-term homeless people "undeserving" of welfare by default. Although government policy could have, for the first time, focused on the overarching issue of homelessness by implementing more inclusive public provisions or policies of entitlement, instead homelessness was characterized as an extension of unemployment issues.

The Creation of Homeless Policy in Seoul

The narratives of policy makers (experts as well as city officials) on the "threat" posed by the homeless are useful to understand the formation of the homeless policy in Seoul at the time of the crisis. First, the discourse of homelessness becomes a lens revealing a changing paradigm for welfare state ideology, from poor relief under developmental regimes toward a workfare regime. The narratives of city officials enunciated neoliberal welfarism by privileging "normal" citizens over homeless people, and the relatively healthy and employable homeless over the long-term homeless. These narratives competed with the narratives of some experts' liberal ideas on equal rights for homeless citizens. Nevertheless, I argue that both city officials and experts insinuated that homeless people should be rehabilitated into normative socioeconomic individuals and family members and, especially in the case of homeless men, into breadwinners.

When it was established in June 1998, the Seoul City Committee for Unemployment Policy (SSCUP) dealt with homeless issues; the city officials confidently presented their immediate responses such as creating a homeless shelter system. The committee was established directly after the election of Mayor Ko Kôn, who became prime minister in 2004 and remained in office until 2006; he was supported by the ruling party and was well connected to the Kim Dae Jung administration. His election pledge included a promise to pay special attention to the metropolitan predicament of unemployment and homelessness. Upon winning office, the mayor kept his promise by creating the SCCUP and the Seoul City Commission on Homeless Policy (the commission), and inviting civil activists and experts to serve as members.

The mayor's invitation to civil activists and experts to participate in the emergency machinery as co–decision makers on city policies, rather than just as consultants, was unprecedented. More significantly, it corresponded to the presidential course for governing the nation through partnerships with civilian groups. Some experts participated in both the SCCUP and the commission. The commission was not a decision-making body; rather, it was a group chaired and composed of religious leaders who managed homeless shelters entrusted to them by the city. In contrast, SCCUP, chaired by a civilian vice-mayor, was actively engaged in decision making, in spite of strong resistance from city officials. SCCUP was comprised of approximately twenty members from NGOs, universities, and government research institutes, in addition to high-level Seoul city administrators. SCCUP's major task was devising plans to solve mass unemployment, mostly by creating jobs and paying short-term wages through the public works program. As a consequence, public works program funding for the staff of homeless shelters and the wages of working homeless people was more effectively executed through SCCUP than through the commission, even though the latter was responsible for running homeless shelters in the city.[8]

In the context where homelessness appeared as a result of crisis-related unemployment, homeless issues became visible and urgent, provoking a great deal of attention from city committees and generating new task forces within the city administration. The Health and Welfare Bureau (Pogôn Pokchi-kuk) was the highest unit responsible for homeless issues, but the practical implementation of the homeless policy was with the bureau's Homeless Policy Division (Nosukcha Taech'aek-pan). Other responses to unemployment in relation to homeless policy, such as the public works program and vocational training programs, were managed by the Industry and Economy Bureau (Sanôp Kyôngje-kuk). Under the bureau, the practical management of unemployment issues was handled by the Industrial Policy Division (Sanôp Chiwôn Chôngch'aek-kwa) and the Unemployment Policy Division (Sirôp Taech'aek-pan), and the Labor Policy Division (Koyong Anjông Taech'aek-kwa) managed the vocational training program.

The mayor also designated three vice-mayors (all of whom were free of military coup connections) to be involved in the SCCUP, with one acting as chairperson. The three vice-mayors attended the monthly meetings of the SCCUP and appeared to elevate citizens' voices over those of civil servants in the process of policy making. It was not uncommon to observe the chair of the SCCUP reprimanding city officials for not complying with the opinions of the civilian members, especially in the first year of the SCCUP. Although the vice-mayors may have been sympathetic to the civilian SCCUP members because they too came from outside the bureaucracy, their show of respect might also have been calculated to enhance civilian leaders' trust in the administration and encourage civilian leaders' coresponsibility in liberal social governing.

THE DANGER OF AND FROM HOMELESS PEOPLE

During a SCCUP meeting in September 1998, Mr. Lee, the head of the Health and Welfare Bureau, presented the city's achievements in dealing with homeless issues. As the top official working on a welfare issue that received enormous attention and support from the new mayor, he confidently presented homeless issues as follows:

> Homelessness is a big problem. It is winter, and they might die of cold (tongsa). It is such a great agony for the city to deal with the increasing

37

numbers of IMF homeless in public places such as the Seoul Train Station Square. The number of homeless amounts to fifteen hundred people. The more homeless, the more spoiled the scenery of the square, the greater the uneasiness (hyômogam) of the citizens who see them. IMF homeless might be violent to the public or might start a riot against the government, as they are angry due to being deprived by the IMF crisis. Therefore, it is dangerous to expose "normal" civilians to them. We tried to persuade them to go to the homeless shelters that the government [temporarily] provided, but they are not docile. They might die of cold on the street during winter. So, we will prevent them staying on the street by making living and sleeping in the streets illegal. When street people are housed in homeless shelters, citizens will not have to see the street people. Already we have housed most of the street people from the square in the House of Freedom.[9] (emphasis added)

Direct services for homeless people in the square were mostly provided by temporary recruits from college social work programs, under the supervision of a few middle- and low-ranking officials. These people did the work of guiding, recruiting, or forcing homeless people to the shelters. Although Mr. Lee, an upper official, did not work directly with homeless people in the square, he gave a lively and animated report of the situation of homelessness, as if he himself had experienced the difficulty of working in the square. In his presentation, Mr. Lee appealed to the SCCUP members by referring to seasonal concerns. For instance, in response to his suggestion that the increasing numbers of the homeless in the square might die of winter cold, most of the committee members showed signs of compassion—nodding heads, worried expressions, and concerned whispers—during his presentation.

While some SCCUP members praised the city's efficient management of the much-publicized homeless issue, others cautiously expressed their worries that the city might violate the human rights of homeless people. As Mr. Nah, a committee member, said, "It sounds like forcing street people out of sight. They are not criminals but victims of the crisis, just like other citizens who suffer from economic difficulty." Mr. Nah complained because Mr. Lee's narrative conveyed a negative view of homeless people when he stated, "it is dangerous to expose 'normal' civilians to them [homeless people]."

Mr. Lee's narrative mobilizes three rationales for homeless policy: possible death due to the cold winter (*tongsa*); an unpleasant environment (*hyŏmogam*) for "normal" citizens; and the potential for violent action (*p'oktong ŭi wihŏmsŏng*). Each references a threat or danger, but to different groups. "Death by winter cold" is the only one of Mr. Lee's rationales that considers a threat *to* the life of the homeless. The other two rationales—"an uncomfortable environment" and "the potential for violent action"—indicate a threat *from* homeless people and the consequent need to protect civilians. The rationale of making a homeless policy for the protection of "normal" civilians explicates the boundary between "deserving" and "undeserving" citizens in two ways. First, it identifies homeless people as distinct from normal civilians, and second, it establishes a need to protect "normal" citizens. In this discourse, there was a twisted application of the binary categorization of "deserving" and "undeserving" citizens. The homeless, who were considered less "deserving" citizens in comparison to normative citizens, would nevertheless be regarded as "deserving" citizens if they were construed as the I M F homeless (short-term street people), as differentiated from *purangin* (the "rootless"; vagabonds or long-term street people). The limited research on homeless people in general, and long-term street people in particular, reveals that most long-term street people are on the street because they don't have housing or because of domestic violence (especially in the case of women and children), and physical and mental disability. We can therefore assume that they are not there as a result of personal failure.[10] Thus, this categorization of homeless people and the privileging of short-term street people illustrates how the homeless issue was fabricated as being caused by the Asian Debt Crisis, rather than being viewed as a social issue that preceded the crisis, such as housing, the mental health care system, and sexual violence.[11]

In other words, when the government implemented its homeless policy, the homeless in general were not considered to be "deserving" welfare subjects; only the homeless with a "normal" life in the recent past and possibly in the near future were "deserving." This particular construction of the homeless as "deserving" subjects during the crisis is strongly related to the efforts to conform the welfare system to the new emphasis on the neoliberal ideas of "productive welfare"—ideas that embraced the potential for rehabilitation, employability, and normative family mem-

bership. It is notable that most committee members as well as city officials took for granted that homelessness was an outcome of employment
loss and associated with the beginning of the crisis. Although Mr. Nah
brought up the subject of homelessness as a matter of human rights,
he participated in constructing homeless people as victims of the crisis,
rather than acknowledging them as a population that had already been
there regardless of the crisis. In spite of the consequences of conflating
homeless issues with unemployment issues, Mr. Nah may have deployed
this rhetoric intentionally to gain financial support for the homeless. This
would have been an effective strategy because unemployment-related
programs were the largest recipients of government funding during the
crisis.

In addition, the "potential for violent action" by homeless people was
perceived to be a threat to state security as well as to "normal" civilians.
This link was crucial because political and social stability are both indis-
pensable elements of a neoliberal economic regime. A fairly common
image of South Korea in the larger world is the picture of mass demonstrations of labor unions, which have been said to hinder South Korean
economic growth (Koo 2001). By prioritizing economic stability, if not
prosperity, the South Korean government effectively pacified the labor
force in the Tripartite Committee of government, conglomerate, and
labor, as noted in the introduction. The city of Seoul, mandated to protect
homeless people and other citizens, was also charged with the prevention
of any possible civil upheaval against the government, particularly by the
growing number of homeless who gathered in the Seoul Train Station
Square.

Through the transformation of the square and the city officials' narratives, we can see two contradictory sides of South Korean society at the
time—on the one hand, the dispossessed citizens and the services established to support them; on the other hand, the passengers who still possessed the means to travel through the square, with full rights as citizens.
The fact that homeless people were driven out of public places during the
day, and later entirely prohibited from the square, reveals how homeless
policy was designed to protect "normal" citizens who might be "harmed"
in some way by the presence of homeless people.

During the crisis, two terms evolved to distinguish the "deserving" home-less from the "undeserving" homeless: "IMF homeless" (*aiemep'û silchik nosukcha*) for the former and the derogatory "rootless people" (*purangin*) for the latter (Song Ch'ang-sôk 1999; Yi Ch'ang-kon 1998). According to Mr. Yang, a mid-level official dealing with homeless issues in Seoul, "IMF homeless are people who came to be homeless due to layoffs after the IMF crisis. *They are normal people, not 'rootless vagabonds.' They have the intention to rehabilitate (chaehwalûiji) and the desire to work (kûlloûiyok).* As opposed to the IMF homeless, 'the rootless' have lived in the streets for a long time. 'The rootless' neither want to work, nor do they have the possibility of resuming regular lives" (emphasis added). Such ideas and assumptions were widely circulated by the mass media, as in the follow-ing article in OASIS, a newsletter created during the crisis for unemployed people in general:

> Although 1998 was the time when the national IMF crisis had all citi-zens breathing hard and tightening their belts, everybody learned how to cope with difficult situations. But, with the severe economic blow that led to the bankruptcy of many conglomerates, and as well to the layoffs of many breadwinners and to the breakdown of families, we find an unprecedented number of homeless people. There are two kinds of homeless people: those originating from the IMF crisis and the rootless homeless. The rootless homeless became street-living due to disease, heavy drinking, family breakdown, and unaffordable living expenses. Most of them are in their late forties to early fifties; they have lost their ability to labor as well as their hope for life; and they move be-tween welfare facilities and street living. IMF homeless, on the other hand, became homeless due to family breakdown related to the IMF period. They are noticeably young and have the capacity to labor and the desire to work.[12]

One reporter's comments summarize the image that was constructed of the IMF homeless versus rootless people:

> Among unemployed homeless people, there are many who used to sleep in the temporary kitchen of a construction site or in restaurant

41

halls downtown. It took at most one or two months for them to end up in the street after becoming unemployed. There are cases when people become homeless immediately after losing employment. However, we should not confuse these people with "the rootless" who wander because they *cannot adjust to a workplace and family life*. IMF homeless are people who would be able to settle down in minutes, as long as they have employment income with which to feed their families, and have a place for their family to spend the night together. (Pak Kûn-ae 1998, emphasis added)

Social workers who met and dealt with homeless people contested this clear division and challenged the image of the IMF homeless as necessarily having a middle-class background and being easily "rehabilitated." A police officer I spoke to in 1998 (who worked in the police office in the square shown in figure 7 in chapter 2) questioned the distinction; he maintained that before the crisis there had already been a lot of homeless people in the square. Interestingly, he did not use any particular word to indicate homeless people. Rather, he used general indicators for persons, *chô saramdûl* ("the people" or "these people"). Although there were more homeless people living in the square during the crisis, he thought most of them were the same kind of transients who lived a street life before the crisis, coming and going as they pleased. His narrative clearly challenged the newly developed view of the IMF homeless.

Nevertheless, the government officially insisted that homelessness coincided with the massive unemployment following the IMF bailout and built its homeless policy upon this premise. The government publicized that it would provide support via work programs and shelters for the IMF homeless, who would soon be rehabilitated. On the surface, government officials denied that homelessness had existed prior to the crisis—though pressure from workers in the field forced them to address the fact that there were homeless people who did not fit the criteria for IMF homeless (see chapter 2). Welfare and shelter systems were developed primarily to support short-term street people who were identified as the IMF homeless; at the same time, long-term street people were pushed away from public attention.

The homeless shelter system in Seoul, established shortly after the crisis, consisted of two categories of shelters: Houses of Hope (Hûimang ûi Chip) and the House of Freedom (Chayu ûi Chip). Field workers were required to sort out the deserving from the undeserving. The House of Freedom was the first stop for all homeless people entering the shelter system. Here they would be assessed, and those who qualified as IMF homeless would be admitted to the Houses of Hope. Many homeless people who did not fit the criteria were left alternating between the House of Freedom and the street. Houses of Hope were small homeless shelters with the capacity to house ten to thirty people; only IMF homeless were allowed to stay. The benefits of staying in a House of Hope included being paid, being able to work in public works programs, getting free meals, and having a place to sleep. IMF homeless who were staying in Houses of Hope worked for particular kinds of public works programs in low-wage jobs, such as construction, cleaning highways and forests, and 3D (that is, "dirty, difficult, and dangerous") factory and garment work. About 60 percent of IMF homeless in Houses of Hope took part in these programs (Kim Su-hyun 2002: 24).

The House of Freedom and the History of Pangnim Textile Factory

When the central state and Seoul city administrations first recognized homelessness as an urgent welfare concern, only the IMF homeless became legitimate welfare subjects; the employability and potential for "rehabilitation" demarcated proper subjects from the long-term homeless. This partial legitimization of homeless people is symptomatic of the selective reconfiguration of "appropriate" citizenship within the recently introduced neoliberal welfare ideology. The dichotomization of Seoul's homeless people was spatially executed and reinforced through the city's shelter system, which highlighted the transformation of the former Pangnim textile factory into the House of Freedom, the biggest homeless shelter, the only place where homeless people were fully "free" of obligation and at the same time "free" of the opportunities to work.

The House of Freedom is a huge building located in the Kuro industrial area of Seoul. The building, then utilized by the city, used to be called

Pangnim factory. It was one of the first and biggest textile factories in the developmental period under the Park Chung Hee regime and symbolized the 1970s economic success attained through light industry, such as textiles. The 1970s in South Korea was a time when the labor movement began its resistance against the exploitation of (primarily female) laborers by factory owners associated with the Park regime. This was the first military dictatorship, which launched a capitalist developmental state (Chun 2003; S. Kim 1997).[13] The Pangnim factory is the site of one of the most memorable labor actions of the 1970s and early 1980s, when women workers' demands for humane working conditions (that is, an end to unpaid night labor) won mass support among labor and social activists (through the Yôngdûngp'o Industrial Mission, Yôngdûngp'o Sanôp Sônkyohoe). Despite their struggles, all of the women workers were fired as a result of an alliance between the factory owner and the Park regime.

By the 1980s, heavy industry, such as automobile manufacturing, began to represent South Korea's prosperity throughout the world (E. Kim 1997; Cumings 1997) and light industry had declined to the extent that the Pangnim factory shut down. The building stood empty for many years before being reopened in 1998 to host thousands of homeless people. Once a symbol of South Korean enterprise, the site now provided shelter to multitudes of IMF casualties with the aim of sending them to work. A locus for economic prosperity in the 1970s, it became a dwelling for the most destitute members of South Korea's citizenry. A place notorious for the exploitation of workers in the 1970s became known as a "shelter" for jobless and homeless people.

The history of the Pangnim textile factory mirrors the history of South Korean state power, which adjusted its way of dealing with labor populations from suppressive to benevolent, while consistently maximizing capitalist interests. The change in the use of the Pangnim factory reflects the history of South Korean capitalism, from the rapid economic development stage to neoliberalism, and the making and unmaking of a "deserving" worker or welfare state subject. During the economic development era (1960 to the late 1980s), the major technology of capitalism was a coercive, draconian state, working hand in hand with expansive conglomerates to exploit low-paid workers (such as the textile factory workers) and discarding them when they were no longer necessary. During the era of neoliberalization (1997 onwards), capitalist technology evolved to subsidize a particular group of the surplus population—employable short-term street people, IMF homeless.

This is an example of the commodification of biopower, a critical problem of neoliberal governmentality neatly identified by innovative Marxist scholars (Kawashima 2005, 2009; Lazzarato 1996, 2004; Read 2002; Sunder Rajan 2006; Virno 2004). They link the Foucauldian concept of biopower as a liberal governing technology with the Marxian concept of the commodification of labor power. Rather than wielding the power of death (suppressive power) over the population, liberal states use their power to keep the population alive (that is, biopower), which can become, if it is not already, an essential buttress to capitalist development.[14] Paolo Virno (2004) argues that Foucault's idea of biopolitics, the politicking of biological life and well-being, is equatable with labor-power in post-Fordism in that the potential of producing labor itself rather than the capacity of manual labor is highlighted (due to a focus on the communication and information industry, market, and social relations).[15] In other words, it is the state that is in charge of the security and welfare of different population groups, including an employable surplus population. This surplus population is crucial for promoting competition among regular workers, precarious workers, unemployed people, and homeless people.

My ethnographic observation also supports the implication of the changes of deserving labor and welfare populations. I visited the House of Freedom in 1999. I had arranged an interview with Mr. Ku, a quasi-governmental employee who ran the shelter and the Homeless Rehabilitation Center, the mid-level civil agency mandated by the government to assign homeless people to the Houses of Hope. In the office where I waited, I sat with a few relatives of homeless residents. Many social work students went in and out of the office, making notes on the board or looking for visiting family members. Repeated announcements over a loudspeaker requested that social workers look for homeless people to provide counseling or to arrange meetings with visiting family. Some announcements also requested social workers from the Houses of Hope to pick up those who had "passed" as IMF homeless: people who were interviewed by social workers could be recognized as IMF homeless if they pretended that they wanted to work to make money and go back to their home or family, even if they were long-term street people. Thus, the boundary was not just ambiguous but ideologically indicative and inducing. An "unemployable"

45

person not capable of undergoing "rehabilitation" meant noncompliance with the normative, as expressed in Mr. Yang's criteria: an "intention to work" and a "desire to rehabilitate."

The House of Freedom's former life as a giant textile factory meant it was spacious, but its industrial past and its long vacancy had left the walls and floor ugly and bare, giving it an empty and chilly feeling. The incessant announcements sounding through the air of the old factory building reminded me of an old train station lobby, where people come and go quickly, much like the traffic in the Seoul Train Station waiting room. The high ceilings and empty space at the House of Freedom caused the announcements to echo. These echoing announcements might have reminded some street people of the train station they were used to staying in. The House of Freedom thus recalled the Seoul Train Station, but with the added dimension of being legitimized as a space in which homeless people were institutionalized and sorted into governable or ungovernable welfare subjects.[16]

Mr. Ku arrived late to our meeting because he had been held up at an emergency meeting dealing with violence among the residents of the House of Freedom. He introduced himself as a devoted student activist in the early 1980s and seemed to feel more comfortable talking with me after discovering that I was also involved in the student movement during the 1980s, though I was his junior. When the subject turned to the IMF homeless, Mr. Ku provided clear insights into the problematic construction of the welfare subject. He attested that the government had made an error in ordering social workers to distinguish IMF homeless from long-term homeless, indicating that the distinction was not so clear and that the rehabilitation of every homeless person would not be accomplished as quickly as the government had promised:

> This is a hell of a battlefield (*asurajang*). Originally, we prepared to receive 300 street people in the House of Freedom, but on the opening day, 1200 people crowded into this building. We don't have enough staff to control them. But the more problematic aspect is the wrong direction of homeless policies . . . The city [officials] might think that they have successfully taken care of homeless issues since they have perfectly managed to hide homeless people from the eyes of the citizenry. However, it is naïve of the city officials to think that IMF home-

less will immediately return to society if only the city offers them a place to sleep and a temporary job for the winter. The problems of homelessness have only just begun.

To analyze the fundamental problems of the homeless and to categorize them in an appropriate way, it is necessary to counsel them in depth for a long time and to conduct qualitative research. But there are few specialists of homeless issues, and any research budget is the first to be cut by the governments, nowadays. This is probably because the city doesn't consider the homeless as a regular welfare subject.

According to Mr. Ku, this was a meaningful time for him and other graduate students of social work to study homelessness as a newly emergent welfare subject. However, he also had pragmatic concerns about the management of homelessness. One big problem for him was the government's requirement that the HRC identify the IMF homeless and provide services only for them. He said that there were many homeless people who had been in the street and in public places such as the Seoul Train Station for a long time. So the requirement to remove all the homeless from the city's public places to the HRC was in conflict with the city's intention to provide services only for the IMF homeless. Mr. Ku said it was difficult to distinguish IMF homeless from long-term street people and indicated that the problems ran much deeper:

> The government might reduce the number of homeless people through providing short-term benefits for them—shelters and work opportunities at a public works program—but those benefits caused an explosion of the population residing in the shelters, and now the government faces the trouble of managing them. Homeless problems should be solved with a long-term plan. The benefits for people who receive governmental subsidy for livelihood are less than those for homeless people. So the House of Freedom intentionally doesn't provide the benefits of the public works program [different from the Houses of Hope]. But without the benefits of the public works program, homeless people tend not to come to homeless shelters.

At a one-year celebration symposium of the HRC, Mr. Ku distanced the HRC from the governmental policies and representation of homeless issues (Sôh Chông-kwôn 1999). He announced that policies designed for the IMF homeless were limited in their ability to address the needs of the rest of homeless people. He also revealed a shocking statistic: he maintained that only 20 percent of the homeless population could be classified as IMF homeless, contesting the governmental premise that homelessness coincided with the economic crisis. Mr. Ku insisted, "Homeless problems in our society have been dormant because of a lack of a social safety net and a meager welfare system. Therefore, it is necessary to reexamine the direction of the homeless policy and consider a long-term plan." This announcement was a blow to the government, which had attempted to dismiss the historical and structural aspects of homelessness by underlining its temporary nature. The HRC's presentation of statistics, traditionally the authoritative domain of bureaucracy, was especially devastating. It brought to public attention the fact that even when a homeless policy was systematically implemented for the first time in Korean history, the pursuit of disciplining welfare citizenship toward workfare or postwelfare citizenship meant the policy did not benefit disenfranchised long-term homeless people.

The changes in spatial arrangements and population of the square and of the House of Freedom embodied the sociopolitical construction of "deserving citizenship," achieved through the distinction of the homeless from normal citizens, and of the IMF homeless from the rootless. Further, the history of the factory building that was later transformed into the House of Freedom reflected the changes in the technology of South Korean capitalist development. This development shifted toward neoliberal governmentality through the biopolitics of commodified labor power—from the exploitation of cheap labor (especially young female workers in the 1970s) to the subsidization of a surplus population (middle-aged male homeless with employability during the crisis). While the welfare state of Kim Dae Jung's administration conveyed an image of successfully "guaranteeing the minimum standard of living" through its inauguration of measures to address homelessness, its offer of "guaranteed" employment was not coming from the state's role as provider to all homeless people, but from the state as a mediator that targets the homeless people whose employability is proven. The Kim Dae Jung administration aimed to mobilize self-governable welfare citizens, a goal that I identify as a product of the emergence of neoliberal welfarism in South Korea.

"FAMILY BREAKDOWN" AND INVISIBLE HOMELESS WOMEN

Two

The method we have employed tries to avoid this danger [of analyzing social governing without questioning the significance of the
family] by positing the family, not as a point of departure, as a
manifest reality, but as a moving resultant, an uncertain form whose
intelligibility can only come from studying the system of relations it
maintains with the sociopolitical level. This requires us to detect all
the political mediations that exist between the two registers (i.e.,
economic and political system), to identify the lines of transformation that are situated in that space of intersections.

JACQUES DONZELOT, *THE POLICING OF FAMILIES*

This chapter examines the particular timing of the Asian Debt Crisis and
its relationships to the reluctance of the South Korean welfare administration to consider homeless women as deserving of state aid, and to the
emergence of a popular discourse on "family breakdown" (*kajŏng haech'e*
or *kajok haech'e*). I seek to elucidate how the discourse of the crisis itself
was a crucial pretext of socioeconomic engineering by amplifying social
anxiety; and how the public discursive operation proved congruent with a
policy of selecting "deserving" homeless citizens, defined as employable
male breadwinners who were capable of being rehabilitated. I argue that,
because of the temporal specificity of the crisis, diverse social actors—
such as journalists, civic leaders, and government officials—effectively
became crisis knowledge brokers, enunciating neoliberal values of employability and the normative family. When these social engineers participated in the governing of homelessness, they relied on the conservative
logic of a gendered division of labor and family values, which they saw
as central for controlling any social chaos deriving from the neoliberal
restructuring of the economy and labor.[1]

Building upon this analysis, I conclude that social governing, particularly of homelessness, is an effective window to understanding the prevalence of neoliberalism in South Korea. Neoliberalism in Korea is not just an economic doctrine promoted by international financial institutions or state administrations. It is also a socioeconomic ethos that gains wide explanatory power from a number of local actors. Although my argument does not imply complicity among the various social engineers, it does indicate that seemingly conflicting social actors can produce powerful alliances under the conditions of a national crisis. In the South Korean case, social activists voiced criticisms of Kim Dae Jung's neoliberal path on the grounds that its restructuring of corporations and finance produced immense layoffs and precarious employment. However, activists' own social relief activities during the crisis echoed government policy. They too emphasized the need for beneficiaries to be rehabilitated within the confines of a normative family ideology. As a result, while the "needy" and protected subjects of the previous welfare regime were predominantly female citizens, especially mothers without family support, the "deserving" subjects of the Kim Dae Jung welfare regime, with the wide support of various civic forces, were breadwinning men with the potential of returning to or creating normative families.

Background of the "Family Breakdown" Discourse

The questions of how and why certain homeless people became "deserving" welfare citizens at the historical juncture of the crisis can be answered, in part, by an analysis of the film Haep'i endû (Happy end), and, in particular, by its ability to illustrate the fear of "family breakdown."[2] In the midst of the crisis, Haep'i endû was one of the most popular movies in South Korea. The film portrays a fictional, scandalous homicide provoked by an extramarital love affair; a man kills his wife for having an adulterous relationship with another man. The husband once worked as a bank teller but became a househusband after being laid off during the crisis. He appears to be unambitious and rather timid, dreaming only of simple happiness for his family. In contrast, his wife, Pora, is an ambitious woman who runs her own "cram school," which provides after-school education for children. Although the film is set during the crisis, when most private learning institutes went bankrupt, somehow Pora manages to keep her business prosperous and maintain her big apartment. The film comes to a climax when Pora drugs her own baby's milk with sleeping pills in order to go out with her lover one night and satisfy her lover's persistent appeals. Pora's husband, who has become gradually more suspicious of his wife's late returns home, finds a remnant of a pill in the baby's milk bottle. He kills Pora. It is, in other words, Pora's irresponsible motherhood, rather than her conjugal betrayal, that justifies the husband's conviction that he must kill her. The police never view him as a suspect, and he gets away with the murder.

The narrative of an emasculated husband justified for killing his wife because she is an "immoral" mother is hardly new in the history of Korean art. Nam Jung-hyun's *Puju chônsangsô* (Letter to father) is another such example.[3] This story narrates a husband's confession to his father; the husband explains that he must kill his wife because she has aborted his son.[4] The use of emasculated husbands as a metaphor for lost sovereignty, or the post–Korean War crisis, was prevalent in Korean cultural texts throughout the twentieth century. However, in contrast with earlier texts, *Haep'i endû* does not depict the female protagonist as explicitly evil. Rather it romanticizes her as an independent woman who can enjoy sexual pleasure but who has momentarily erred. Thus, *Haep'i endû* reveals the changed expectations of women in South Korean social history. The film shows how South Korean feminism blossomed in the 1990s pursuant to civil rights activism that emerged after the liberalization of the post-1987 democratized era.[5] Pora, in this regard, emerges as an independent woman aspiring to gender equality.[6] Distinct from the pre-1987 political movements that featured collective opposition to the military dictatorship's political oppression and to capitalist exploitation of low-income laborers and farmers, the post-1987 sociopolitical movements cultivated diversified civil activism. This diverse agenda focused on individual happiness, rendering the middle class a legitimate target of social activism.[7]

During the crisis and in its immediate aftermath, however, the feminist discourse on women's independence was severely contested, if not subsumed, by the resurgence of collective activism in the face of the "national emergency." Not only did the women's movement recede, but women were reprivatized—forced to retreat to private domains—after having enjoyed a liberalizing social environment during the decade leading up to the crisis. This is the social context in which the discourse of irresponsible mothers or wives as the cause of "family breakdown" increasingly appeared in newspapers, editorials, novels, public forums, and films such as *Haep'i endû*.[8]

The discourse of the "family breakdown" presumes employed men as the breadwinners of the family, women as the keepers of the hearth and supporters of their working husbands, and the nuclear family as the core of social well-being.[9] This fundamentally conservative family ideology demonized sexual relations outside of marriage, sex work, rising divorce rates, and emerging same-sex unions.[10] For example, newspaper editorials took note of families of same-sex couples (*tongsôngae kajok*) and divorce among "silver" (or elderly) couples (*hwanghon ihon*) as signs of family breakdown.[11]

"Silver divorce" was not common but it was an emerging social phenomenon that generated a lot of discussion and controversy in the media. In one prominent instance in 1997, an elderly woman sued her abusive husband (both were in their eighties) for divorce and alimony. The woman had been abused by her husband both verbally and physically. Although he was well off financially, he controlled the money without sharing it with his wife. When he began to develop senility, he became insistent that she was having affairs and was increasingly abusive.

With support from women's organizations, such as the Korean Women's Hotline and the Korean Sexual Violence Relief Center, the woman won her suit in the municipal court in 1998. However, the decision was reversed by the high court in 1999. Although the court agreed that she had been mistreated by her husband for a long time, it stated that she could not leave her husband when he was sick—because a wife should be responsible for taking care of her husband. The court also argued that "it looks better" for a couple to grow old together, to keep the family peace. The court decision reveals how marriage law prioritizes the duty of women in marriage (to serve a husband) over the rights of women in marriage (to be protected from domestic violence). Here again, women are held responsible for preserving the superficial stability of the normative family, even to the point of sacrificing their individual safety.[12]

The specific ways in which the insecurity of the normative family is imagined and guarded are also revealed by the Hong Sôk-chôn incident. Hong is an actor who used to regularly appear in children's programs, such as the Korean versions of *Sesame Street* and *Teletubbies*. Although never the protagonist, he is famous for his unique hairstyle (a shaved head) and for portraying "peculiar" personalities. He typically presents a somewhat effeminate voice and gestures. In one television drama, he played a fashion designer who showed interest in men, although he was not explicitly identified as gay or a "same-sex lover" (tongsôngaeja).[13] In the summer of 2000, during Hong's heyday as an actor, a tabloid journal revealed that Hong was gay and that he frequented gay bars.

Hong's response to the exposure of his private life was to make a public announcement, admitting that he was gay. He expressed his agony about revealing his gay identity because of both the social taboo and his concern for his family. Yet he demonstrated that gayness is not or should not be a shameful issue. Hong was the first Korean gay actor to come out openly about his sexuality. However, after his "coming out," the broadcasting company fired him because he was supposedly setting a bad example for children. When activist networks (including lesbian and gay organizations, some feminist groups,[14] and human rights groups) supported Hong and protested the broadcasting company's decision, the spokesperson noted that it was not a decision made solely by the company, and that they were responding to the complaints of parents and pressure from the Broadcasting Ethics Committee (Pangsong Yulli Wiwônhoe) that called Hong's presence on TV an "obscenity."

Resonating with the conservative Broadcasting Ethics Committee's statement, editorials of major newspapers deplored the threat posed to family security by the appearance of gays in South Korean society. They associated the existence of gay people in South Korea with a negative Western influence on the "new generation" and implied that gayness was critical evidence of family breakdown.[15] Although Hong was able to work with smaller cable companies, he could not get back into children's programs at the major broadcasting companies because of resistance from corporate boards of trustees, who declared that they did not want to upset the public during a time of national crisis, and that the timing was not good.

The question of timing is important. Was it the timing, namely the concurrence with the crisis, that somehow justified laying off a gay employee from his job in a children's program? Was it the timing of the crisis that motivated the court to rule that an elderly woman must put up with her abusive husband for the rest of her life? Was it the timing of the crisis that encouraged the judgment that Pora from Haep'i endû deserved death?

These discourses of family breakdown are critical for understanding how women's layoffs were taken for granted and how homeless people were perceived along gender and class lines at the particular historical juncture of the crisis and the Kim Dae Jung presidency.[16]

The Korean Farmer Association Bank's Layoffs of Women Employees

In late 1999, the Korean Farmer Association Bank (Nonghyôp Ûnhaeng) laid off 688 women employees whose spouses were also employees at the bank. The company's documents listed the criteria for the dismissal as "spousal employees" (*sanae k'ôp'ûl*). The women were told that their husbands would be fired if they did not "volunteer" to leave. The bank engaged in numerous tactics to compel the women to quit their jobs. These tactics included putting pressure on the women through the authority of their parents-in-law. Some of the parents reprimanded their daughters-in-law for being inconsiderate of the male breadwinners' position. Others persuaded the women to leave because their husbands had higher wages. In general, men get higher wages than women in South Korea because of the universal draft for male military service, a product of the cold-war ideological division between North and South Korea. Despite the women's movement's challenge to the privilege resulting from the gendered conscription policy, the crisis-induced mass layoffs produced violently defensive responses even from young men against the campaign to remove the credit given to men for mandatory conscription (*kun'gasanjômje p'yeji undong*).[17] After receiving their letters of resignation, the bank rehired the laid-off women as part-time, short-term contract employees. A few of the 688 women had higher salaries than their husbands and the husbands willingly agreed to be laid off instead—and subjected to the negative patriarchal social response. However, most of the women gave up their jobs.[18]

According to a documentary film, *P'yônghwa ran ôptta* (There is no peace),[19] the Korean Farmer Association Bank was not bankrupt but in the black, unlike most of the giant Korean banks that collapsed during the crisis. Further, the number of employees laid off exceeded the number that the bank managers announced as necessary. The bank, like many conglomerates, turned to precarious and cheap labor, taking advantage of an opportunity to decrease costs, and excusing their action under the motto of "sharing national suffering." In other words, the bank claimed to be participating in the national policy of structural adjustment. The state government and the mass media were silent on the issue and did not discuss the fact that women were being laid off first among spousal employees.

Many members of the team (the Youth and Women Unemployment Monitoring Team, introduced in the preface as my ethnographic locus) participated in a rally in support of the women workers. Most of the team members were young feminists and former student activists who were underemployed college graduates. It is useful to recall that the official statistics of women's unemployment were similar to men's because they did not include women at home seeking jobs outside the home (Chang 1998; Cho Soon-Kyung 1998, 1999). Cho Soon-kyung notes that in reality the women's unemployment rate would have been about 20 percent (1999).

The support rally for women workers began with a chant: "Don't tell whether I am married or not" (Na ûi kyôlhon ûl alliji mara):[20]

I want I want to work (really?)
I don't like the Nonghyôp [Korean Farmer Association Bank]
    (me too)
What should I do if I get fired 'cause I'm a woman (no way)
I want I want to work (really!)

I want I want to work (really?)
Why does it matter if I'm married or not (exactly!)
I'll work regardless of whether I'm single or married (will you?)
I want I want to work (really!)

I want I want to work (really?)
It's hell to get a job (exactly!)
What's left are only irregular jobs (no way)
I want I want to work (really!)

I want I want to work (really?)
What Kim [the bank's president] did is nonsense (exactly!)
Are you (men) relieved to stay in the company? (funny!)
I want I want to work (really!)

The team members joined a small group at the square of the Ewha Woman's University in the early afternoon of November 3, 1999. It was a sunny but cold and windy day. The rally banners said, "It is a clear transgression of gender equality that the Korean Farmer Association Bank first laid off women whose spouses were employees" (Nonghyôp sanae k'ôp'ûl yôsông usôn haego nûn myôngbaek han sôngch'abyôl ida). The rally was followed by a peaceful street demonstration and parade to a central branch of the Korean Farmer Association Bank.

The event's coordinators were graduate students in women's studies programs in Seoul and undergraduate students from the campus feminist group, the University Women's Committee (Yôsông Wiwônhoe). The event was sponsored by the Korean Women Link Equal Employment Committee (Yôsông Minuhoe Koyongp'yôngdûng Ch'ujinbonbu). Two team members, Ussha and Nolja, were in women's studies and took central roles in the series of demonstrations. Ussha was also active in Women Link, and Nolja had been a leader of the University Women's Committee, as well as an active member of a new feminist self-help network for unemployed women (FRɛE-WAR). At the rallies, they performed a scene of cutting up their Farmer Association bankbooks while shouting slogans such as "Don't tell whether I am married or not," and leading chants. At another peaceful demonstration, they went into the bank to withdraw their funds. Although the front door of the bank was firmly shut and surrounded by policemen, somehow several participants managed to penetrate the guard line and enter through the back door.

Nolja proudly told me what had happened. When Nolja moved to the front of the line and asked a bank teller to make her balance zero (her bankbook originally recorded less than a dollar), the teller immediately understood the meaning of this unusual act as a protest against the bank. However, the teller knew that her managers kept a close eye on her and the other tellers, especially women. So, returning my colleague's bankbook and money without making eye contact, the teller furtively but sincerely said, "Thanks a lot" (komawôyo). This was a meaningful moment for Nolja and others who participated in the rallies. It meant that although the bank's women employees put up with the unfair situation and were publicly silent for their individual and family well-being, they supported the noisy rally and demonstration.

I see the event as a symbolic gesture, signaling an attempt by radical, unmarried, young feminists to be allies with diverse groups of women, including married, white-collar female workers. Team members were aware of the emerging changes and challenges dubbed "flexible labor" that turned many workers, especially women workers, into the working poor. In addition, unmarried women who were unemployed needed these alliances with married women workers because their reputations as radical feminists isolated them from the mass population of women who were mothers and wives. This isolation comes because of the normative expectation for women to be married and mothers. Unmarried women's difficulties in the job market tended to be scorned not only by the majority of corporations but by women's organizations that focused mainly on the employment difficulties of working and middle-class married women.

The Korean Farmer Association Bank's actions embodied neoliberal reasoning by forcing women to "volunteer" to be laid off and then rehiring them as unstable part-time workers.[21] As the idea that some workers had to leave the workplace to benefit the majority of workers (i.e., "somebody should sacrifice") gained explanatory power in society as a whole, the people who left or were laid off were consigned to categories of people who were assumed to have resources within normative familial and marriage institutions.

The young feminists who rallied in front of the Korean Farmer Association Bank hardly met with mass support. Although their ideas of women as individual units and independent workers conformed to liberal ideology, their focus on the equal rights of women did not hold as much explanatory power as the neoliberal discourse that highlighted the virtue of women volunteering to retreat to the domestic sphere.

Homeless Politics and Family Politics

In chapter 1, I noted that the primary criteria that demarcated the International Monetary Fund (IMF) homeless as deserving subjects and "the rootless" as undeserving were the "desire to work" (kûlloûiyok) and the "intention to rehabilitate toward a normal life" (chôngsang saenghwal e ûi chaehwal ûiji). I demonstrated that the homeless were effectively equated with or subsumed into the category of the unemployed so as to exclude long-term street people. Issues of homeless women further uncover the ways in which the definitions of who deserved welfare subsidies were streamlined. It is notable that, from the very beginning of the homeless policy, city officials assumed that there were no homeless women. Indeed, they went so far as to omit gender in their statistics of homeless people. When TV reporters approached city officials dealing with homeless issues to discuss the existence of homeless women, the officials vehemently denounced the reporters' findings as false and rejected offers to exchange information.²² When pressed through the Seoul City Committee for Unemployment Policy (SCCUP), city officials later claimed that the number of homeless women was negligible. They reported only 120 women out of a total of 4,000 homeless. Mr. Yang, the mid-level official who offered the criteria for distinguishing IMF homeless from the rootless discussed in chapter 1, said this about homeless women: "There is no such thing as homeless women. . . . I have become friends with IMF homeless, and sometimes I even drink with them. So, I know their agony very well. They lost their jobs, houses, wives, children, families, friends—everything. You won't find any homeless women, I'm sure . . . [short pause] . . . There are a few female rootless [purang yŏsŏng] among the male homeless. But they are not IMF homeless; they are mentally ill." In this narrative, Mr. Yang imagines the IMF homeless as previously stable, home-owning male workers who sustained "normal" lives: they were married (to a woman), had a normative family, and a stable employment before the crisis hit. This portrait is congruent with the media representation of IMF homeless as having middle-class or faltering middle-class backgrounds, as indicated in one article from the Han'guk kyŏngje (Korean economic newspaper):

> The middle class is falling—it has lost its wings. Salary reductions, layoffs, property deflation, and sky-rocketing living expenses are chasing the South Korean middle class to the edge of a cliff. Until November 1997, the middle class was full of hope. Newlyweds renting a single room in other people's apartments imagined that after ten years of saving, they could buy a sizeable apartment. They bought cars dreaming of themselves as rich people. The stock market went up steadily until the IMF crisis. According to the Korea Chamber of Commerce and Industry, with the crisis, salaried workers have experienced on average a 32.6 percent wage reduction. Workers cannot afford to pay back the interest on their loans, let alone save money. And they have given up the idea of ever owning an apartment. The faltering middle class is most vividly revealed in the phenomenon of homeless people.

Mr. Koh (thirty-four years old), who began living in Sôsomun Park, used to be a middle manager in a big conglomerate. He was laid off last December. At the time, his wife began working as an insurance saleswoman. She ended up having an affair with the branch head of her insurance company and often did not return in the evening. Mr. Koh asked his wife to quit her job, but she instead asked for a divorce. He then left home, without divorcing his wife, on account of his children. In the Seoul Train Station, the Yongsan Train Station, and the City Hall subway station, there are many street people like Mr. Koh, the so called "IMF homeless." The fact that these homeless men still intend to work differentiates them from foreign homeless who have ended up living on the street because of alcoholism, escapism, and mental problems. Many South Korean homeless are "involuntary" street people, the victims of bankruptcy or the sufferers of shame in front of their family members. The South Korean middle class is losing hope. The bedrock of our society is in crisis. (Chông Tae-ung 1998)

Homeless women, on the other hand, were epitomized as part of the rootless, the undeserving homeless. The dismissal of homeless women cannot be accounted for merely by gender discrimination because not all homeless men were considered deserving homeless either. However, it is interesting that while long-term homeless men were considered to be part of the rootless by virtue of being lazy or resistant to normal life, homeless women were considered to be members of the rootless because of their pathology or immorality. I turn now to the comments of Ms. Pang, a low-level city official in the Team for Women in Need (Yobohoyôsông T'im) of the Social Welfare Division. Ms. Pang's office was responsible for managing four types of shelters that accommodated specific categories of women, which included victims of domestic and sexual violence (sông p'ongnyôk p'ihaeja shimt'ô), single mothers (moja poho sisôl), unmarried pregnant women (mihonmo sisôl), and women with no place to stay who were housed at the Temporary City Shelter for Women (TCSW, Ilsi Sirip Punyô Pohoso). Ms. Pang explained that the TCSW's clients included mentally challenged older women and dementia patients (ch'imae halmôni) who were either lost or abandoned by their families, but not homeless women.[23] When I asked her about homeless women, she stated, "I don't know anything about homeless women. It is not my responsibility. But, do you really think that there are homeless women? I can't imagine (*sangsang halsu ka ôpsô yo*) there being any homeless women. How can women with children run away from home and leave their children? Mothers cannot be that irresponsible. Women who do that could only be insane. And in the case of single women, they can live by prostituting. So why would they have to live on the streets?" I was speechless. I tried to find a relevant response without showing my emotion, yet I felt something between unease, insult, despair, and indignation. I told her that the team that I belonged to was interested in minority groups among the diverse homeless people, including women, the disabled, families, and old people. She maintained her stance, saying: "It is meaningless to conduct separate research for women or disabled homeless because it is unlikely that they would live on the street."[24]

With this moralistic and presumptuous comment, Ms. Pang judges women who have left their children to be inhumane and insane, regardless of their reasons for leaving their children or for not returning to their home. It is impossible for her to imagine that a single woman without a family would choose to live on the street. That much is clear from her blunt assertion that women are either sacred mothers or prostitutes. Ms. Pang reflects a resurging conservative view that refuses to legitimate the possibility that a divorcée or a widow might decline to remarry, or that a woman might prefer to lead a single life.

Her comments are especially striking in light of the fact that she was responsible for dealing with destitute women who had nowhere to go, including battered women and mothers out of wedlock (the Team for Women in Need under the city's Social Welfare Division). Had she known that women who run away from home often endured domestic violence, perhaps it would have been easier for her to imagine that some runaway women had become homeless because women's shelters and religious retreat centers had failed them. Under the previous welfare system, "mentally ill" women without family were the "needy" objects of protection in the name of maternalism. Under productive welfarism, maternalism remains.[25] Ironically, however, by using maternalist ideology to pathologize homeless women, governmental officials have become unable to count homeless women as legitimate welfare subjects. This type of selective deployment of moralistic maternalism is a symptom of the neoliberal welfare state that has shifted its definition of deserving welfare citizenship from "needy" (that is, dependent and in need of protection) to "productive" (independent and self-sufficient) subjects. From the perspective of the state, productive subjects are those people whose activities result in the maximization of capitalist profit.

This shift from needy to productive subjects seems to dismantle the stereotype of the gendered welfare subject in the history of the South Korean welfare system, introducing the idea that men can be protected and economically supported by the state. I argue, however, that this gender reversal of the "proper" welfare subject did not challenge South Korea's gendered division of labor: namely, that of the male breadwinner and female homemaker—a dualistic gender paradigm based in heteronormative familism (Butler 1990; Fraser 1989; Koven and Michel 1993; Mink 1995; Sedgewick 1990; Warner 1993; Weston 1991). I define *heteronormative familism* as certain forms, functions, and values of families that are normalized, including heterosexuality, marriage status, work and house-ownership, gendered division of labor, and maternalist morality (that valorizes women's caretaking positions in both the "private" and "public" spheres). Further, I argue that it is (neo)liberal market principles that promote a male breadwinner's labor into "self-reliant" and "independent" wage work by mobilizing the gendered division of labor within the normative family. This resonates with Eva Feder Kittay's challenging question about whether our very desire to be independent is the embodiment of (neo)liberal thinking. She points out that "no one escapes dependency in a lifetime, and many must care for dependents in the course of a life." Kittay continues, "Rather than denying our interdependence, my aim is to find a knife sharp enough to cut through the fiction of our independence" (Kittay 1999: xiii).

I would like to return to my central argument by noting that state functionaries were not the sole social agents who contributed to the moral regime of deserving welfare citizenship and the normative family. (Neo)liberal social governing relies on a wide social consensus or moral authority drawn from civil forces to legitimize democratic state decision-making processes such as homeless policy. The cultural and political logic entailed in the demarcation of welfare subjects was widely shared by the media, academics, and civil activists, as well as by state elites. I discovered in the process of my fieldwork that many homeless shelter managers, even though they worked in the nongovernmental sector, shared this conservative family ideology.[26] They too blamed homelessness on non-normative family situations and promoted the "normal family" as the best way to prevent homelessness. Newspapers and public forums reported that the biggest concern of homeless people was related to family matters (27 percent), followed by finding a job (22.4 percent), and securing food and a place to stay (0.3 percent) (Sôh Chông-kwôn 1999). The majority of homeless people were reported to be suffering from fragile family relationships, which included those who were single parents and divorced, unmarried, and widowed individuals.[27]

By privileging conjugal relationships in heterosexual marriages, the above reports reveal cultural assumptions that middle-aged men cannot live alone and should be attended by female sexual partners. Because the family, and its breakdown, was alleged to be the cause of homelessness and other social problems, the homeless welfare agency responded with a variety of rehabilitation programs aimed at creating and reinforcing conservative familial norms. For instance, homeless shelters offered matchmaking, sponsored joint wedding ceremonies, organized reunion events with relatives, and provided transportation and presents for visits to families or hometowns for holidays (Homeless Rehabilitation Center 1998, 2000). The objective was to motivate homeless people to resume normal life and to promote the type of family that is ideally suited for functioning as the basic unit responsible for social needs.[28] Marriages between homeless people living in homeless shelters were presented as success stories. High-level government officials and prominent politicians as well as civil leaders repeatedly and eagerly visited those few homeless shelters that housed newlywed homeless couples or families, while ignoring other homeless shelters that could not boast wedding ceremonies or family ties. This suggests that it had become politically valuable to idealize homeless men and women who created normal families.

Some South Korean scholars noted that the sociocultural fragility set in motion by the crisis was rooted in long-standing, latent issues connected with compressed modernity and rapid industrialization (Chang 1997, 1999; Yoon 1999). In a way, the ideology of disciplining family is not new to South Koreans. It was pivotal in managing Koreans' national loyalty during the realm of neo-Confucian ideology, most conspicuously since the late Chosôn period of the seventeenth century (Deuchler 1992; Haboush 1991; Janelli and Janelli 1982). The South Korean family was also promoted as the basic unit of survival and social mobility through the Japanese colonial era (1919–1945), the Korean War period (1950–1953), and the developmental regimes (1960–1987) (Kwon 1999). Even the civil liberties celebrated during the democratized era promoted women's rights only in the direction of heteronormative maternal protection. As Wendy Brown succinctly shows, civil liberty is founded on "masculinist liberalism," which recognizes equality but is precisely predicated on and does not challenge naturalized differences, such as gendered roles and characters (1995: 155–57). In particular, the affective labor assigned to and provided by women in the construction of the ideal bourgeois family is a core foundation of liberalism (Anagnost 2000).[29]

It is important to note that most mass media as well as governmental and civil documents presented family breakdown as largely the product of the crisis. In other words, condemning irresponsible motherhood and female caregivers at home became conspicuous in an unprecedented way during the crisis.[30] The flip side of such moralistic maternalism celebrates the female homemaker who maintains domestic cohesion through her responsible motherhood. In September 1998, an article in the Han'gyôre sinmun, a progressive newspaper in South Korea, used John Steinbeck's The Grapes of Wrath to equate the South Korean Crisis with the Great Depression in the United States and to underscore that mothers are the central axis for holding the family together in dire times. The editorial's emphasis on maternal strength is congruent with the anxiety and fear of family breakdown discourses and the tacit blame assigned to undutiful mothers, wives, and daughters-in-law (Pak Kûn-ae 1998). Privileging the notion of responsible motherhood, the government implemented a policy that promoted women's self-employment by providing small business loans only to exemplary mothers who did not have a capable male breadwinner in their households.

However, even these exemplary mothers could not access loans and benefits if they failed to get financial sponsorship from their closest male kin. Women's legal eligibility has obviously been bound to the patriarchal structure even when mothers are eulogized as central figures in the family.[31] Policy and governing of the family have been crucial tools used by neoliberal projects to produce independent social members, that is, those who do not depend on the state (Anagnost 2000; Stacey 2000). In responding to various social problems, such as juvenile delinquency and public hygiene issues, Western welfare states shifted their role from regulator to mediator by encouraging liberal values (free civilians with self-responsibility) and supporting the family as the self-regulating unit morally liable for unruly social members (Donzelot 1979; Foucault 1991). Civil society activists with long-standing histories of antistate activism were no exception. They also contributed to promoting the moral economy of a conservative normative family. Although some voiced criticisms of Kim Dae Jung's welfarism, primarily because of its insufficient support for poor people, their own activities emphasized the capacity of welfare beneficiaries to rehabilitate within the confines of a normative family ideology. From the onset of the crisis, *chaeya*, the long-standing political dissident collective, mobilized a huge donation campaign within the "national movement to overcome unemployment" (NMOU, *sirôp kûkpok kungmin undong ponbu*). The NMOU inherited its nationalist motif from the gold-collection campaign (*kûm moûgi undong*) that was launched at the onset of the crisis for repaying the national debt to the IMF. The NMOU undertook various charity distribution activities throughout the crisis in 1998 and 1999 based on recipients' capacity to rehabilitate and their commitment to self-sufficiency. Those activities include the "pan-national network movement" (*pôm kungmin kyôryôn undong*) and the "movement to survive winter" (*kyôulnagi undong*), which provided cash allowances and food to the unemployed. Families, rather than destitute individuals, were the beneficiaries of the two programs. The fact that women's nongovernmental organizations (NGOs) were assigned to take care of beneficiary families suggests that not just individual women, but also women's organizations, were assigned to have moral responsibility as caretakers of the family. This aspect of returning women and women's organizations to the domestic site can be seen as a consequence of recognizing women's affective labor as "productive" and as necessary for sustaining individualism with its "selflessness" in the very construction of liberal political ideology (Brown 1995: 149–57). In short, neoliberal welfare principles and the conservative side of liberalism's gender ideology operated as synergetic components of social engineering in civil activism.[32]

My fieldwork provides examples of the ways in which civil society activists were inadvertently complicit in moral governing through the discourse of family breakdown. In May 1999, the mass media reported that the rate of domestic violence had drastically increased after the crisis. It is interesting how some issues, such as those of homeless women, were made invisible, while others, such as domestic violence, appeared anew. These reports were based on information provided by respected NGOs that ran hotlines and shelters for victims of sexual harassment and domestic violence. I was astonished to hear these reports because when I had called the same agencies three months earlier, executives had denied any relationship between the rates of domestic violence and the crisis. Ms. Hyun, the acting director of a leading domestic violence hotline, had previously told me: "Well, I haven't observed any influence of the IMF crisis on domestic violence. I am a little bit frustrated by everybody's talking about IMF [crisis]. Domestic violence has existed for a long time independent from the IMF crisis. I don't understand why people try to connect issues of domestic violence to social tides, like the IMF crisis. We are busy enough counseling battered women on the phone, how can we worry about who is an IMF victim or not?"

In those early days of the crisis when I called Ms. Hyun, these important civil organizations for women's rights were not paying attention to the crisis's impact on women, except in the case of women's labor issues. Within a few months, I observed a huge change in attitude: the crisis and domestic violence had become intimately linked. I suspect that the funding provided by the NMOU to women's NGOs through the "movement to survive winter" pressed the NGOs to reconceptualize their social welfare concerns in relation to the crisis. Issues under the discourse of family breakdown began to be seen and interpreted differently by various social actors. This does not mean that women's NGOs and feminists disassociated women from the family in the 1990s, during the lead-up to the crisis. However, if we consider the background of family breakdown discourses, 1998 and 1999 were historic years when a revived conservative, collectivistic family ideology superseded a decade-long feminist contest between women's independence and privatization in domestic spheres. I do not want to give the impression that responses to the crisis were consolidated by complicity and conspiracy among various social forces. We have already seen that civil groups used multiple strategies other than direct opposition to negotiate democratic social governing with the Kim Dae Jung government. The condition of national emergency offered civil forces the optimal context for participating in the implementation of social policy, because the Kim Dae Jung government actively promoted partnerships between governmental organizations (GOs) and NGOs, such as the preceding example of the women's hotline. Domestic violence, which was initially perceived as a separate issue from unemployment, became effectively staged as a crucial consequence of the crisis and deeply related to unemployment.

A Return to the Square

My visit to the Seoul Train Station Square in 1998 revealed the gendered aspect of the spatial construction of the welfare subject. A police station was situated at the far outskirts of the southeast corner of the square (see figure 7). Across from the police station was a small, old one-story building with a sign that read, "Women's Welfare-Counseling Center (WWCC)" (Yôsông Pokchi Sangdamso) (see figure 8). I wanted to know what the center's function was, but its doors were firmly closed. I looked around and saw a policeman smoking outside the police station. He was looking in the direction of the square, filled with homeless people. From everything I had heard, policemen aggressively drove homeless people from public places or urged them to go to homeless shelters. But this officer was not staring at the homeless people in a negative way. He was in a meditative mood, like an old man smoking at the village gate with little to do but think and silently observe his neighbors' trivial actions.

When I asked him if the WWCC was temporarily closed, he told me that it had been closed for months. He explained that a woman (the only staff member at the WWCC) used to bring food to the police station, but that without notice she had stopped coming. He seemed to have enjoyed her visits and was perplexed by their abrupt ending. Shortly after she stopped appearing, the WWCC was closed. He didn't know why. I learned that the WWCC had been administered by the district office where the train station was located. In an effort to find out what had happened, I called the district office and found out that it had laid off the only person responsible for women's and family welfare, a position created in 1997 under the Kim Young Sam regime.[33] The person discharged was the woman the policeman had been friendly with. An employee at the district office implied that she was a casualty of voluntary layoffs (myôngyet'oejik) in state and local governments.

Apparently the local government had been under pressure to "restructure" the administrative system immediately after the South Korean gov-

Figure 7 The police station (left) and the former Women's Welfare-Counseling Center (middle background) in the square. PHOTOGRAPH BY JESOOK SONG

Figure 8 The shut-down Women's Welfare-Counseling Center, with its sign covered. PHOTOGRAPH BY JESOOK SONG

ernment received the IMF bailout funds. With a new emphasis on efficiency, the Seoul government laid off workers who did not have good
records or whose duties were not considered necessary. This was another
example of the tendency to lay off female workers first, an illegal discrimi-
natory practice. The central government administrator for women's affairs in the Ministry of Health and Welfare did not know of this incident
when it happened. When she heard about it later, she lamented, "We told
them [Seoul city and districts] not to discriminate against female employees, especially public social workers. But see, they didn't listen to us." As I
made my inquiries with district social workers, I also tried to gather data
on the situation of deprived women during the crisis. I asked how many
times they had received phone calls or visits from women whose destitute
situations, or homelessness, could be a result of the crisis, and if they
knew of any homeless women's shelters supported by the city. I could
not find out anything from the workers I spoke to because the laid-off
employee from the WWCC was the only person responsible for maintaining this information. Not only had the services for women been spatially
relegated to the outskirts of the square (figure 7), but the only worker
responsible for this service had been eliminated—and with her went all
records of the women the WWCC had assisted.

When I revisited the square in October 2001, the former WWCC had
been transformed into the Homeless Counseling Center (Nosukcha Sangdamso), now run by a religious organization (see figure 9). This change
from "women's" service to "homeless" service in the title and function of
the district office building is significant because it signals a welfare subject constructed differently in successive regimes—women and mothers
in the Kim Young Sam regime and homeless men in the Kim Dae Jung
regime. During the crisis, a man in need was entitled to immediate help
and considered a more deserving welfare citizen than a woman in need.
As before, the center was understaffed during the day, and the building,
still shabby and locked, stood out in stark contrast against the rest of the
square, which had been radically upgraded.

The historic and allegorical welfare space of the square is not constructed as gender-free, but in accordance with the mixed (neo)liberal-
and-Confucian principle of reprivatization of women. It is marked by the
gendered division of liberal space into the public versus the private, epitomized in Choi In-hoon's Kwangjang (The square) (1960); the gendered rela-

Figure 9 The former Women's Welfare-Counseling Center, now known as the Homeless Counseling Center. PHOTOGRAPH BY JESOOK SONG

tionship between homeless men and homeless women; and the gendered perception of neoliberal policy makers regarding who is deserving of state or social support. In *Kwangjang*, the intellectual space for the ideological competition between liberalism and socialism is inhabited exclusively by male protagonists, whereas heroines Yun-ae and Ŭn-hye exist merely to physically and emotionally comfort the male protagonists, who want to escape from the ideological battle, as if male intellectuals are the only true victims of the ideological space. In the novel, the female characters are equated and overlapped with the image of the cave, the spatial symbol of the private, the nonpolitical, the erotic, and the emotional, in contrast to the square, the novel's primary spatial symbol of the public, the political, and the rational. Likewise, the Seoul Train Station Square and other public places that sheltered masses of homeless people are not for homeless women: simply, these places are too violent and unruly (see chapter 3 for more discussion of the square and the safety of homeless women). The square, the site that revealed (or was used to represent) South Korea's democratic aspirations, similar to the public space in *Kwangjang*, simultaneously liberates and silences different social agents, a process that is deeply implicated in gendered spatiality. The moment the protagonists (Yi Myŏng-jun in the novel and homeless men in my ethnoscape) became

69

victims or heroic subjects in response or resistance to the larger dominant political-economic context, they silenced the cry against the violence done to other victims in Korean history. That the protagonist victim/hero in *Kwangjang* was male while the silenced victim, or heroine, was female is an allegorical concurrence in the novel as well as in my research.

The Role of the Experts

South Korean experts played the part of arbitrator in debates on family breakdown, a position not unusual in the process of (neo)liberal knowledge production in other social and global contexts (Goldman 2000; Peck and Theodore 2001; see chapter 5 of this book). For instance, women's policy experts discussed changes in family structure to highlight the unrecognized and underserved needs of women and families and to connect these changes to the development of "family welfare." To an extent, they criticized and negotiated fixed concepts of family at a time when the public and policy discourse of family breakdown was in flux (Kim Kyông-dong 1999; Pyun Hwa Soon 2000; Yi Mi-kyông 1999; Yim In-sook 1999). However, the experts contributed to moral conservatism by not challenging the direction of rehabilitating normative families.

At the "Han'guk kajok kinûng ûi kyôlson kwa taech'aek pangan mosaek" (Symposium for the solution to the dysfunctional Korean family), hosted by the city of Seoul and the South Korean Women's Development Institute in July 2000, a keynote speech about the reality of and solutions for dismantled families introduced the idea of changes in the concept of family. It is worth noting how the oral representation of the speaker, a leading feminist expert working for the government on gender and family policies whom I'll refer to as Dr. Han, differed from the written text of her speech. In her speech, Dr. Han mentioned the necessity of recuperating family *function* rather than emphasizing ideal family *structure*. Asserting the possibility of diverse forms of family, she illustrated her point by referring to an international news report of a Western lesbian couple who had won adoption rights in court. She interpreted this decision to signify that parenting means having *two responsible adults* to take care of children, regardless of the adults' gender. She said, "The changing concept of the family is a global trend. Therefore it is problematic to consider the family's failure to preserve its traditional form as a *crisis* of the family. Instead, we have to do our best to revitalize the *function* of the family.[34] And state, society, and family should share the responsibility" (emphasis added). The written text of her speech, however, did not include these alternative comments. Whereas her oral presentation implied that crisis was an inaccurate representation because the notion of family itself was being reconstructed, the written text indicated that family crisis was a result of conditions contributing to the debasement of family. While her presentation recognizes the changing and diverse forms of family, her presentation handout presents the family crisis as a matter of fact and provides a prescription for strengthening the normative family.

The difference between Dr. Han's written and oral texts should be understood in the context of her effort to address the government's interest in family crisis. On a practical level, she probably realized that a remedy should be provided for the suffering that many people go through, regardless of their position in relation to the boundaries of family. Ironically, Dr. Han's double texts called for less stigmatization of alternative family forms while at the same time constructing non-normative families as those that were in crisis. If she intended to highlight the function of family to denaturalize the presumptive boundaries of normative family, she could have further deconstructed the mythical association between the normative family form and the image of a well-functioning family by indicating the prevalence of nonfunctioning "normal" families.

The focus of her presentation was not to question the normative family institution but to provide answers about how to solidify and restore the meaning of the normative family. Her presentation implies that experts' intervention in family breakdown discourses did not digress from the neoliberal project of securing and engineering society through disciplining family. Dr. Han's argument was similar to that put forward by other social engineers and crisis knowledge brokers, such as civil activists, journalists, novelists, filmmakers, and quasi-governmental workers. Like the discourse of family breakdown in the courts, mass media, and social relief campaigns, Dr. Han's argument reflected multifaceted intentions and interactions in the rhetoric of crisis employed in the name of liberalization of the society.

ASSUMPTIONS AND IMAGES OF HOMELESS WOMEN'S NEEDS

Three   The various agencies comprising the social welfare system provide more than material aid. They also provide clients, and the public at large, with a tacit but powerful interpretive map of normative, differentially valued gender roles and gendered needs. Therefore, the different branches of the social state, too, are players in the politics of need interpretation.

NANCY FRASER, "STRUGGLE OVER NEEDS: OUTLINE OF A SOCIALIST-
FEMINIST CRITICAL THEORY OF LATE-CAPITALIST POLITICAL CULTURE"

In the previous chapter, we saw how the discourse on the "family break-down" operated in the making and unmaking of gendered welfare and labor subjects in neoliberal social governing. Homeless women became invisible and women's layoffs became justified in the climate of charging "irresponsible" mothers and female caretakers for "faltering" family solidarity. If city officials, journalists, and experts—as crisis knowledge brokers and social engineers—employed the concept of family breakdown to define who was deserving of welfare, how then did shelter managers and city officials who dealt directly with homeless women understand homeless women's needs?

Nancy Fraser's notion of "needs-talk" is useful in understanding the different positions of the "need" of welfare subjects in microscopic contexts (Fraser 1990). I investigate the gendered assumptions embedded in these narratives of need and argue that, in the continuum of the macro discourse on family breakdown, microscopic narratives of homeless women's needs evince gendered assumptions that render homeless women as either invisible or citizens unworthy of welfare. Although the narratives of city officials and shelter managers were in many ways in conflict, they were nonetheless contributing to establishing homeless women as "undeserving" subjects of welfare.

"Needs-Talk"

Feminist scholars have developed pathbreaking analyses of the gendered welfare state by critically examining discursive representations of social welfare policy in specific historical contexts.[1] In particular, feminist scholars have shown that the workings of the welfare state are linked to an unequal welfare system and the production of deserving and undeserving citizens.[2] Related to this analysis is Fraser's framework for interpreting needs-talk, which helps delineate the boundaries of deserving welfare citizenship and maps out various positions and dynamics among the various actors involved in the creation of welfare policy.

According to Fraser, the U.S. social welfare system can be divided into two gender-linked and unequal subsystems: (1) workmen's compensation, an implicitly "masculine" social insurance subsystem that is tied to primary labor force participation and geared toward white male breadwinners, and (2) mothers' allowance, an explicitly "feminine" social relief subsystem that is tied to household income and geared to homemakers and mothers and their "defective" (that is, female-headed) families (1990: 208; see also Kingfisher 2002:15). For Fraser, women who receive state subsidies are considered needy, and welfare policies accordingly reflect heavily gendered assumptions—in particular, that women's labor belongs to the (unpaid) domestic sphere. Additionally, Fraser (1990: 213) links various interpretations of "needs" to the positions of different social actors: social activists ("oppositional"), administrative officials ("reprivatizational"), and professionals ("expertizational").

My analysis builds upon Fraser's framework by taking this characterization of needs-talk as a departure point for discussing the production of deserving welfare subjects and the positions of various actors participating in the process of homeless policy making in South Korea. However, Fraser's approach is not wholly transferable to the South Korean context. First, her initial argument regarding the masculine social insurance subsystem and feminine social relief subsystem does not adequately describe the welfare system that existed in South Korea during the crisis. While it reflects the system of the precrisis era (from the late 1980s to the mid-1990s), in which male workers of large business corporations received employment benefits, it is important to recognize that subsequent to the crisis (1997 to 2003), the South Korean welfare system changed significantly. In this period, men became the *unprecedented* recipients of state subsidies—unprecedented because it was the first time in state history that welfare as an institution acquired a gendered gloss, in this case by targeting specifically male recipients. South Korean men who received social relief were not framed as being needy in the same way that Fraser's American women were. However, this new welfare system—in which social relief was exclusively provided to South Korean men—nonetheless reproduced the gendered assumption of male as breadwinner and female as homemaker. Despite the varied applications of gendered assumptions in different national policies,[3] gender operates as a key axis of the neoliberal conceptualization of binary personhood—between the nonpoor as "controllable" and "independent" (associated with the masculine) and the poor as "uncontrollable" and "dependent" (associated with the feminine) (Brown 1995; Smith 2007; Smith 1990, cited in Kingfisher 2002).[4]

Another limitation of Fraser's framework in the South Korean context is her rather static characterization of social actors' positions on the interpretation of need. For example, I do not see the position of South Korean social activists as purely oppositional and that of South Korean administrative officials as solely reprivatizing. Instead, I wish to highlight the ambiguous and ambivalent positions of activists and shelter managers that I interviewed as not necessarily in opposition to the city officials. In particular, I analyze how the narratives of various social activists and state administrators were subsumed within the political logic and cultural ethos of neoliberalism, which includes a high regard for employability and rehabilitation.

Two Homeless Women's Narratives: Ms. Kim and Ms. Pak

Although homeless people were not the subjects of my primary research, I am including the narratives of Ms. Kim and Ms. Pak, two homeless women with whom I met briefly. Their narratives are not representative of all homeless women, but they provide an important glimpse into individual women's lives, especially in the absence of research on homeless women beyond an indirect and short-term survey (Seoul City Youth and Women Unemployment Monitoring Team 1999a; Kim Kwang-rye 2001; Kim Su-hyun 2001).

I encountered Ms. Kim in the winter of 1998 at the square. I was speaking with an employee of the Telephone of Love when I noticed Ms. Kim. She was a slim, neatly dressed woman at the front of the line at the service desk, carrying a light backpack. She appeared to be in her late thirties. I asked the welfare agency employee, "How many homeless women have you seen in the square?" She curtly replied, "I have never seen a homeless woman." I was taken aback by the conviction in her voice and pointed to Ms. Kim at the front of the line. The employee seemed irritated by the sight of Ms. Kim and said, "Well, there might be some, but the numbers are small."

I noticed Ms. Kim was completing the agency's questionnaire without assistance, which distinguished her from many other patrons who required help reading and completing the forms. Ms. Kim nervously asked the volunteer if it was necessary to write down her name. After hearing that it was required, she paused for a moment and then wrote down a common Korean woman's name. After submitting her forms, Ms. Kim obtained some supplies from the agency. I saw that she was about to leave and approached her. I asked if she lived in the square. She said, "No, people in the square are not nice. Most women do not stay here. It is really rare for me to come here, but I came today because I heard that some free goods would be distributed. . . . I sleep in W Station,[5] which is warmer. Mostly women gather there, and the guards at the station are much nicer to us."

Ms. Kim told me that approximately thirty women had stayed in W Train Station for years, but that there were often more of them. She herself had been there for over three years. When I asked Ms. Kim if she had a family, she said yes and continued, "I graduated from college and was once married, but I couldn't stand it. I like to live by myself. It's freer to live like this." She also mentioned an experience at a government shelter. She attempted to stay there but left almost immediately because shelter regulations prohibited her from smoking. She stated, "People gave women shit for smoking. It's suffocating there," and again stressed, "I am much freer living by myself like this." Ms. Kim described how she would rather sleep leaning on another woman's back in W Station—even during winter months—than stay at a homeless shelter because of the strict regulations. When I asked her about the other homeless women,

Ms. Kim said their ages ranged from about thirty to fifty and that most were single. However, younger women and teenagers sometimes stayed there for short periods. She then emphasized, "We don't ask about each other's personal stuff. So I don't know about their family situations." When I asked her how she managed to make a living, she said, "It is difficult to get a part-time job these days. I used to work at a small restaurant, washing dishes and doing various errands. But now I can't find anything." After a pause, glancing around the square, she mumbled quietly to herself, "It is amazing to see the change in the way these [government and private welfare agency] people treat us. Who could have known this kind of public welfare [e.g., basic medical treatment, free meals, places to sleep, clothes] would someday be provided? Seeing these changes has made my life 'worthwhile' [Sesang ch'am salgo pollil ida].[6] Huh, it's all due to the IMF crisis, I guess."[7] All of a sudden, she seemed to remember my presence and asked, "Do you have a place to sleep? Do you need help?" I politely said no and she said goodbye and hurried away.[8]

According to the homeless shelter social workers whom I met and interviewed during my research, long-term street people were notorious for "lying," or using various tactics, which included disguise and pretense, to protect themselves and other homeless people they associated with from street violence. From this perspective, some might say that the information relayed by Ms. Kim is neither reliable nor representative of the reality of women living on the street in South Korea. However, following other feminist ethnographers who scrupulously examine the "deception" and "betrayal" of socially marginalized informants (see, for example, Haney 2000; Nelson 2000; Visweswaran 1994), I am interested in looking at how Ms. Kim's story represents the fragmented reality of homeless women living in Seoul.

How should we think about the predicament of homeless women, in particular independent homeless women who do not want to stay in shelters, when an emerging neoliberal welfare regime was being implemented in South Korea? As a long-term street person, Ms. Kim was surprised at the apparent outpouring of attention that was being given to homeless people. What did she think about the distinction that was being made between the IMF homeless and long-term street people, or *purangin*, according to the criteria of "desire to work" and "intention to be rehabilitated"?

Would Ms. Kim's desire to be independent from the state be acknowledged? Would she be recognized as a deserving homeless person since she
clearly expressed a desire to work?

Many of the Seoul city officials and social workers I interviewed in my
study conveyed compelling yet unsettling justifications that ultimately
categorized homeless women as rootless people—even if they (either
single homeless women or homeless mothers) expressed a desire to work.
These justifications were strongly based on gendered assumptions about
men's and women's labor and space—men's productive labor as wage
workers versus women's reproductive and care labor as unpaid workers.
Thus, gendered assumptions were reinforced through the emerging and
pervasive neoliberal welfarism, which was reflected in the homeless policies created during and after the crisis.

Ms. Pak, a homeless woman caring for her two children, resided in a
homeless women's shelter. When I made my second visit to the shelter,
I was introduced to Ms. Pak as she returned from her work at a public
works program. Ms. Pak was a tiny woman with several broken teeth that
hampered her speech. Although she was a little nervous about talking to
me, she was calm, expressive, and consistently portrayed herself as fortu-
nate to be living with benevolent shelter managers. The head of the shelter proudly noted that Ms. Pak was much healthier than before she had
started living at the shelter. When the shelter head added that Ms. Pak was
not fully recovered, but was industrious and responsible for her children,
Ms. Pak modestly said, "I just can't rest all day long inside. To survive and
rear my kids, I have to work. Since I have dealt with sewing machines
(mising irŭl haetta) for ten years, I'm good at it. And most of all, I can work
now, thanks to the staff of this shelter who have treated me well. So I
feel much better. My children and I are so lucky. I would like to tell every
woman in my situation to come here."[9]

Ms. Pak and her children had stayed at an east end subway station for
six months after leaving her home in a big harbor city. For more than ten
years, her husband had been threatening her and her children with death.
Her parents-in-law also participated in the domestic violence.[10] When she
asked officers in the local police branch (p'ach'ulso) for help in preventing
her husband's violence, they did not treat her concern seriously.[11]

Ms. Pak ran away several times, but there were few places in a southern
harbor city where mothers (aegi ŏmmadŭl) and their children could go for

protection. Although there was one shelter for women who suffered from domestic violence in her home city, she was afraid that "the father of [her] children" (aedûl appa) would find them.¹² This caused her to leave the city and stay at several different prayer houses (kidowôn), which are mostly located in the remote countryside or in mountainous areas. When I asked Ms. Pak to tell me about the prayer houses where she stayed, she listed many of the largest ones, the corporate-style churches with huge memberships (sôngdo). Ms. Pak said, "I stayed at all different prayer houses, such as K, N, S, C, and L.¹³ You know these are huge places. Have you been to kidowôn, too?" I answered "yes" after a long pause,¹⁴ and her eyes brightened as if she were now more comfortable telling me about her experience in kidowôn. She then said:

> Each kidowôn has a different system, you know. S kidowôn is open 365 days but does not provide meals. L kidowôn has several branches and makes people commute. For example, on Thursdays a branch of L offered a service and free meals but kicked us out on Fridays and on Mondays the other branch has the same thing. I heard that they even have branches abroad, but not just anybody can go there, though. . . . There were buses to move people in from big cities to kidowôn or from one branch to the other in the case of L kidowôn. I saw many homeless people using the buses and staying at S kidowôn for free meals and sleeping. Once I stayed at C kidowôn—you know, the famous Reverend Lee made it—for a month with my kids, but I couldn't stay longer than that because of saving face [nunch'i ga nômu poyôsô]. After all, if we don't have money to pay for meals at least, we actually could not afford to stay there as long as we want. I mean, there is a limit to staying at kidowôn, too. So, I came to Seoul.¹⁵

Ms. Pak's story demonstrates that domestic violence can be a major reason for women leaving and losing their homes. For women without economic and social resources, there is no safe place to stay long enough to arrange employment and to set up their own households. As noted earlier, research on homeless women is very limited. According to reports from shelter managers, temporary layoffs were not the cause of women going to shelters (Seoul City Youth and Women Unemployment Monitoring Team 1999a; Kim Kwang-rye 2001; Kim Su-hyun 2001). Their reasons for being homeless were similar to those of homeless men in that they had very few socioeconomic resources. However, while homeless men find street living a relatively viable option, homeless women view it as a last resort because of the danger of being exposed to sexual violence (Kim Su-hyun 2001: 4). A government-affiliated report from 2001 that surveyed sixty-one women in homeless women's shelters found that the average single woman was in her forties and women with children were on average in their thirties (ibid: 32). Women stayed from two to twenty-five months at the shelter, although the official limit for homeless shelters is nine months (35). Health assessments by a doctor showed that of 61 women in the shelters, 52.4 percent were physically healthy and 47.6 percent suffered from chronic disease. Only 47.5 percent were mentally healthy; 27.9 percent had a mental disorder; 18.1 percent had a mild emotional instability; 4.9 percent were addicted to alcohol; and 1.6 percent had unspecified problems. Domestic violence was the top reason for being homeless among the sixty-one women (52). The other reasons cited for leaving home, in descending order beginning with the most frequently given, were mental disorders, domestic disputes, "family breakdown," economic difficulty, and desertion by parents when young (53).

We can recall from chapter 2 that the women's hotline for domestic violence did not immediately make a connection between domestic violence, the crisis, and homeless women. However, once unemployment became a major social issue and involved government funding for nongovernmental organizations (NGOs), the hotline announced rocketing rates of domestic violence and an effort was made to link domestic violence to the crisis. The hotline was not the only NGO that lacked awareness of homeless women's issues. Many other women's shelters and agencies—such as shelters for victims of domestic and sexual violence (sŏng p'ongnyŏk p'ihaeja shimt'ŏ), shelters for single mothers (moja poho sisŏl), and shelters for unmarried pregnant women (mihonmo sisŏl)—also internalized mass media and government projections on homelessness and assumed homeless people referred only to men. For example, in the winter of 1999, the Seoul City Youth and Women Unemployment Monitoring Team, the Homeless Women's Shelter Network, and the Temporary City Shelter for Women (TCSW, Ilsi Sirip Punyŏ Pohoso), organized an education session for social workers from women's crisis hotlines and shelters. The educational session was sponsored by a high official in the City Women's Affairs Division. Many of the ninety participants did not know about the existence of homeless women, which indicates a disconcerting unfamiliarity with the very concept of homeless women on the part of workers who likely encountered them daily.[16]

After making phone calls and paying visits to several of these women's shelters in 1999, I became aware that they were overcrowded even before the crisis and could not possibly provide assistance to all the women who knocked on their doors. According to TCSW and homeless women's shelter managers, most homeless women fell through the cracks of the social welfare system either because of the lack of care facilities or because they were unaware of the existence of those agencies (Seoul City Youth and Women Unemployment Monitoring Team 1999a: 99–112).[17] When the Unemployment Monitoring Team suggested to the Seoul City Committee for Unemployment Policies (SCCUP) that the capacity and tenure of various women's shelters should be increased and a connection made between them for long-term housing of homeless women or women in need of protection in general, the City Women's Affairs Division argued that none of the city-sponsored women's shelters were over capacity. However, the city-sponsored shelters for women in need were in a compromised position; due to their need to maintain city funding, they could not complain to the city about deficient facilities. Similar contexts in homeless women's shelters are later exemplified in the narratives of shelter managers.

The History of Social Policy for Women in South Korea

An understanding of the history of South Korean social policy in general and support for women in particular is useful in grasping the context that drove women to the streets, prayer houses, and shelters. Before the crisis, four welfare programs formed the backbone of the Korean welfare system: industrial accident insurance, national health insurance, the public assistance program, and the national pension program (Kwon 1999: 24). Industrial Accident Insurance was introduced as a compulsory program in 1964, and by 1990, 41 percent of employed people were covered by the program. National health insurance was introduced in 1965 as an experiment; by 1977 it was made compulsory and in 1989 it became universal. The public assistance program was enacted in 1965, and the national pension program was introduced in 1988.

In the broader welfare structure, a governmental transformation in conjunction with the Asian Debt Crisis made the welfare state a focal point for reformation. Compared with the previous welfare system, which was superficially and partially developed, the emergency welfare scheme under the Kim Dae Jung regime developed a concrete and balanced plan for a welfare state, accompanied by rapid implementation. The Kim Dae Jung administration did not merely enliven existing programs, but made major changes to the largest welfare programs. In particular, the health insurance, national pension, and employment insurance systems were nearly universalized, requiring a sweeping expansion of human and financial resources. Service distribution was effectively rearranged, although it created conflicts among various social-interest groups (for example, between the doctors' association and the pharmacists' association, between local health insurance agencies and private health insurance agencies, and between the taxpayers and the government [H. Song 2003; Wong 2004]).

Despite these significant developments, the responsibility of family units for their members' economic and welfare security was not reduced. Rather, during the crisis, the discourse of family breakdown tended to intensify the duty of family responsibility (see chapter 2). However, the regime claimed to deal with the double focus of economic prosperity and a welfare society through a cost-effective welfare system with optimum coverage, namely productive welfarism.

The public assistance program, dubbed "cash benefits," has neither expanded substantially nor changed, retaining means-tested applications with the addition of a homeless policy as an emergency measure. The history of constructing the public assistance program before the crisis was more likely an addition of legitimized groups entitled to receive subsidy (for example, veterans, children, women—mostly mothers without male breadwinners, the disabled, adolescents, and the elderly). Although employment insurance was dramatically expanded during the crisis (the insurance began by covering workers employed in small workplaces with more than five employees), it was too late to benefit workers laid off from small companies who did not begin their insurance payments long enough before the crisis. In addition, temporary or part-time workers were not included in the program expansion, which had enormous effects on women, who made up the majority of those in irregular and unstable jobs.

The public assistance program is a means-tested program providing benefits to low-income people. The program classifies recipients into four categories, according to earning ability. The first category includes those who have no earning ability and have to stay in public residential institutions (either temporarily or semipermanently) because of old age, mental disability, unwed pregnancy, domestic and sexual violence, or "vagabondage." The second category refers to people who have no earning ability but live in their own homes. The third category indicates working poor who can earn but live in poverty.[18] Single mothers with children and women arrested for prostitution are in this category. Finally, the fourth category includes people who are beneficiaries of free medical treatment. In principle, the first and second categories receive monthly income support (in 2008, approximately $370 for single households and $1,050 for households with four members); the third category receives an amount that is between the amount of the recipient's income and minimum living expenses; and all four categories receive limited medical support and educational support for children up to the middle-school level.[19] However, most eligible people in the first category do not manage to receive cash benefits because information about their benefits and medical and educational support is not widely publicized.[20]

Notably, people in the third category (the working poor) are entitled to job-training programs, food support, family allowance, and extra cash for the transitional period between training and getting a job. Participation in job-training programs increased up until the late 1980s but tended to decrease in the 1990s due to the unpopularity of these types of training programs (for example, low-skilled blue-collar, 3 D — dirty, difficult, and dangerous—jobs, and typically gendered jobs, such as sewers or needle workers, cooks, and bakers). The job-training program, one of the most featured elements of the government's unemployment policy during the crisis, was heavily criticized from the moment it was introduced.

There are two stages in the application process. First, the potential beneficiary makes his or her own claim. Then, the smallest unit of local administration, the ward office (tong samuso), officially verifies the claim. However, awareness of the public assistance program was low among poor and illiterate people. Therefore, informal contacts through social workers or between local governmental administrators and residents played a significant role in claims and the verification of recipients.[21] In particular, homeless women who move around a lot, in order to hide, have little access to these resource networks. Without a broad promotional campaign and systemic support through long-term shelters for homeless women, outreach for these transient women is difficult.[22] Even for those who managed to register, the cash benefits were far too little to survive. Although there were four distinct categories, some eligible people received mixed benefits. For instance, single mothers in poverty and women who were arrested for prostitution were either provided with an opportunity to stay in a public residential institute (for the single mothers) or compulsorily housed (for sex workers).

Here, it is critical to note that one of the major characteristics of the public assistance program before the crisis was its gendered nature; women were additionally protected by the maternalist social policies.[23] This is the context in which I mark South Korean social policy, in particular the public assistance program, as maternalist. Yet it also makes sense to call it a "paternalist" welfare regime, according to the state's provision of benefits to mostly female-headed families without male breadwinners.[24] However, during the crisis, when the weak foundation of social policies exploded, productive welfarism seemingly changed the gendered objects of public assistance without adding a regular entitlement group. The previous female-centered public assistance and male-centered work compensation programs changed during the crisis through a homeless policy designed basically for men, with no expansion of support for the increased numbers of women in need. Instead of expanding the regular entitlement group within public assistance, the government administration implemented emergency welfare policies. In other words, the way in which the government dealt with the issues of livelihood protection was not by expanding the public assistance program, but by utilizing emergency funds for public works programs (that is, workfare).

The Needs-Talk of Government Officials

Seoul city officials used the rationale of numbers to legitimize their indifference to homeless women in need. During a SCCUP meeting in September 1998, a member of the Subcommittee on Youth and Women's Unemployment inquired about the population of homeless women in Seoul. Mr. Lee, the chief official of the Health and Welfare Bureau, replied that there were no homeless women in South Korea. He declared that although there might be some homeless women belonging to IMF homeless families, there were no single homeless women living on the streets. When asked if the city knew how many women were included in the homeless families, Mr. Lee said that there was no way of knowing because the city had not collected numbers and personal records according to gender. He added that he could only determine the number of homeless women by phoning every homeless shelter "one by one," implying that the work would be very onerous and therefore impossible to carry out. However, the chair of the SCCUP, who was also a vice-mayor of Seoul (recruited by the new mayor, who was strongly connected to the Kim Dae Jung administration), requested that Mr. Lee give an answer to the question at the next monthly meeting.[25] The vice-mayor's support for the SCCUP member's demand implies that the partnership between GOs and NGOs, a major neoliberal technology of social governing, was ushered in within the context of a democratizing administration under President Kim Dae Jung and Mayor Ko, as chapter 1 describes.

At the next meeting, Mr. Lee begrudgingly revised his remarks about the nonexistence of homeless women, stating: "There are homeless women but there are only a few and their numbers are nothing compared to those of homeless men" (original emphasis). He added that the city government had generously created four shelters for homeless women, which were not and never would be fully occupied.[26] I later discovered that the four shelters had been established through the efforts of people such as Reverend Kang, a feminist religious social activist and a member of an association of NGOs known as the Council on Homelessness, rather than by the Seoul city government.[27]

Mr. Lee's trivialization of the numbers of homeless women conflicted with the new welfare state policy, the Law to Guarantee a Minimal Standard of Living to National Citizens (Kungmin Kicho Saenghwal Pojang Pŏp). Those who were designated as IMF homeless were to receive public benefits, regardless of being a small percentage of the unemployed. In fact, Mr. Lee's "few" homeless women amounted to 125 people out of the 4,000 people housed in homeless shelters in 1999. The number of women living on the street was about 3 percent of the reported number of homeless people in Seoul during the crisis. However, the total number of homeless people reported was less than 1 percent of the number of working poor who lived under the poverty level (about 500,000 people) and were in need of immediate cash support but neglected.[28] Apparently, the designation of numbers as the critical basis on which to verify the significance of welfare subjects was selectively used to promote short-term homeless men as deserving welfare citizens.

It is problematic to measure the significance of homeless women's issues based upon their limited attendance in homeless shelters. Social institutes for vagabonds reported that more than 30 percent of their clients were women (Kim Su-hyun 2001).[29] Counting only sheltered homeless people follows the logic that distinguished the deserving homeless from rootless people, which remained the primary rationale for failing to address and acknowledge the needs of homeless women and the rootless as legitimate homeless people.

By contrast, the numbers of IMF homeless, homeless men who had supposedly been laid off, were interpreted to be significant. Yet these numbers were small in comparison to the number of jobless people whose subsistence level was precarious and who were living in poverty. This kind of reasoning enabled the city government to present its new policy directives as a timely response to the crisis. At the same time, the emphasis on addressing the needs of the IMF homeless enabled the government to deflect attention from the massive problem of the working poor.

The Needs-Talk of Shelter Managers

The city officials' inability to conceive of women living outside of normative family and gender roles prevented them from viewing homeless women as potentially valuable contributors to society, at least in terms of paid work. However, shelter managers' narratives regarding homeless women's need were not homogeneous. In this section, I provide narratives of four shelter managers who spent a considerable amount of time working with homeless women in Seoul. All four were involved in running shelters for homeless women and women in need.

DIRECTOR WON AND MS. HAH: HUMANITARIAN VIEWS
OF HOMELESS WOMEN'S NEEDS

Director Won was the head volunteer of Swallow House, a shelter for homeless women created during the crisis, largely funded by a Buddhist organization and run by Buddhist social activists. I was introduced to Director Won through Reverend Kang, who had been my initial contact as the leader of the network of homeless women's shelters. At the onset of the crisis, Reverend Kang had submitted a proposal to the city government requesting the creation of separate shelters that addressed the needs of diverse groups of homeless women. Her proposal was rejected. As a result, the Homeless Women's Shelter Network discussed how they could serve different kinds of homeless women more effectively. In the early fall of 1998, members of the network decided to designate separate shelters for women who were accompanied by children, and for those who were alone. Two shelters were allocated to women with children and two, including Swallow House, for women on their own. Each shelter was managed differently, in terms of regulations on smoking, drinking, dating, and curfew. Like many other homeless shelters formed during the crisis, Swallow House was run by an NGO but received subsidies from the city (such as wages for temporary managers in the shelters) under the same regulations applying to public works programs (see preface). In addition, to receive subsidies the shelters were required to house a minimum number of homeless people (twenty to thirty).

While Director Won was acting as head of the shelter, Ms. Hah was the actual manager and lived at the shelter. Director Won indicated that the lack of visibility of homeless women was likely related to the increased risk of sexual harassment faced by single homeless women.[30] She explained that homeless women who were independent and more experienced living on the streets would avoid places frequented by homeless men to avert the threat of sexual violence. Director Won's comments were consistent with those of Ms. Kim, who avoided the train station due to the hostility of men there.

Director Won said that despite the risk of sexual abuse, there was a lack of supervision at most homeless gathering places. She used the expression mubôpchidae to describe these unregulated places, which literally means "lawless." Director Won also noted that homeless women who stayed with homeless men were often pregnant as a result of either consensual sex or rape. She said that it was necessary for her to "recruit" homeless women because city officials repeatedly checked the numbers of homeless women that used the shelter and threatened to discontinue the subsidy if the shelter was not full.[31] However, the staff at Swallow House refused to depend entirely upon the government system, particularly upon the public works program, in order to subvert these regulations. For example, they often referred job-seeking homeless women to personal networks (such as small companies rather than to public works programs). Ms. Hah, who was hired as a temporary manager with a public works program subsidized by the city, also said they tried to link homeless women to small businesses because the relatively higher wages offered by the public works programs would "spoil" homeless women. Although Swallow House staff assisted homeless women in finding work, they nonetheless deemed them to be deserving only of limited wages.

In contrast to the views expressed by many of the city officials, Director Won was relatively positive in her evaluations of homeless women's "sanity." Rather than explicitly pathologizing homeless women, Director Won claimed that their capacity for self-management was demonstrated through their personal hygiene and their strategic decision making around issues of safety and protection from the threat of sexual violence. For example, she said, "They protect themselves from those men or others by looking dirty. However, despite their filthy faces and outer clothes, we found that independent, homeless women's underwear was really clean and they kept their bodies pretty clean." On the other hand, both Director Won and Ms. Hah spoke about the "deception" and "unreliability" of homeless women. They remarked that because homeless women lied so frequently, shelter managers had a difficult time taking them seriously. In particular, Director Won stated, "In order to prevent [homeless women] from misusing us, at least some kind of regulation, such as no smoking or alcohol and curfews, is needed." Thus, although Director Won and Ms. Hah mentioned some positive attributes of homeless women, their perceptions were still largely consistent with the more negative perceptions held by city officials in terms of seeing homeless women as deceivers, and therefore undeserving of full welfare services.

MS. CHIN: STANDBYS AND THE TERMINALLY ILL

Ms. Chin was the director of the Temporary City Shelter for Women (TCSW), a shelter funded by the city government with a capacity of 250 beds. I contacted Ms. Chin to explore the situation in women's shelters after my conversation with Ms. Pang from the Team for Women in Need at the city administration (discussed in chapter 2). Ms. Chin told me that at the outset of the crisis, her biggest challenge was to maintain the TCSW as a public service and retain her employees. She said the TCSW was one of the primary city-sponsored agencies being targeted for privatization and the reduction of personnel. Ms. Chin had only recently heard of the term IMF *homeless* and it was not as familiar as the category of the rootless. She noted that the majority of women who stayed at the TCSW did not match the image of homeless people that was portrayed by the government and in the media. About 90 percent of women staying at the TCSW were older women who had been diagnosed with a mental disorder or dementia (*ch'imae halmôni*); the other approximately 10 percent of the residents were runaway girls (*kach'ul sonyô*) and terminally ill women in their thirties and forties.

When I asked Ms. Chin to describe the inhabitants of the TCSW, she identified two categories of women. She termed the first group "rootless women" (*purang yôsông*), or women who had no option other than staying in a shelter because they were incapable of looking after themselves. She referred to the second group as "homeless women" (*yôsông nosukcha*), who were seeking shelter but left the TCSW almost immediately after realizing that they did not belong among rootless women. Ms. Chin explained: "Those independent women just know right away that they are different from the *ch'imae halmôni* (senile, older women) or 'rootless women' here." Ms. Chin said independent homeless women did not want to stay at the TCSW because they were "standbys, people who sojourn until they can resume their normal social life." Interestingly, Ms. Chin used the rhetoric of "standbys waiting to reenter society" to describe homeless people, which was similar to how Mr. Yang from the Homeless Policy Division described homeless people in chapters 1 and 2. Both Ms. Chin and Mr. Yang presented these as qualities that distinguished IMF homeless from rootless people. However, Ms. Chin's and Mr. Yang's descriptions of "appropriate" subjects and their "proper" places differed. For example, Ms. Chin indicated the possibility of including women in the category of IMF homeless, surmising that independent homeless women who did not find the TCSW suitable for their needs would eventually find ways to resume their former lives. By comparison, Mr. Yang did not consider the possibility that street women could become self-sufficient.

Throughout my interviews, subjects of homelessness were dichotomized by gender, and "appropriate" places of belonging for women and men were differently imagined. Ms. Chin's portrayal described independent homeless women as wanting to pursue their lives on the street, rather than being confined to public institutions. This contrasted with the perceptions of Mr. Yang and Ms. Pang, who ascribed independence and employability as characteristics that distinguished deserving from unde-serving homeless subjects, necessarily excluding homeless women be-cause they fell outside of normative marriage and family structures. Both Mr. Yang and Ms. Pang promoted the idea of homeless men as deserving welfare recipients by describing their potential to be rehabilitated—that is, to live in normative families as primary breadwinners.

What is particularly striking about these narratives is how they all share a high regard for domestic living. This assessment was applied to both genders; overall, men were promoted as wage earners and women as docile homemakers. However, the narratives given by city officials fo-cused on rehabilitation into a normative family structure more than on self-sufficiency and employability for homeless women. Thus, in the face of the drive to rehabilitate women into docile homemakers, women's independence and desire to work was not counted as a qualification for becoming a neoliberal welfare recipient. The fact that the attainment of a normative domestic lifestyle was a requirement gauged specifically for women is a clear example of how neoliberal welfare social governing was built on and reinforced the gendered division of labor in the heteronor-mative family.

REVEREND KANG: MOMMY'S PAIN

I met Reverend Kang through a colleague, and immediately recognized that she was someone who could help me understand the politics of home-less women in and outside of the city administration.[32] She had ten years' experience as a minister serving in an industrial area, during which she observed and shared the destitution of women living and working in the area. A female reverend—an unusual vocation for a woman—Reverend Kang was the first "social safety net" activist to raise homeless women's needs in Seoul in the spring of 1998. A member of the City Commission on Homeless Policy, which consisted mostly of community activists, Rev-erend Kang volunteered to run the first emergency shelter for homeless women. She organized the Homeless Women's Shelter Network (Yôsông Nosukcha Shimtô Yôndae), which consisted of eight homeless women and family shelters (six shelters sponsored by the city government and two additional shelters without government support). Women's shelters belonging to the network were run mostly by civil activists, religious orga-nizations, or private welfare institutes, whether or not they received government funding. Her exposure to the collective grievances of clients of the Homeless Women's Shelter Network gave Reverend Kang an insight into the invisibility of homeless women. Her tentative explanation was that many abused women came to be homeless after wandering between relatives' houses, inns, all-night church services (ch'ôryayebae), and prayer houses (kidowôn).

In the name of partnership between civil society and government in the Kim Dae Jung regime, the city of Seoul originally planned to entrust the responsibility of managing homeless shelters to renowned NGOs and nonprofit organizations (NPOs). The city relied especially on religious groups, including the Chogye Order (the largest Buddhist denomination in South Korea), the Roman Catholic Church, the Anglican Church, and the Protestant Church. However, within a month of the start of the homeless policy, due to the need for an immediate response to the crisis, the city changed its strategy and opted for a bureaucratic top-down process.[33]

The city subsidized homeless shelters run by about one hundred welfare agencies that had been connected to the city welfare structure. Although some civil groups volunteered to open shelters, the city did not help them overcome any bureaucratic difficulties. For example, when Reverend Kang found a place for the shelter and needed to sign a one-year lease,[34] the city did not provide the down payment in time, as city officials had promised: the "proper procedure" (chôlch'a) of bureaucratic process resulted in six months' procrastination.[35]

Reverend Kang went to various levels of local government for assistance with this financial problem. However, none of the city (sich'ông), district (kuch'ông), and ward office (tongsamuso) officials were helpful. Reverend Kang interpreted the situation this way: "I do not think all city, district, and ward office officials intended not to help us. But unfortunately ward office officials, who more closely understand the situation we are in, do not have enough authority to exert control over this issue [unsin ûi p'ok i chopta]. And city officials, who have the power, just don't understand our difficulty."

Although the city invited civil activists to help manage homeless issues in the name of "partnership between governmental organizations (GOs) and NGOs," the two were not necessarily equivalent in the power structure. When entering an unfamiliar working relationship, civil activists had a tendency to experience bureaucratic gatekeeping from governmental officials. The new relationship was hard on civil activists, especially when they were subjects of the officials' financing and auditing. This is an example of a consequence of neoliberalization in that the state's administrative authority was not diminished, despite involving more civil powers than the previous interventionist state regime.

In addition to difficulties occasioned by unequal power dynamics between the administration and civil activists, Reverend Kang said that she faced barriers in making government officials understand the diverse needs of homeless women. Reverend Kang asked city officials if she could run separate shelters for lone women and for women with children, such as two adjacent units in a building, or multiple rooms in a house. According to Reverend Kang, homeless women who left their children at home suffered from "mommy's pain" (emi pyông).[36] She said that homeless women who had left their children were upset and psychologically worse off when they had to live in the same room as homeless women and their children.

However, the city refused, instead lumping all homeless women together as rootless, implying that they did not deserve much funding. Reverend Kang's maternalism, which understood homeless women who have left their children as still in the realm of proper motherhood, contested the city officials' maternalism, which framed them as improper mothers.

Reverend Kang also noted the gendered impasse of the city officials' understanding of homeless women's needs. The officials' measurement of numbers of homeless people per shelter was inaccurate because they standardized the capacity and equipment based upon the condition of healthy men who merely needed a place to sleep and food when they came back from work.[37] Many homeless women, she said, also had a "desire to work" (kûlloûiyok), but they needed to rest and regain their health first, which took some time. They needed special care in what she called a recovery/rehabilitation shelter (chahwal/chaehwal shimt'ô).

Reverend Kang thought that most homeless women living on the street had strong characters and had lost the ability to express their emotions. She also said that many of them had serious blood circulation problems from the cold that would cause harm to their reproductive organs. Her shelter made a rule requiring shelter residents to attend morning prayer services to motivate them and prepare them to recover. Reverend Kang strongly recommended government aid to foster both their psychological and physical recovery. She mobilized the governmental discourse of rehabilitation and employability to tap into the special funds available for homeless people. Reverend Kang is a good example of Korean intellectuals whose dilemma I discuss in detail in chapter 5: intellectuals with liberal intentions who ended up consolidating neoliberal welfare society. By labeling needed homeless women's shelters as recovery shelters, Reverend Kang not only took advantage of the official catchphrases of "rehabilitation" and "employability," but reaffirmed the official representation of homeless women as pathological and not inherently deserving.[38]

On the one hand, Reverend Kang contested the productive welfare regime's gendered valuation of employability and its negative deployment of maternalism. Her gender-specific concerns and recommendations included attending to "mommy's pain," establishing "recovery shelters," and educating children who were in shelters with their mothers. On the other hand, her endorsement of the emphasis on "desire to work" resulted in excluding the possibility of street life as an independent way of living. When she maneuvered governmental financial support by suggesting a recovery shelter as the solution for homeless women, she confirmed the pathological view and the logic of the rehabilitation of homeless people. In addition, the way Reverend Kang located the "proper" motherhood of homeless women within the image of the normative family strongly corresponded to the broader concern for family breakdown. In a sense, Reverend Kang's narrative supports the Korean welfare system, in which family functions as the primary institution responsible for social and individual wellness (particularly for mental health).[39]

The connection Reverend Kang draws between family support and the need to build a social support system for individual well-being is symptomatic of the liberal ideas that burgeoned among civil activists after the democratization movement in 1987 and culminated in social management during the Asian Debt Crisis. Reverend Kang, a pioneering civil activist, also relied heavily on the long-standing normative family institution as the foundation of social management during the crisis. Like governmental officials, she employed crisis discourse as a device to orchestrate emergency social governing.

Gender and Neoliberal Welfarism

My analysis of needs-talk by city administrators and shelter managers reveals their varying perceptions of homeless women's needs and competing assessments of whether homeless women were deserving welfare subjects. While these narratives differ in terms of how homeless women's existence was perceived, they are consistent in ascribing significant moral value to women's place in the home. In this particular historical context, such moral judgments helped reconfigure welfare policy in South Korea, reflecting a gendered neoliberal logic that constituted homeless women as undeserving citizens. Simultaneously, the new category of IMF homeless served to differentiate homeless men, who subsequently were deemed to be deserving welfare subjects. City officials and some social workers in shelters for homeless women assessed homeless women's legitimacy as welfare citizens by applying the criteria of employability, which was the same parameter used to identify deserving homeless men. City officials' narratives also pathologized independent homeless women as improper or immoral subjects and therefore irrelevant, whereas self-sufficient homeless men were considered the most deserving subjects. In this manner, homeless women were not considered deserving welfare citizens because they represented the antithesis of gendered norms, even if they were employable.

City officials and homeless shelter workers relied heavily on moral scripts that confined women to the domestic sphere. I maintain that such narratives reveal their support for the traditional family norms in South Korea, including maternalism. The high value placed on maternalism is not a new social value in South Korea; rather, it is a long-standing ethos that is based on a Confucian patriarchal social structure (Cho 1986, 1988; Haboush 1991).[40] However, while previous welfare regimes employed similar gender norms as a way to extend welfare benefits to mothers and women who fell outside of traditional marriage and family structures, Kim Dae Jung's productive welfarism deployed standards of maternity and other gendered norms to limit the extension of state benefits to homeless women. In this context, statistics, moralistic judgment, and pathologization were deployed to justify the relegation of homeless women to the status of undeserving welfare citizens.

Four

If there is a common thread linking the many late twentieth-century projects of neo-liberal reform, both within particular states and in the international arena, it lies in the attempt to introduce not only market and quasi-market arrangements but also empowerment, self-government and responsibility into areas of social life which had hitherto been organized in other ways—the corporatisation and privatisation of state agencies, the use of financial markets (and credit-rating agencies) to regulate the conduct of the states, the promotion of competition and individual choice in health, education and other areas of what Western states once regarded as the proper sphere of social policy, etc.

BARRY HINDESS, "LIBERALISM: WHAT'S IN A NAME?"

I will now focus on the relationship between welfare society and labor population control in the neoliberal discursive formation of "self-manageable," "self-enterprising" subjects. This chapter traces the social governing of underemployed young adults in relation to the way South Korean conglomerate-centered industrial capital is challenged by finance capital based on venture business and investment markets. The late 1990s were the time of the dot-com boom, when start-up companies financed by venture capital were on the rise in the United States and other technologically advanced countries. South Korea went through this trend in the middle of the Asian Debt Crisis and took advantage of growing finance capital to resolve the country's economic recession. Along with industrial and financial restructuring during the crisis, the Kim Dae Jung government also coordinated welfare programs for young adults. Youth were envisioned as a central work force in the future information and communication technology industry that would enable the national economy to survive in global capitalism.[1]

I have shown how the making of the neoliberal homeless subject during the crisis is a good example of welfare-labor coordination, in that governing homelessness (that is, distinguishing "deserving" homeless people through criteria of employability and capacity for rehabilitation) was a technology for managing a surplus labor population. Simply put, the neoliberal welfare governing of homelessness was synchronized with controlling an unstable population and molding a component of that population into commodifiable labor power. However, whereas governing homelessness was a *reactionary* welfare measure to prevent a bottom-class threat to social security, governing youth underemployment was a *proactive* attempt by the South Korean capitalist state to nurture and organize a post-Fordist labor population.

Throughout the democratized period and especially during the crisis, individual-centered work aspirations (that is, formation of venture companies)[2] and sociopolitical spaces (for example, identity politics or the consumer movement) were no longer regarded as "selfish" or "destructive," as they had been labeled in large conglomerates and in the antistate political movements in the past (see chapter 5; Abelmann 1996; Janelli 1993). The crisis, and the subsequent neoliberal governing, concluded the transformation of the mode of South Korean capitalist production. New markets, industries, entrepreneurs, and labor populations were sought to replace the developmental state, and adjust to post-Fordist global market competition. Venture companies and businesses emerged as an alternative to the mass-production, industrial form of large conglomerates; continuously changing jobs in small enterprises emerged as an alternative to stable employment in a big company. Venture capital boomed as a new finance capitalist method of investment through domestic and international short-term funds and bonds.[3]

Through using the Internet, industries of service, information, and knowledge prevailed over the manufacturing industry's use of personal sales representatives. Praise was heaped on those who engendered new ideas and cultured new markets by opening their own small businesses, risking instability. They were regarded positively as "creative" (ch'angjojôk), and as "new intellectuals" (sin chisigin). In a similar vein, people who were exposed to cosmopolitan communication skills, such as the Internet,

English, and traveling abroad were dubbed the "new generation." They were touted as a generation that had the potential to survive continuously challenging times, and thus, to undertake and potentially overcome an unstable employment environment and lifestyle.

In this context, "underemployed young adults" conjured up the image of a new generation and "new intellectuals" who deserved a welfare subsidy through public works programs specially designed for them. This was in distinction from idling underemployed youth labeled "good-for-nothings" (paeksu). New intellectuals were deserving welfare subjects who presented the possibilities of being transformed into entrepreneurs or workers in venture businesses and companies that represented a new mode of capitalist production. Here, the object of entrepreneurship was not just the small and innovative businesses they would open. More importantly, the object of entrepreneurship was their individual selves, whose very bodies became subject to the autonomous terrain of self-governing (thus, "entrepreneurship of the self"). This is where the subjectification of the individual through discourses of "self-management" (chagi kwalli) and "self-cultivation" (chagi kyebal) operated as a pivotal technology of neoliberal governing (Seo 2005).[4]

This chapter aims to show how the discursive engineering of neoliberal subjectivity into the "self-governable" (that is, independent, flexible, and creative) subject facilitated the connection between the welfare programming of underemployed youth (in tension with the trope of "new intellectuals") and the capitalist state's appropriation of a labor population for "venture industry." The neoliberal governing, through entrepreneurship of the self, linked welfare to labor and industrial domains. A concrete example of this is the way in which the members of the Youth and Women Unemployment Monitoring Team experienced being state subjects (as underemployed youth working in a public works program) at the same time as being state agents (as government temporary researchers on the subject of underemployed youth) in the production of deserving underemployed young adults.

Entrepreneurship of the Self:
Between Productive Welfare and Precarious Labor

If the homeless population was imagined as the bottom rank of unemployment and engineered as potential labor for low-paid, unstable work, then underemployed youth were envisioned and mobilized as promising laborers for high-income, flexible labor in the era of a technology- and knowledge-centered global market. While homeless people were assigned to the lowest-income public works programs, such as cleaning highways or natural environments, underemployed youth were assigned work in higher-income public works programs such as the data digitalization project (*chôngbohwa saôp*) or offered work doing research to promote new markets or public goods (for example, the work of the Unemployment Monitoring Team).

To be deserving welfare citizens in neoliberal social governing, both welfare populations (the homeless and underemployed youth) were encouraged to be self-sufficient, rather than dependent on the state, and were appropriated and forced to join precarious job markets. However, the way in which self-sufficiency was implied and imposed on underemployed young adults was different from its meaning for and projection onto homeless people. For the homeless population, self-sufficiency was reduced to simply being "employable" at the bottom of existing low-waged, unstable job markets and capable of being rehabilitated by accepting the heteronormative family order as male breadwinner or caregiving mother (see chapters 2 and 3). For the underemployed youth population, who were exposed to cosmopolitan media and technology such as the Internet, self-sufficiency was aimed at enhancing and presenting oneself as being self-employable through creating new businesses and markets (that is, venture companies) or being employable in a rapidly evolving, irregular job market within the knowledge industry. In addition to the promotion of this entrepreneurship of the self and of creativity with commercial value, flexibility and adaptability to a risky and unpredictable lifestyle and employment were imposed on the underemployed young adults. Their labor power was acknowledged as promising and valuable rather than seen as diminishing the male breadwinner's authority and the normative social order.

The nature of the precariousness of each of these two welfare-labor populations was distinct. The instability of minimum wage work that homeless people were engineered to participate in, as competing disposable workers, derived from the operation of the marginal job market. Minimum wage workers themselves had no control over the marginal job market and did not cause the instability. However, the precariousness of venture company workers or entrepreneurs originated in the very way in which their employment depended on their own capacity for maneuvering, inventiveness, and adaptation. Therefore, they themselves became implicated in their own precariousness.

The precariousness engendered through "entrepreneurship of the self" illuminates the relevance of a limitation of Foucauldian governmentality. On the one hand, as Akhil Gupta notes, "the goal of 'good government' is not merely the exercise of authority over the people within a territory or the ability to discipline and regulate them but the fostering [of] their prosperity and happiness" (2001: 67). Foucault (1990) illuminates the liberal invention of governing technologies through biopower—the notion that governing power is legitimized through protection of life rather than threat of death. Examples of such liberal governing technologies include the regulation of health and the promotion of the quality of living. Foucault notes that this form of governing operates through quasi- or non-state agencies, and particularly through individuals that decenter state power by constructing self-regulation and correction from inside (that is, "subjectification of the body," "conduct of conduct"), rather than by direct intervention of the centralized state machinery (Burchell 1996; Gordon 1991). Thus, self-governing, such as entrepreneurship of the self, is a key technique for diffusing power and garnering social members' consensus in the liberal governing of a population (Foucault 1988).

However, when Foucault asserts a "positive" sense of power as opposed to a "domineering" sense of power (that is, surveillance), he does not go into the connection between nurturing populations through a welfare state and the effects of a nurtured population in a capitalist labor market. A liberal state operating in a market economy (that is, a capitalist state) is not only benevolent but also coercive, because it enhances the commodification and exploitation of labor power (Brunhoff 1976; Perelman 2000). Productive welfarism in a South Korean neoliberal welfare state fostered a particular welfare subject (such as underemployed youth) as an investment in and cultivation of a "productive" labor population that would maximize national capital in the post-Fordist capitalist production mode. With empowered individual agency, individuals became responsible for their own employment and survival. These autonomous individuals became micro-engineers of "productive" labor as a whole and involved themselves in the appropriation and exploitation of surplus labor power.

The South Korean welfare policy and public discourse on underemployed young adults explicates the process of neoliberal subjectification of the "entrepreneurship of the self." Specific public works programs (for example, the data digitalization project) and the discourses of "new intellectuals" and "venture company and capital" are concrete examples.

An underemployed youth or young adult did not simply stand for a young person in need of emergency welfare benefits. The components of creativity, flexibility, and capacity for self-management were considered the key features of an individual who could devise new commodities for the global market or advanced cost-effective technologies of production and distribution. This enabled a reorganization of the value of labor power in various sociopolitical domains, including the education system. Since democratization, notions of "autonomy" (*chayulsŏng*), "creativity" (*ch'angŭisŏng*), "individual character as an asset" (*kaesŏng*), "citizen's rights" (*simin ŭi kwŏlli*) or "human rights" (*inkkwŏn*), "ownership" (*onŏ*), and a "new generation" (*sin sedae*) have become prevalent markers describing liberal individuals, and thus have affected the direction of the education system (Abelmann 1996; Park and Abelmann 2004).

During the crisis, with the democratization grounding of a liberal social ethos, "management of self" (*chagi kwalli*) and the "entrepreneurial spirit for successful self-realization" (*ch'angŏp chŏngsin*) became the salient rhetoric beyond the existential recognition of the significance of the liberal self. This aggressive cultivation of the liberal self through self-disciplining processes was prescribed as a way of breaking through the difficulties in the job market and in business and industry during the crisis. The management of self entailed beautification of the body with physical exercise, regardless of gender or vocation; development of skills for the efficient organization of time and scheduling (for example, by use of the Franklin Planner, a professional daily calendar, as a way of building the self to be an efficient enterprise); presentation of a professional and marketable self-image; further education for proficiency in computer and Internet technology as well as in languages, such as English (and in some cases, Japanese and Chinese); and exposure to cosmopolitan culture and media through travels abroad and watching foreign TV programs (Arai 2005; Muraki 2003; Takeyama 2005). By and large, notions of self-sufficiency framed underemployed youth as a population responsible for their own success or failure.

During the crisis, I attended an event that illustrates the diagnostic use of the liberal rhetoric of self-management in the context of a neoliberal imposition of a limited job market. The Presidential Commission for Women's Affairs (PCWA, now the Ministry of Gender Equality) hosted a seminar, "Realities and Problems of Female College Graduates Looking for Jobs, and Solutions through Alternative Policy-making," in November 1998. It was celebrated as the first official function of the PCWA after its historic launch; its very establishment came across as a sign of gender democracy in the Kim Dae Jung administration. This event marked the first government recognition of the difficulties of young adult women facing severe gender discrimination in job markets. Following the PCWA director's opening remarks about the significance of gender equality, two of the panelists failed to address women's unemployment as a structural issue. One of the panelists focused in detail on how to "decorate a resume in a feminine manner." Rather than encouraging female college students to strengthen their professional skills, her presentation urged young women to comply with gendered norms of self-representation. In a similar vein, the other panelist was proud of having introduced a class on "women and employment" at the coed college where she was an associate professor. Her main goal for the course was to teach female college students "appropriate manners," such as the respectful greeting of elder male colleagues. Her message was clear. Highly educated women cannot get jobs because of their "problematic" attitudes toward their superiors, who are almost always men (problematic attitudes referred to not greeting superiors or greeting them without full respect). The two women panelists focused on the importance of women's individual effort within a traditional patriarchal framework, without pointing out structural/policy-level limitations that disproportionately affected women. Their understanding of "being employable" sustained and reproduced conservative gender norms. In spite of the seminar's focus on solutions through alternative policy making, the panelists ignored the issue of accountability at the level of the state administration.

The PCWA officials who organized the event failed to acknowledge the problem of individualizing the issue of young women's unemployment and the contradictions between the presentations and the founding mandate of the PCWA. In addition, the audience itself did not disagree with the speakers' approaches (perhaps due to the fact that, as I discovered later, many students were given course credits for attending the event by professor panelists at the event). PCWA officials were satisfied with the fact that they had held the first PCWA-sponsored seminar. In a follow-up phone conversation with a PCWA official, I learned she was a labor policy specialist who believed that a rise in the employment rate would solve the other social issues of the crisis (including women's issues) and that men and women faced the same difficulties entering the job market. She said not one gender discrimination complaint had been recognized by the Ministry of Labor so far. In this context, the PCWA official believed that individualized tips for self-management were convenient and practical ways to address issues of young women's unemployment. This focus on achieving self-sufficiency, regardless of the structural issues, was a prominent symptom of neoliberal governing during the crisis.

The "New Intellectuals" Campaign

The logic of productive welfarism is to optimize liberal social governing by launching a welfare state at a minimal cost. The first welfare state in South Korea, deploying neoliberal techniques, designated not only the "working poor" (sômin) but the middle class (chungsanch'ûng or chung'gan kyegûp) as the objects of welfare provision. It was the first time that the middle class had been recognized as being deserving of the welfare state's attention and benefits. The inclusion of the middle class as welfare beneficiaries seemed absurd to lower-level state administrators because they had been accustomed to the idea that the government could only afford to provide for destitute people, a philosophy compatible with the principle of the developmental state that prescribed austerity in every sphere. However, Kim Dae Jung's reform of welfare citizenship corresponded to the liberal view of deserving welfare citizenship: it focused on employable and taxable citizens, populations that do not normally depend on public provisions.

The idea of employable and self-governing people as deserving welfare citizens is resonant with the idea of youth being recognized as a valuable resource under the Kim Dae Jung regime. During the crisis, the interest in young people increased primarily for two reasons. First, because of the shrunken job market for young people, they became a major unemployed population and dominated public works programs, particularly the data digitalization project (*chôngbohwa saôp*). The purpose of this project was to enter central and local governmental documents into a computerized database. Because computer skills were required for this job, most of the project workers were young people at ease with personal computer (PC) technology. However, the job was relatively straightforward and required only basic computer skills. This raised questions about the importance of computer literacy, as well as about the effectiveness of utilizing the skills of highly educated people for undemanding entry-level jobs.

Second, young people who were innovative enough to create their own jobs and new service and knowledge commodities were promoted and tokenized as a model for the government campaign of "new intellectuals." The term referred to knowledge workers who were aware of their own marketability, responsible for their well-being, and continuously upgrading themselves to be better commodities (Kim Hyo-kûn 1999; Seo 2005). "[New] Intellectuals were not only erudite university professors, but also people who elevated the price of their labor commodities [momkkap sûl nop'i nûn saram] through improving, developing, innovating their work" (*Maeil kyôngje* 1998: 51, quoted in Seo 2005: 63). The significance of the new intellectuals was announced, in tandem with productive welfarism, in one of Kim Dae Jung's first presidential speeches. Starting in 1999, the presidential Committee of the Second Foundation of the Nation (Che i ûi Kôn'guk Wiwônhoe) annually granted a "new intellectual award" (*sin chisigin sang*). The development of the award signaled that the neoliberal Kim Dae Jung government had become a postdevelopmental rather than a protectionist state, developing human capital with advanced information technology (IT) skills that could compete globally and be incorporated into the global market (Ong 1999; Ong and Collier 2005).

In addition, there were many smaller awards for new intellectuals in ministries and local government offices: the new intellectual award from the Ministry of Industry and Energy, the new intellectual award from the Ministry of Culture and Tourism, the Seoul new intellectual award, the Inchôn City new intellectual competition, and the new intellectual award from the Kyônggi Province Education Bureau. While productive welfarism reshaped *unemployment* policies (by creating public works programs and the vocational education program), new intellectuals discourses invoked the need for *industrial* policies (that is, policies promoting small-

and middle-sized businesses including startup and dot-com companies) aimed at overcoming the crisis. Many reports noted that public works programs contributed to reducing and stabilizing unemployment rates.[5]

Discourses on new intellectuals and industrial policies portrayed "independent" subjects who created jobs not only for themselves but for others. Further, both productive welfarism measures and the new intellectuals discourse were predicated upon the need to produce neoliberal state subjects. The "new intellectuals" slogan of the Kim Dae Jung regime was adopted and manipulated by experts in various ways. New intellectuals frequently appeared in governmental documents, as well as in experts' and journalists' narratives in the mass media. Academics, researchers, nongovernmental organization (NGO)/nonprofit organization (NPO) leaders, journalists, reporters, and even unemployed welfare subjects actively deployed the rhetoric for their own interests. Members of the Seoul City Committee for Unemployment Policies (SCCUP) and the Youth and Women Unemployment Monitoring Team serve as examples of this process. "New intellectuals" became an idiom for indicating promising underemployed youth who deserved financial support through public works programs.

Dr. Oh, the head of the Subcommittee on Youth and Women's Unemployment and one of the team's supervisors, was an academic researcher and expert on youth who employed the government's new intellectual campaign to support youth culture. She became an expert social engineer in the (neo)liberal governing of the youth population during the crisis.[6] She was in charge of managing an alternative school, sponsored by the city, for incubating creative youth who did not adjust well in regular secondary educational institutions. Team members also adopted the term "new intellectuals" though they were aware of the danger of opportunism and of the neoliberal baggage of the rhetoric. Team members worried about Dr. Oh's imposition of "flexible labor" as the rationale for promoting underemployed youth as deserving welfare subjects. This push for flexible labor failed to consider the exploitation of people in the marginal labor market (women, the disabled, the working poor). Team members, however, decided to use the discourse of "creativity" and "new intellectuals" as a means to legitimize unemployed young people as viable subjects of new presidential projects.

Young people's creativity, intrepid spirits, familiarity with computer technology, and participation in individual or small-scale enterprises (that is, small office or home office operation, SOHO), were well regarded and touted as values that older generations should embrace. Yet underemployed young people, such as team members, were much more adept at deploying the "new intellectuals" discourse than the city officials.

Many city officials straddled conflicting perspectives on youth during the crisis. On the one hand, young people received less attention from the welfare state because, unlike their parents, they were not deemed breadwinners in normative families. When young people requested access to governmental provisions through public works programs, they were easily devalued as "good-for-nothings" (paeksu), lacking the discipline to become independent citizenry. Government officials housing young-adult public works program workers in their workplace were deemed to be wasting national funds on "dependent" citizens. For instance, Mr. Cho, a mid-level official in the Seoul Women's Affairs Division, bluntly asked team members if they knew that their work was paid for with "blood tax" (hyŏlse), meaning that their wage came from taxing hardworking and frugal people like him. This provocation should be understood in the context of city officials' own financial difficulties. However, the official's insistence that he and other governmental workers sacrificed their salaries to budget public works programs is not only inaccurate but it also exposes the attitude that young adults were initially not a legitimate priority for government workers' attention.[7] In contrast to their unyielding position on middle-aged homeless men as deserving welfare subjects, the idea of unemployed young adults posed an enormous challenge to city officials. The controversy around recruiting youth as neoliberal welfare subjects is best seen through the activities of the team's research on and recruitment of unemployed young adults.

The Report on Unemployed Young Adults

The team defines *unemployed young adults* as "people in their twenties and early thirties who belong to the mass of unemployed (those who had been laid off or who never had a chance to enter the job market after graduating from high school, college, university, or graduate school due to the crisis), who are not just waiting for instant relief, but are attempting to create ways of helping themselves through a kind of self-employment, such as freelance and contract work" (Seoul City Youth and Women Unemployment Monitoring Team 1999b: 2). The team's rationale for researching young unemployed or underemployed people stressed that young people were citizens who could contribute significantly to economic prosperity and make a difference in global competition, but whose sociological attributes were little known.

The team chose its research topics in consultation with the Seoul City Subcommittee on Youth and Women's Unemployment and reported to the SCCUP. The research topics included the situation of homeless women's shelters and the referral and shelter system for women in need of special protection; problems of government support for female breadwinners' small businesses; Internet resources for unemployed women; creative ideas of underemployed young adults' small entrepreneurship; and problems of public works programs in general. Topics related to youth were taken up under the advice of Dr. Oh, head of the subcommittee, who asserted that youth-related issues were relevant to government initiatives and would not conflict with the interests of city offices and officials. The team's category of "unemployed young adults" covered a wide range of youth from the completely "good-for-nothing" (paeksu) to young entrepreneurs—because, as the team noted, "the [reality of] self-supporting underemployed young people was hardly captured by the concept of 'unemployment'" (Seoul City Youth and Women Unemployment Monitoring Team 1999b: 10). In other words, they might not have been people who were desperate or well acknowledged within the system of unemployment registration.

Throughout the three rounds of research, several categories were identified. In the first round (April–May 1999), the team used various media, including newsletters, magazines, the Internet, and PC networks, to make contact with young unemployed or underemployed people attempting creative ways of making a living. The team listed four categories of self-help groups for "unemployed young people" and one category of groups that financially or institutionally supported them. The self-help groups included networks or organizations among unemployed young people, small business preparation groups, small business support groups, and sociopolitical movements organized around the unemployment issues of young people. The other category referred to governmental organizations incubating small startup and dot-com companies, quasi-civil associations linked to governments, and grassroots organizations supporting the working poor and the dispossessed.

In the second round (June–July 1999), the team selected seventeen groups from the list of the first three categories; these seventeen groups were based on the criteria of self-sufficiency and creativity so that the selected groups would fit the city government's definition of *new intellectuals* and possibly attract financial support. The team then started to conduct interviews and do participant observation. This was one of the most dynamic and energetic periods for team members as they experienced, shared, empathized with, and represented the struggling young people. The team finally selected ten groups consisting of three artists' groups, five small business groups, and two networks of unemployed young people. In the third round (August 1999), the team conducted a workshop with concerned city officials, experts, and unemployed young adults on the application of the research results for utilizing and activating various policies.

It is notable that the three rounds of subject selection had different foci. While the first round was a mix of groups that were looking for governmental support and groups that were not, the later rounds were more focused. The groups invited to the third-round workshop tended to propose the creation of public works programs in connection with programs promoting "creative capital" and "public good." These criteria were employed to accommodate the way in which productive welfarism promoted self-sufficient welfare subjects who were also responsible for others by pursuing the common good and goodwill. In this process, unemployed young adults' groups that did not seek government support were excluded because they expressed discomfort from their previous experiences of being belittled by government officials as indolent or needy. Thus, the team recruited panelists from the groups of young people who had concrete suggestions for remedying their unemployment problems by utilizing public works programs. The team was attempting to create an encounter where city officials might debunk their own derogatory notions of unemployed young adults as idle and spoiled.

The team used the discourse of "creative capital" and "new intellectuals" to mediate different needs: unemployed young people's financial needs, city officials' administrative needs, and Dr. Oh's political-

107

ideological needs (to give youth the same citizenship rights as adults). The team devised terms and criteria that would justify groups of unemployed young people as deserving or productive subjects eligible to receive governmental support, such as public works program positions and work placements in NGOs. Groups invited to the third-round workshop were described as having "art-oriented cultural resourcefulness" and the "intention of contributing to the public good." The participating groups proposed various plans with strategic reference to the discourses of "creative capital" and "new intellectuals." For example, the National Good-For-Nothing Association (Chôn'guk Paeksu Yônhap), a group of young people who assert their unemployment as a viable lifestyle, suggested creating a public works program to develop a walking-tour map (wôk'ingt'uômaep) of Seoul. The group detailed their plan for making the map, referring to their rich knowledge of subcultural and hidden places.[8] The organizing committee of the Independent Festival or Seoul Fringe Festival (Tongnip Yesulje) proposed using public works programs to sponsor street festivals as a subcategory of the Independent Festival.[9]

The underemployed youth who had not been considered to be deserving of public assistance entered a new phase of making ends meet through state provisions, by trying to prove their value as resourceful human capital. They began to find ways of refashioning their noninstitutionalized life experience and perspective as "creative cultural capital," thus accommodating the needs of experts (such as Dr. Oh who theorized the value of youth with creativity and cultural capital) and governmental officials.

In the process, team members exhibited multiple and fragmented subjectivities in their guidance of the selected groups of unemployed youth. The team generously gave advice to young people about how to write proposals and represent themselves at workshops with city officials. I interpret this as evidence of the team members' subjectivity as semiexperts, doing the actual labor of translating youth into investable human capital within a neoliberal market paradigm. In addition, the fact that the team initiated surveys and selected young unemployed groups to enact governmental policies indicates the subjectivity of team members as quasi-state agents. Although the ideological effects of the team's position as a semiexpert entity might not have conflicted with its task of collecting data as a quasi-state agent, the nature and communicative codes of these two positions toward their clients were different. One was an expression

of a potentially positive consultation, the other an expression of arbitra-
tion and potentially restraint. Accordingly, it brought complexity to the
communication between team members and their clients. At the same
time as team members pioneered ways of providing subsistence, they also
maintained their cultural and political identities as young people in general, and as young unemployed feminists in particular, by grounding their
claim that youths are also deserving citizens.

Despite the team's efforts, they were not successful in gaining significant attention from city officials, who said that the city and the state administration could not afford to satisfy young people's "whims." However,
as will be demonstrated, youth came to be seen as deserving or produc-   109
tive citizens by the same city officials through a somewhat unexpected
series of incidents related to a town project: the Seoul youth-culture venture. Even giant bureaucratic corporations, much less public works programs such as the data digitalization project, could not compete against
the "venture wind" (bench'yô yôlp'ung)—the emergence of dot-com-style
small startup businesses—in terms of popularity among highly educated
or technologically adept young people.

Here, I would like to note that it is unclear if youth itself was commodified. Rather, it is a process of making a new mode of production in
conjunction with creating a new mode of subjectivity by targeting youth
as a priority surplus population for nurturing and exploiting their potential computer and Internet skills, and commercializable ideas in the process of constructing infrastructure for immaterial postindustrial capitalism. My fieldwork data show how a certain kind of youth was projected
as "productive" labor power in the South Korean neoliberal welfare state.
Similar to homelessness, some of the youth population was fantasized
as a surplus labor or reserve army to be exploited. The youth who were
imagined by government and mass media to have productive exchange
value were young adults who were equipped with IT technological skills
and were capable of making new commodities out of their creativity and
moving around flexibly. The value of deserving youth was imagined by
active dissociation from "good-for-nothings" who do not make efforts
to use themselves (their body, ideas, and differences) as commodities. In
this context, the object of capitalization was the capability of translating
and instrumentalizing ideas or items into commodities in the IT-satu-
rated markets, rather than youth itself. Although youth was targeted as

a population for having more potential of such a value ("creative cultural capital") than the older generation, it is hard to generalize that youth as a whole in South Korea was capitalized in my ethnographic context, which shows menacing distinctions between the deserving and undeserving for both youth and homelessness.[10]

Mr. Yu and His Two Sons

Mr. Yu's story provides a good sense of how neoliberal subjectivity prevailed in everyday life in South Korea during the crisis. I met Mr. Yu, a white-haired taxi driver and owner, in Seoul early one morning in March 2001. He was a gracious elderly person who seemed more like a high-level manager than a taxi driver. (It is not uncommon for people retired from long-term stable jobs in government or large conglomerates to become small business owners, such as independent taxi drivers.)

As soon as I got into his taxi, he suggested that I pay double if he could guess where I was headed—if he guessed incorrectly, then I would ride for free. It was an unusual suggestion, but he sounded sincere, and I felt that I had nothing to lose by agreeing to his offer because I was doubtful that he could guess my destination.[11] I was right. He thought I was heading to nearby Hanyang University. As he said, all youthful people looked like college students, like his youngest son who had only recently graduated.

In spite of missing a chance to earn a double fare, Mr. Yu was cheerful and talked ceaselessly. He talked about the difficulties young college graduates faced in finding jobs due to the crisis. He followed this line of discussion by bragging about his youngest son, who had graduated in engineering from Yonsei University, a prestigious private university founded by Protestant American missionaries.[12] Despite the worsened job market, his son was hired by Samsung SDA, a leading producer of digital display software and one of the most popular workplaces for South Korea's college graduates. Samsung is one of the three largest conglomerates (chaebôl). While Hyundai and Daewoo, the other two largest chaebôl, were divided into smaller enterprises during the crisis because of state intervention and restructuring, Samsung remained close to its original scope.[13] His son quit his enviable Samsung job within a year and announced to his parents that he had accepted a proposal from a startup company that offered a higher salary. After only eight months at his new job, the son moved to another venture enterprise. Mr. Yu said that he and his wife were worried about their son losing a stable job in a big company because of his zeal for money (ton yoksim). His son's most recent decision tried his father's patience most of all. Just the night before I met Mr. Yu, his son had confessed to his parents that he had quit the second start-up company after only a month there. He aimed to become the founder of a venture company (bench'yô ch'angôp) of his own along with several friends.

The taxi driver told me, "As a father, I was shocked when my son said this last night. 'What the heck is he doing?' I thought. Life isn't a soap opera, is it?" He continued,

I yelled at my son, saying, "Hey, do you think anybody can be an entrepreneur? Running your own business is very unstable even though you might think you can earn big money really fast that way. Life is a long-distance race, you know?" I expected my younger son to be a normal salaried man who would marry soon. His marriage cannot but be delayed as he takes such risks in life. My wife and I stayed up all night worrying about our son. Although my wife isn't comfortable with this yet, I've made up my mind to help my son because he will do it anyway. I will give my money to him whether or not he succeeds. For him, it's all or nothing now [to animyôn mo da].[14]

Mr. Yu invoked a Korean maxim to describe neoliberal materiality in everyday life—the unpredictability and precariousness of the job market and the ascendancy of finance capitalists with short-term investments such as "venture capital."

Mr. Yu also told me about his eldest son. He was in his forties, leading a successful life as a professor in Japan, after studying at a prestigious graduate school in the United States. Mr. Yu made a clear contrast between his two sons. He presented the first as an obedient son who never caused any trouble for his parents and smoothly attained prestige in life, while the younger son was an obstinate and adventurous person who often shocked his parents or made them uneasy in spite of his amazing capacity to survive. In a sense, Mr. Yu's older and younger sons represent the virtues of those who have thrived in the last decades (due to their persistence, patience, and stability) and those who will likely succeed in the coming decades (due to their flexibility, dynamism, and risk-taking). At the same time, Mr. Yu noted that his sons both had negative feelings about

South Korean society. His sons did not want to stay in Korea—his elder son skeptical of Korean academia, and his younger son frustrated with big conglomerates. He said he understood them, "because South Korean society was not built upon 'rationality' (hamnisông i kyôryôdoen sahoe da)." Humbly referring to himself as an ignorant old person, he said that he encouraged his sons not to feel obliged because of filial piety to live in South Korea as they had to make their own choices to adjust to the global era (kûllobal sidae).

Mr. Yu's narrative demonstrates competing but converging generational perspectives about living with globalization as well as job security in the emerging venture market. He and his sons devised different strategies for survival depending on their personal historical contexts. Mr. Yu, likely a person of the post–Korean War generation who came of age in the austerity of the developmental military regime, pursued a stable job for social and financial security. His sons, belonging to a relatively affluent generation, pursued adventurous or ambitious jobs as an investment for a better quality of life in an ever-changing world. Although Mr. Yu was grappling with different ways of managing life, he was open to the rationales of a new historical context (sidae) belonging to the liberal ethos and liberal way of reasoning that had infiltrated South Korean society over the decade and culminated during the crisis.

Venture Industry, Venture Capital, and Venture City

A high-level official in the Seoul Industry and Economy Bureau confirmed the meaning of venture in a meeting with the team to discuss drafting a white paper for the Seoul youth-culture venture. He said, "Venture literally means high-risk, high-return" (Bench'yô nûn mal kûdaero hai risûk'û hai rit'ôn iya). For him, venture included management of investment, business, industry, and government projects that create maximum profits for the entrepreneur who risks instability and failure. This approach was markedly different from an earlier emphasis on stability in managing companies.

During the crisis and the dot-com boom, venture business (bench'yô saôp) emerged as an alternative type of commerce in the conglomerate-oriented South Korean economy. While conglomerates (chaebôl) had been perceived as the leaders of South Korea's economic miracle during the three precrisis decades, after the crisis, the chaebôl's uncontrolled expansion and accumulated debts were considered to be the culprit behind the economic collapse. As these corporations became increasingly unstable, many technically adept people in their twenties and thirties sought alternative employment by opening their own dot-com-type businesses or looking for jobs in the dot-com industry. The mass media reported on the short-term successes of many such endeavors. The number of startup companies increased, as did the volume of venture capital that came from both individual investors and investment agencies.

The city government and the central government were also active participants in promoting venture companies (bench'yô kiôp), mainly because of the urgent need to recover from economic recession and the optimistic expectations regarding startup companies' taxpaying capacity. Seoul, the biggest metropolitan government with the biggest debt, designated the "venture industry" (bench'yô ôpkye) as its central strategy. Immediately after the mayoral inauguration in July 1998, the city formed the Seoul Industry Promotion Commission of civil experts. In December 1999, the city administration heralded the Overall Plan for Startup Company Promotion. In an announcement launching the Seoul Venture Center, the venture industry was proclaimed the "center for industrial competence in the information society of the twenty-first century."[15]

Before the Seoul Venture Center was opened, the city had already planned a support system for startup companies comprised of public and commercial organizations (higher education institutes and venture capitalists), and these measures coincided with similar efforts from the central government. Some of the locations were dubbed "incubators" for small and medium businesses, specifically for startup companies (Seoul City Youth and Women Unemployment Monitoring Team 1999b). Small companies were supported by the city and the central government to an unprecedented extent; twenty university-based incubators were financially supported by the Ministry of Information and Communication, and the most prestigious national university opened its own incubator with the help of Seoul. In this arrangement, universities provided space and human resources while governments provided equipment and financing. Tenant groups that opened startup companies at the incubator facilities paid a reduced rent, subsidized to three-quarters of the usual rent.

The Seoul Venture Center was located on Teheran Road, which came to be known during the crisis as the Silicon Valley of South Korea because of the high concentration of startup companies, including information- and communications-related companies (so-called IT companies). Teheran Road is in the heart of the Kangnam area, where solid upper-middle-class Seoulites came to reside after the establishment of new apartment complexes in the area.[16] Moreover, the building where the venture center was located was designed as an "ultra-smart building" (ch'ômdan int'ellijyônt'û pilding), which included a self-regulating artificial intelligence system, a LAN system for fast Internet connection, and up-to-date equipment for virtual conference rooms.

After 2001 venture companies and venture capital investments became less popular than they had been at the beginning of the crisis. However, the ascendancy of the venture market at this time carved a new direction for chaebôl. Investors endorsed the idea that they were both most profitable and most risk-tolerant. Chaebôl had often advertised themselves during the crisis as the biggest venture companies while at the same time the most reliable venture capital investment. Many chaebôl attempted to resolve the dilemma of losing elite employees to sprouting venture companies by sponsoring or founding venture capital companies as sister companies. They too found that the venture capital market could offer high returns, while fierce competition in other areas drove profits down.

"Venture" and Youth

The Seoul youth-culture venture was initiated by a high-level official of the Seoul Industry and Economy Bureau. After successfully launching the Seoul Venture Center project, he had the inspiration to connect "venture" and creative youth in synergy with the presidential mandate of promoting the "new intellectuals." There are several interesting aspects of the Seoul youth-culture venture. The city project aimed to develop a cultural business center by mobilizing young avant-garde artists' groups, modeled after the Pompidou Center in Paris. The Industrial Policy Division under the Industry and Economy Bureau first contacted the team to request help in designing the project and writing the proposal.[17] The proposal was to be modeled along the lines of the Seoul Venture Center but with distinguishable "youth" and "cultural" characteristics and themes. The expected budget for launching the project was about 1 billion won (about $10 million).

The Industrial Policy Division was not responsible for any other activities of the team, so the team could get additional payment for the work that was not related to the SCCUP projects.[18] The Industrial Policy Division became aware of the team through the recommendation of Mr. Pae, a mid-level official of the Labor Policy Division. Although the Industrial Policy Division and the Labor Policy Division offices were next door to each other within the Industry and Economy Bureau, the team had not been introduced to the Industrial Policy Division—a sign that the team members were not viewed as legitimate workers in the city offices.

Mr. Pae's recommendation was exceptional because it represented a dramatic change of attitude on his part. As a city administrator responsible for youth vocational schools, he had previously undervalued unemployed youth both as researchers and as legitimate welfare subjects. He had also been involved in the team's transfer from the Labor Policy Division to the Women's Affairs Division by bluntly stating that the team was useless to him. He had said that he did not want to see "green youngsters like unripe radishes" (*saeparatk'e jôlmûn aedûl*) around his office.[19]

However, the high-level official in the adjacent Industrial Policy Division was looking for a creative think tank to prepare a proposal on a Seoul youth-culture venture to present to the mayor. When Mr. Pae learned of this proposal, he seemed to realize that the direction of governmental policy had changed in terms of how it defined its deserving subjects and its attitudes toward younger generations. Mr. Pae later self-consciously told the team that he had not realized the importance of the team's report on unemployed young adults until after the Seoul youth-culture venture's town project was espoused by the Industrial Policy Division. With this new understanding, Mr. Pae suggested that the Labor Policy Division take on the financial responsibility for printing and distributing the team's report on unemployed young adults without interfering in the project. It was a marvelous moment; few officials at that time of frequent administrative audits or censure were willing to take on the financial responsibility for new projects. Further, city officials previously had meticulously screened every detail of how the team compiled, published, and distributed its reports. Thus, it was remarkable that he agreed not to interfere in the process.

According to Mr. Pae, his proposal to financially sponsor publication of the team's report on youth was the "right procedure" (*chôlch'a* or *ch'aegim sojae*), because the research on unemployed young adults was conducted while the team was working in his office, even though the team had moved to another division by then. Mr. Pae did not follow up on the team's report until he recognized its value in his own attempts to make himself useful to his upper official.

However, the mayor turned down the Seoul youth-culture venture's town project in spite of the support of the vice-mayor and the Industrial Policy Division top official. The mayor's reluctance to promulgate the project was possibly a result of growing concerns about the "bubble" economy tied to the venture boom. Since the crisis, industrial policy makers, including ones in the city administration, had prioritized support to startup companies that had the potential to create cultural capital with creative ideas or artistic talents, so-called creative cultural capital. It was not a coincidence that venture replaced chaebôl as a preferred capitalist production system. A flexibility-oriented labor market replaced a stability-oriented labor market, from the perspective of both job-seekers and policy makers. This corresponds to the taxi driver's narrative, which illustrates how the venture market was an alternative career path for young adults who could not find satisfactory work in big corporations.

The South Korean government campaigns for the new plan emphasized the relatively greater value of young people, whose potential for taking risks, engaging in flexible labor, and creating creative cultural capital was thought to derive from their new way of thinking and living. Creative "new intellectuals," "venture companies," and "flexible labor" were the core concepts of the campaign rendering young people the target of new economic policies. It is not surprising that some of the team members went on to work at startup companies. The experience of the team members — translating labor power and human qualities into creative cultural capital, comprehending the value of risk-taking in a capitalist world, and surfing the precarious terrain of an unstable job market — provides us with a window through which to observe South Korea's rapid adjustment to neoliberal governing through the production of "self-sufficient" subjects.

THE DILEMMA OF PROGRESSIVE INTELLECTUALS

Five

Many social commentaries on 1990s activisms are posed against the past. They reveal a widespread social fatigue and even disgust with that culture of dissent. Many people distance themselves not only from the military authoritarian culture of the recent past but also from the righteousness and drama of dissent—from the total-izing projects of both the Left and the Right. Recalling the 1980s, what comes to people's minds are the infringements of personal life imposed by both military authoritarian rule *and* the culture of dissent. People remember: *when* urban spaces were consumed by the violence of demonstrations and their suppression; *when* the govern-ment demanded sacrifice and restraint in the name of political sta-bility and economic development; and *when* the moral prerogatives of the Left made those with progressive inclinations feel guilty that they could not do more.

NANCY ABELMANN, *ECHOES OF THE PAST, EPICS OF DISSENT: A SOUTH KOREAN SOCIAL MOVEMENT*

This chapter aims to problematize how even progressive social forces inadvertently joined the intensification of (neo)liberalism in South Korea during the crisis. On the one hand, I affirm the significance of the consciousness-raising tradition of South Korean intellectuals who spear-headed the democratization: social change requires awareness of how the capitalist-state ideological apparatus is internalized in our minds and structured in society. Louis Althusser's influence on Korean intellectuals is still effective in critiquing and responding to neoliberalism when ap-plied together with Michel Foucault's idea that (neo)liberal social govern-ing regulates the population through and while producing individuals as self-governable subjects. Despite their different ways of understanding the regulating power—state machinery (for Althusser) versus multiple social engineers (for Foucault)—Althusser and Foucault both consider social change and social governing to necessitate the involvement of not just the state institutional terrain but the social and the cultural arena as well.

On the other hand, I argue that former student activists (including many of the informants in this book and myself) were not fully aware of their own roles as (neo)liberal social engineers during the crisis, caught between the liberal pursuit of common wealth and the enduring leftist quest for just redistribution to the deprived. It is difficult in general to distinguish (neo)liberal thinking that promotes capitalist values and interests from the embedded "good" liberal thinking that pursues democratic actions (Mitchell 2004). But it was particularly confusing to Korean intellectuals who had experienced a decade of a liberal regime (1987–1997), where the exercise of individual liberty, privacy, and the right to property exploded as signs of democracy, rather than of neoliberalism. I aim to demonstrate this difficulty of countering (neo)liberalism in South Korea by drawing on literary and cultural texts that describe the problematics of Korean neoliberalism and democracy, as well as on the narratives (recorded in my field research) of intellectuals involved in homeless policy. Concrete examples of the confusion and difficulties in dealing with neoliberalism during the crisis are prefaced by a brief history of South Korean intellectuals' participation in the democratization movement in the 1980s and 1990s.

History of Social Movements in the 1980s and 1990s

A 1970s worker-intellectual alliance was inspired by the self-immolation of Chôn Tae-il, a garment factory worker who cried out, "We are not machines!" when light industry, such as textile production, was the focus of the developmental state. In the 1980s, thousands of South Korean university students (vanguard "organic intellectuals" [Gramsci 1971: 6]) joined forces with laborers and peasants by becoming laborers and peasants themselves (S. Kim 1997; Koo 2001; Lee 2005, 2007; Ogle 1990).[1] Although the Gramscian idea of organic intellectuals is found in other countries (for example, Frantz Fanon during the Algerian revolution, Subcomandante Marcos of the Zapatista revolutionary movement in Mexico), South Korean student activists in the 1980s risked more than the privilege of college life and good job prospects by becoming organic intellectuals under the cold-war military dictatorship.[2] They jeopardized the well-being of their families, lost normative social connections, endured lifelong trauma through torture and imprisonment, and succumbed to physical injury, even death (Cho 2002).

In the early 1980s, the military dictatorship increased repression to prevent unionization and deter leftist influences in the labor movement. The government limited the age and education of factory workers, making it illegal for college students to work in factories. Thus, to obtain a factory job and avoid surveillance, student activists needed to obtain fake identification cards and to disconnect from families and friends. It is difficult to know how many students worked in the factories in greater Seoul, but it is estimated to have been around three thousand in the early 1980s and ten thousand in the late 1980s (Park 2002: 10).

The vigorous alliance between workers and intellectuals was strengthened in part because the union movement was growing in the context of the developmental state's changing focus to heavy industry, such as automobile manufacturing (Koo 2001), and in part because intellectuals felt a sense of responsibility for not "saving" the Kwangju people from the 1980 massacre by the military junta (Lee 2005). The worker-intellectual alliance was a crucial background that led to democratization in 1987. The regime's torture of student activists who became laborers and labor activists, or of student activists on campus who supported the labor movement, inflamed resentment toward the regime among factory and office workers and other progressive people. Pivotal incidents that propelled the demonstrations of 1987 include the sexual torture of Insook Kwôn (a female student-worker activist who courageously sued the police who tortured her) on June 4, 1986; the torture and murder of Pak Chong-chôl (a male member of a student activist organization) on January 14, 1987; and the death of Yi Han-yôl (a male student who died of a tear-gas pellet gunshot by riot police during a street demonstration) on June 9, 1987.

However, after the official end of the military junta in 1987, university students' political organizations either collapsed or were at a loss due to international, national, and internal turmoil. Internationally, the fall of the former Soviet Union and Eastern bloc ruled out socialist revolution as a viable option, and was a big blow to South Korea's student movements.[3] Nationally, civilian support and solidarity for oppositional

THE DILEMMA OF PROGRESSIVE INTELLECTUALS

resistance movements crumbled, along with the official disappearance of the dictatorship, "the enemy" that prompted wide networks of pre-democratization solidarity. Student organizations gradually moved away from the labor union movement following the emergence of a labor union leadership that did not welcome student intellectuals in the union, especially after the victory of the heavy industry strike in 1987 (the Workers' Strike, Nodongja Taet'ujaeng). This tendency displaced many intellectuals as spokespeople for the labor movement (similar to French intellectuals in 1968 [Foucault 1977] and Chinese intellectuals after the Tiananmen incident in 1989 [Wang Hui 2003]). Student activists changed their focus to internal campus democracy, demanding the transparency of private university governing structures and boycotting increases in tuition fees to sustain the support of the student masses. Despite the changed focus, activist groups struggled to recruit new members, because the majority of students found street demonstrations unnecessarily violent and confrontational. Thus, support for student and labor activism was hard to gain after democratization.[4]

The new civilian government conducted less surveillance of the mass media, with the resulting exposure of previously censored history, such as the Kwangju massacre and anticommunist persecutions.[5] Television dramas scripted by Song Chi-na, such as *Moraesigye* (Sandglass) and *Yŏm-yŏng ŭi nundongja* (Eyes of sunrise), portrayed the previously hidden histories of collective memory (Seoul Broadcasting System 1995; Munhwa Broadcasting Company 1991).[6] The more these emotionally appealing mass media productions restored the collective memory of suppression by past military regimes, the more the mainstream population became indifferent to radical movements in the democratized era. A harmonious relationship—between the state and its subjects, between employers and employees—was presented to the public as a viable method of social governing, eliminating the need for the mass demonstrations that had caused a tangible loss of commercial activity and business revenue.

The liberal attitude toward how to govern society was gaining political power over a militant leftist attitude of saving the society from a military government. The promotion of harmonious relationships cultivated the civility or docility of social members as responsible for self-control (Hindess 2004). This social matrix bifurcated into two genealogies of sociopolitical movements. On the one hand, it enhanced civil society movements that instigated consumer-based or identity-centered issues to make society less harmful and more inclusive (for example, the anti-corruption movement, hotlines for sexual and domestic violence, anti-discrimination against minorities movements). On the other hand, many radical leftist intellectuals and former student activists who had devoted their lives to the collective cause lost their raison d'être with the emergence of individualistic liberal movements that criticized past collective activism as dogmatic and confrontational. Although there is some debate about whether leftist movements (minjung undong) continued to grow despite the ascendance of civil society movements (Sonn 1999), it was not uncommon for many former student activists to experience inertia, escapism, or cynicism as the radical ideals of collective social change were replaced by the liberal pursuit of individual liberty and security.

Kong Chi-yông's novel, In'gan e taehan yeûi, literally "civility toward human beings" (published in translation as Human Decency), depicts the dramatic changes in the life of a former student activist through the narrator's self-reflection:[7]

> "Things around us, things inside us, things that seem trivial—those are the things we'll tackle first, all right?" He said this with a smile on his face and a glow in his good-natured eyes. And then he fought those trivial things and went to jail, the sight of him dragged into court, gagged, in white traditional prison garb bringing us to tears . . . and he worked in a factory and married a factory girl with only a middle-school education. And here I was, five years later, going to see this man, a man now quoted as saying, "there was no use risking one's life for something trivial," a man who had inherited his father's bus company, who fathered two daughters and then separated from the factory girl with the middle-school education, after which she was committed to a mental hospital. (Kong Chi-yông 1997: 68–69, emphasis added)

What are the dual meanings of trivial in this passage? Under the fascist capitalist state (1960s to 1980s), trivial things referred to anything that upheld inequalities and oppression, such as compliance with the expectations of teachers and parents who disavowed students' antistate activism, reluctance to help activists chased by police or who participated in street demonstrations, and general aspirations of bourgeois life. To 1980s student activists, such as the protagonists in Kong's novel, these trivial things led them to "plunge into the world of the factory worker, forgoing university diplomas, job prospects, and middle-class lives" (Lee 2005: 912). Then, less than a decade after the democratization in 1987, those devoted revolutionary actions of the past were turned into a different kind of "trivia," something no longer worth risking one's life for. Some leftists and student activists became typical salarymen or company owners, such as the man in Kong's book, losing hope for radical social change and championing individual liberty and wealth. Other intellectuals turned to grassroots movements, party politics, or government administration, often in cohesion with civil movements for the common goals of making society better and safer.

How should we understand this changed perspective? If liberalization was the reason that radical activism was losing ground, then what was the reaction of people who still aspired to radical social change? What is the connection between the changes during the democratizion period (1987–1996) and the neoliberalization of social governing during the crisis? If civil movements became conservative and capitalistic after the democratization (Sonn 1999), then people who carried leftist ideals through the democratization movement would not easily fit into either liberal or leftist categories. I posit that these ambiguous and ambivalent identities of intellectuals were widespread throughout the democratized era and especially during the crisis—in part, for practical reasons, to continue to support the dispossessed.[8]

The Fine Line Between "Good" Liberalism and "Bad" Neoliberalism

There is a propensity to see a distinction between "good" liberalism and "bad" liberalism, with neoliberalism designated as bad. Wendy Brown and Janet Halley in *Left Legalism / Left Critique* (2002) dissect two different meanings of *liberal*: liberal as indicating politically progressive; and liberalism as politically conservative and economically market-centered, a conventional understanding of liberalism in scholarly literature. The focus of Brown and Halley's book is left liberalism (leftists involved in legal and institutional struggles such as the civil rights movement of African Americans and the legalization of gay marriage). David Harvey (2005), a leading leftist critic of neoliberalism, employs the terms *liberal* and *embedded liberal* in a positive sense, as if *liberal* is inherently the counterforce of *neoliberal*. Katharyne Mitchell (2004), a leftist geographer who interrogates the genealogy and limitations of liberalism, also suggests battling the "fantasy of neoliberalism" by establishing "good" liberalism, in the context of the complex geography of different liberalisms in Vancouver (that is, a neoliberal joint force consisting of financially affluent Hong Kong migrants and Canadian politicians to develop monster housing blocks versus a white liberal local population keen to protect the quiet suburban environment). She writes, "Liberalism's constant 'failure' to live up to the promise of universalism is not merely an accident of implementation. . . . Citizenship and liberalism historically have been shown to foster not equality and inclusivity but internal differentiation and hierarchy. . . . There exists, however, a 'promise' of social liberalism. . . . Perhaps the pretensions of social liberalism and enlightened modernity toward the principles of universality have been irrevocably damaged, 'punctured from the moment of their conception in the womb of colonial space.' Nevertheless, I am hopeful that some vestige of the promise remains" (2004: 219–20).

I question if it is just neoliberalism that needs to be demystified. What about liberalism? Is not our fantasy of liberalism—a wish to establish "good" liberalism or a "good" market that would not promote capitalist value or interest—dangerously confusing? Foucault and post-Foucauldian writers helped us to understand neoliberalism as an advanced liberalism sharing core characteristics of political liberty and freedom of private property. So why does the fantasy of a good liberalism persist? In the South Korean context, leftist and progressive intellectuals in the democratized era, particularly during the crisis, found it difficult to distill liberal democratic ideas and actions from the structure of the market economy and private property. A good example of this is "small shareholder activism" (*soaekchuju undong*) led by the People's Solidarity for Participatory Democracy (PSPD, Ch'amyôyôndae). PSPD is a civil society movement organization that emerged in 1994 with the motto "dedicate[d] to promoting justice and human rights in Korean society through the participation of the people."[9]

Small shareholder activism was a campaign to buy small quantities of the stocks of big conglomerates to participate in the democratization of corporate structure. As the previous chapters detailed, South Korean conglomerates were central to national economic growth and capitalist exploitation, and garnered the support of the military state. In particular, the conglomerates' monopolization of corporate governance by kin-centered owner groups went relatively unchallenged even after democratization. Then the crisis revealed that weaknesses in their financial structure (that is, nepotism at the management level and misuse of bank loans) were a major cause of national debt. From 1997 to 1999, PSPD focused on the undemocratic management of the big corporations by becoming stockholders in those corporations.

PSPD is more progressive than other civil society movement organizations. For example, the Citizens' Coalition for Economic Justice (CCEJ, Kyôngje Chôngûi Silch'ôn Yônhap, or Kyôngsillyôn), established in the early 1990s, appealed to the middle class (Nelson 2000). However, PSPD attracted support from radical intellectuals, including orthodox Marxists (Sonn 1999), especially when it criticized CCEJ for its "department store" style, and for not attempting to fundamentally reform society.[10] Small shareholder activism gained wide support from progressive and leftist forces because it continued the antidictatorship, antimonopoly (pan-tokchae, pan-chaebôl) spirit of the democratization movement in a realm untouched by democratized regimes—that is, the reform of the monopoly structure of big conglomerates. It appeared at a vulnerable moment for the big corporations: they had to sell their property and make new value through stock markets when the Kim Dae Jung government pressured them to restructure and downsize during the crisis.

Small shareholder activism became controversial when Ha-Joon Chang, a prominent Cambridge University economist, criticized the campaign as neoliberal (Jang 2006; Chang, Chông, and Yi 2005).[11] Chang notes that antistate and promarket actions are promoted by neoliberalism; becoming stockholders in big conglomerates (chaebôl) to break down their financial structure implies replacing the ownership to monitor property management and profit making. According to Chang, the global market economy, which has been dominated by advanced nation-states, left only a few options to South Korea for surviving and achieving economic growth, such as state protection for big industry and a state-chaebôl alliance. Supporting the reduction of state intervention and destroying the chaebôl ownership and management implied eliminating obstacles to the neoliberal push for a free global market. Finally, replacing the ownership of the big conglomerates by becoming stockholders promotes the neoliberalization of the South Korean economy, especially since South

Korean small shareholders and foreign investors as big shareholders had to work together to fight the Korean chaebôl ownership (Chang, Chông, and Yi 2005). Chang points out that the democratic attempts, through buying shares and aligning with profit-making individuals and foreign investors, ironically work against the interests of national prosperity. His argument makes sense of the ascendancy of finance capital as a neoliberal characteristic distinct from industrial capital-dominated liberal regimes. The cultivation of various financial markets, especially short-term loans, hedge funds, and stock markets, led not only to the national debt crisis but to individual bankruptcies. Individuals in the financial crisis are not just victims of neoliberalism, but active contributors to it in their own entrepreneurial attempts to manage their lives and be affluent and self-sufficient.

125

Although Chang positions himself as a critic of neoliberalism, his argument is built upon nationalist interests in competition with the global market, itself a key foundation of liberalism. Further, his premise of liberalism as an effort to reduce state intervention is not based on historical research. Both classic liberal regimes and neoliberal regimes have selectively deployed the "invisible hand" (that is, free market) and state intervention (Hindess 2004). Examples of the classic liberal regime's state intervention include the British enclosure movement that privatized public land to change peasants into wage laborers (Perelman 2000), and the Japanese colonial state that regulated Korean day laborers' entrance to labor markets in the early twentieth century (Kawashima 2009). Neoliberal regime examples include the recruitment of young female domestic workers and factory workers through the post-Mao communist party agency (Yan 2003; Pun 2005), and South Korean policies for making the homeless and underemployed youth employable and flexible labor. In summary, posing as pro-state does not provide sufficient grounds to counter (neo)liberalism.

Small shareholder activism vividly exemplifies the fine line between "good" liberal actions for democratization and "bad" liberal actions for neoliberalization. It is hard to differentiate the political goals from the economic effects when liberal subjects are navigating different liberal options, even with good intentions. The liberal options are varied but lead to a common ground for making decisions: the need to protect and promote wealth through welfare. Pro-state advocacy could be simply a question of "*whose* capital do we care about?" and "how do we rationalize the need for and use of wealth in connection to redistribution or welfare?" Advocating pro-state for national wealth and welfare takes the side of national capitalism against the global capitalist movement. South Korean intellectuals' discussions on both welfare and democracy reveal their ambiguity about what constitutes democracy and good liberalism (Pak Kyŏng-tae 2008: 110–113). Were progressive intellectuals in South Korea, including leftists, aware of their participation in neoliberal social governing despite their critique of neoliberalism? What if the liberal discourses that inevitably buttress neoliberalism are embedded in activists' well-intended efforts to achieve democratization and a welfare society, in spite of themselves?

Contradictions in the Liberal Critique of the South Korean Welfare State

In chapter 2, we saw how volatile remarks on "family breakdown" became an effective tool of social engineering and the production of neoliberal homeless subjects. Street women were not considered to be "deserving" homeless citizens because they were seen as irresponsible mothers/housewives who contributed to family breakdown. Yi Tŭk-chae, a professor in a private university in South Korea, was one of only a few outspoken critics of family breakdown discourses during the crisis, calling the family-centered solution of social welfare "barbaric." In his book *Kajokchuŭi nŭn yaman ida* (Familism is barbarous) from 2001, he urges South Korean society to change from a familial society (*kajok sahoe*) to a civil society (*simin sahoe*).[12] He directs his criticism at both the state administration and citizens. He calls the Korean state fascist for handing public responsibility solely to male breadwinners in the name of familism, reckoning that this burden pushed many male patriarchs to the edge of suicide during the crisis. At the same time, he reproaches Korean citizens for not noticing the state's evasion of its responsibility.[13]

In his challenge to the family breakdown discourse and familism in general, Yi is certainly a liberal agent who wants to improve social conditions. His criticism of Korean society and the state as barbaric is shocking to many South Koreans. However, when he affirms that the family is sacred but familism is disturbing, he does not challenge normative ideas of the family itself as a crucial ground for producing conservative familism in collaboration with the neoliberal regime. Despite his demand for state accountability, his act of highlighting civil duty for social governing inadvertently supports the neoliberal welfare state's technique of encouraging partnerships with nongovernmental organizations (NGOs) to economize on costs and responsibilities. While he urges the increased autonomy of civil society, he also advocates for the welfare citizen's right to depend on the state, entrusting the state administration with the role of welfare provider, and legitimizing the state's right to regulate. His logic of creating a "civilized" way of living by building "civil society" rather than relying on the state is contradictory to his argument on the need for full state protection.

Yi introduces the British welfare model as the ideal, recalling a scene from his sojourn in Britain. He records being impressed by seeing old people waiting in line to receive their old-age pensions. However, he omits the context of the British welfare system's change to means-tested workfare (that is, neoliberalism) during the Thatcher regime. Although it might have been the United Kingdom's universal pension system that Yi wants to highlight, Kim Dae Jung's productive welfarism, modeled after the British "third way" neoliberal welfare state, promulgated a national pension system in 1999 (two years before the publication of Yi's book). Yi is unsuccessful in debunking "family values" as an engine of neoliberal social governing during the crisis. Instead, he bolsters neoliberal governing through his liberal idea of civil society.

What about researchers and public intellectuals who were directly involved in the welfare state practices, such as implementing homeless policy? I introduce three examples from my fieldwork: Dr. Uh, Mr. Ku, and Reverend Kang.

Intellectuals Involved in Welfare Governance During the Crisis

DR. UH, A LEFTIST EXPERT ON HOMELESS ISSUES

I met Dr. Uh, a former student activist and an independent researcher, in 1998 when I was assessing the needs of homeless women for the Seoul City Committee for Unemployment Policy (SCCUP). He was a consultant on urban unemployment issues. We met at a time when state administrators were claiming that the government could only afford to assist short-term homeless men. I encountered great difficulty trying to convince state administrators to pay attention to the broader spectrum of homeless people, including homeless women. In this context, Dr. Uh's research on long-term homeless men and men at risk of homelessness (mainly day-laborers) was influential in the creation of the first homeless policies in South Korean history.

From 1998 to 1999, Dr. Uh and I often worked together, carefully challenging state administrators to reconsider the narrowly defined category of deserving homeless citizens. Dr. Uh admitted that he had little knowledge about women's issues, including homeless women. He candidly expressed his prioritization of class oppression over gender oppression, a position that reflected his background as a student activist in the 1980s, when South Korean activism was largely focused on labor exploitation and the military dictatorship at the expense of other social issues. Dr. Uh was nonetheless sympathetic to the plight of homeless women, recognizing the city officials' bureaucratic dismissal of their needs.[14]

As homeless issues emerged as a showcase subject of the neoliberal welfare state, Dr. Uh grew to be an important resource. In early 1999, he became a full-time researcher in a state-sponsored research institute. Within four months, he was an expert member of the Presidential Secretary Planning Committee to Improve the Quality of Life under the Kim Dae Jung government. This group of experts produced a white paper on productive welfarism in the summer of 1999. After joining the committee, Dr. Uh changed his perspective on social governing. He published a report on homeless women that concludes that homeless women's issues are not necessarily the domain of government social policy, and that civil society should actively share the responsibility for taking care of homeless women.

Dr. Uh had not necessarily supported Kim Dae Jung's neoliberal welfare policies prior to joining the Presidential Secretary Planning Committee. He expressed his confusion by stating he could not understand why the middle class as well as the working class was a target of the welfare state. As a researcher who had been involved in leftist student movements, Dr. Uh was accustomed to focusing on the working poor. Therefore, he may have expected Kim Dae Jung's welfare regime to reflect more social democratic views, according to which the working poor would be considered the only or the most deserving welfare citizens. However, rather than assigning the responsibility for homeless issues, including homeless women's issues, to the state, Dr. Uh relegated such responsibilities to civil society, following the logic of neoliberal welfare governing along the lines of his own priority of class over gender.

MR. KU, THE HEAD OF THE HOUSE OF FREEDOM

As noted in chapter 1, I first met Mr. Ku when I visited the House of Freedom as a temporary researcher for SCCUP to gather information on the homeless shelter system. Mr. Ku served as a liaison between civil representatives of the Commission on Homeless Policy and city officials from related divisions. In addition, he headed the Homeless Rehabilitation Center (Nosukcha Tasisôgi Chiwônsent'ô, HRC), an NGO set up as an emergency response to the crisis. He also mediated between 120 homeless shelters (that is, Houses of Hope) and the government office responsible for developing policies on the homeless. Like Dr. Uh, Mr. Ku was a student activist leader in the 1980s. When I met him, he was a Ph.D. student of social work at a renowned university. Readers might remember that Mr. Ku seemed more at ease with me after learning that I also had been involved in student activism during my college years.

He said, though, that the student movement of the 1980s had been intense and difficult, especially during the early to mid-1980s, implying that student activists of the 1990s, like me, could not possibly imagine the experience. This reveals the way in which student activists from the predemocratization era differentiate themselves from the next generation of activists.[15] The period from 1990 until 1997 (before the Asian Debt Crisis coincided with Kim Dae Jung's presidency) is when the pursuit of individual freedom became the predominant ethos, including in student activism. When liberalization—political liberty and the freedom of the market—carved a space for individuality, many student activists had difficulty coping with the changes.

It is notable that Mr. Ku did not immediately understand my conflicted status as a temporary researcher in Seoul, for I was neither a regular city official nor a government-affiliated researcher. Rather, I had an ambiguous status as a citizen receiving workfare subsidy through a public works program. However, Mr. Ku and I were in somewhat similar positions. We were both Ph.D. students who had reluctantly but nevertheless seriously undertaken government-related work—work that we had hardly imagined ourselves doing because of our antifascist views. Despite the recent democratization, the collective memory of a three-decades-long era of fascism remained strong. We were both attempting to carry out the militant leftist guerilla tactics of the 1980s, working in quasi-governmental agencies as an activist strategy. At the same time, our sense of achieving an ambitious goal, regardless of what other people would think, would be the embodiment of liberal individuality. The lives of South Korean leftist intellectuals such as Mr. Ku and myself in the democratized period could not but be fragmented.

As noted in chapter 1, Mr. Ku questioned the dichotomy between deserving homeless people and undeserving homeless people. Yet the HRC where he worked is a salient example of the privatization of the public sphere. Outsourced groups, such as the HRC, are agencies that are neither grassroots organizations nor parts of the state bureaucracy. The HRC works with the Commission on Homeless Policy in addition to various levels of government. It also runs the House of Freedom and officially determines which homeless people can reside in the Houses of Hope. Interestingly, however, very few operating shelters willingly complied with the HRC's regulations because most of the Houses of Hope were small welfare agencies funded by religious groups with minimal state support. For social workers who worked for the welfare agencies, running a homeless shelter was an additional burden unrewarded by tangible benefit. Thus, Mr. Ku's critical views of government management did not necessarily indicate his solidarity with civil activists. His position of managing homeless issues by controlling 120 homeless shelters was similar to that of democratized neoliberal state officials, in terms of being responsible for maintaining a healthy and harmonious population and minimizing suppressive governing methods. His position in a quasi-governmental agency to buffer the intervention of the state authority in the name of enhancing homeless people's health and life is a good example of Foucault's concept of biopower, the modern liberal tendency to control a population through its well-being rather than through the threat of punishment or death (Foucault 1990).

Furthermore, Mr. Ku was inadvertently complicit with neoliberal social governing when he drew upon arguments that reinforced conservative gender and family norms by endorsing the idea of rebuilding middle-class stability and social morale.[16] It is true that Mr. Ku challenged government authority over homeless citizenship. During the first annual HRC ceremony, Mr. Ku announced that the premises of the government policies on homelessness were false. He questioned whether IMF homeless were clearly discernible from long-term street people, especially regarding them being able to resume a normal social life easily. Yet, at the same public event, Mr. Ku said that 55 percent of the total homeless people at the HRC were classified as suffering from a "broken family." These people's experiences included not only abandonment or losing family members but also being unmarried or divorced, information which upholds a strict normative sense of family.

Overall, Mr. Ku maintained the normative ideas of family and household by privileging conjugal, heterosexual relationships, relying on the cultural assumption that a middle-aged man cannot live alone and should be attended by a wife. In the context where the mass media represented the family — and its breakdown — as the cause of pathologized social phenomena, such as homelessness, divorce, homosexuality, and teen prostitution, Mr. Ku and homeless welfare agencies acted upon and confirmed the media portrayal that family breakdown had triggered various social problems. For instance, HRC sponsored a variety of rehabilitation programs primarily aimed at creating normative families, including matchmaking, wedding ceremonies, and reunions with relatives (see chapter 2; Homeless Rehabilitation Center 1998, 2000).

Much like Dr. Uh, Mr. Ku appeared to undergo a transition from leftist to liberal "democratic" views, which is symptomatic of neoliberal governing in democratized South Korea. As a leftist, he produced policy for subalterns, in this case, homeless people; as a liberal, he acquired and employed a managerial position to effectively control and manage homeless issues. Ultimately, Mr. Ku's strategies for managing the homeless converged with dominant neoliberal rhetoric — perhaps most significantly by relying on conservative gender and family discourses. His complicity in neoliberal social governing is illustrated in his reiteration of normative family ideology, which contributed to the discourse and subject formation of deserving homelessness. In other words, it is not a coincidence that only "employable" male breadwinners, those who could be rehabilitated to assume a normal family life, emerged as deserving welfare subjects.

Reverend Kang comes from a different activist background than Dr. Uh
and Mr. Ku. She was a student activist as an undergraduate but also at a
Protestant graduate school where she was part of a liberation theology
(*minjung sinhak*) movement. Reverend Kang was a charismatic female minister who was the first "social safety net" activist to attend to homeless
women's needs in Seoul in 1998. In 1999 she passed on to me her personal
notes about how former student activists coped with trauma in the process of democratization:

> Actually in my personal family history, my brother, at the time [of the
> Kwangju massacre] a freshman in the economics department of Chôn-
> nam University [located in Kwangju], was tortured by the emergency
> army. He is the only boy of seven siblings and the second generation
> with only one son. My parents had to send him to a mental hospital
> several times [because of his schizophrenia caused by the torture]
> and they felt very guilty about it. Although my brother received some
> compensation so that our family could buy a house,[17] he was confused
> and upset our family for a long time. He is psychologically unstable—
> even expelling our mother and sisters from the house on a cold win-
> ter day—making my father, an education official awarded the Order
> of President, an insomniac. But when his friends visited our home, he
> sounded normal. Because of my brother's inconsistent behavior, our
> family couldn't understand him and suspected him—wondering if he
> had lied to us. But it took us ten years to figure out that he acted that
> way in front of the family because the family are the only people who
> he could rely on and show his real character to. . . . Therefore society
> should warmly embrace and support these traumatized people instead
> of giving those responsibilities to individuals.

Many former student activists have experiences of police violence, being
arrested, and witnessing the bloody injuries of comrades (and some riot
police) in street confrontations. Others have heard emotionally volatile
firsthand accounts. For instance, an unforgettable memory for me was
hearing of Yi Han-yôl's death by tear-gas gunshot from a senior student
who had held the dying Yi in her arms. Kong Chi-yông's novel describes

several characters affected by the violence, including one who died of self-immolation, as Chôn Tae-il did in real life, and one whose decade-long experience in prison made it hard for him, once released, to find direction in his life. Militarized state violence against students, laborers, peasants, squatters, and villagers in anti–nuclear waste demonstrations was not just a relic of the 1980s but continued until the early 1990s (Cho 2002) and revived in 2005, when Taechu-ri, a South Korean southern village, protested being the new location for a gigantic U.S. army base.

The family institution had been the only source of caregiving to individuals who did not have secure employment, not to mention people who were under state surveillance when the social policy and welfare system was minimally established (see chapter 3). There was a strong taboo against people with mental illness, and mental health services were regarded as a luxury. In the South Korean context, it is still uncommon to resort to a mental hospital unless the symptoms are extreme, though there is compensation provided for the victims of state violence.[18] This is the historical and personal context in which Reverend Kang realized the significance of the "social safety net" for people in need of support beyond the boundary of the family. Working as a minister in an area of garment factories and the working poor, she was not involved in any massive class struggle, but she initiated a small grassroots movement to help people, such as homeless women, who were not being cared for by their families. The way she carried out her predemocratization ideal in the democratized liberal context was to reconstruct the meaning of the collective political history under the military dictatorship as an individually and psychologically hurtful trauma that needed healing.

I interpret Reverend Kang's reference to family not necessarily in contradiction to her aim of encouraging social responsibility for individual well-being. Rather, the connection she draws between family support and the need to build a social support system for individual well-being was symptomatic of liberal ideas that burgeoned among civil activists after the democratization in 1987 and culminated in social management during the crisis. Reverend Kang, as a pioneering grassroots activist, took a position of crisis knowledge broker, heavily relying on the longstanding normative family institution as the foundation of crisis social management and intensified neoliberal governmentality.

Would Dr. Uh, Mr. Ku, and Reverend Kang agree with neoliberalization in terms of opening Korean industry, education, and farms to the global market in the name of free trade? Would they have gone to a rally in Seoul to show their solidarity with Korean and other national peasants opposing a World Trade Organization (WTO) meeting in Hong Kong that was pursuing the full opening of the global market? Were they oblivious to how they contributed to South Korean neoliberal welfare governance? Or is it inherently difficult to detect the convoluted nature of neoliberalism? Dr. Uh, Mr. Ku, and Reverend Kang had all been ardent student activists and had not lost their hopes for social change. All of them kept their passion and support for the bottom socioeconomic strata and worked for the homeless during the crisis. Yet when we exercise our political freedom to make decisions for ourselves and to pursue economic profit and property in a market-centered political economy, it is not easy to see the way we are embedded in liberal thinking and actions in our daily lives. Foucault's passage gives a hint of a discursive and ethnographic way of looking at liberalism: "What should we understand by 'liberalism'? . . . I tried to analyze 'liberalism' not as a theory or an ideology—and even less, certainly, as a way for 'society' to 'represent itself . . .'—but, rather, as a practice, which is to say, as a 'way of doing things' oriented toward objectives and regulating itself by means of a sustained reflection. Liberalism is to be analyzed, then, as a principle and a method of rationalizing the exercise of government, a rationalization that obeys the internal rule of maximum economy" (1997: 73–74). The amplification of the (neo)liberal ethos and economy during the crisis was possible, not only because of the coincidence of the crisis with the Kim Dae Jung presidency, but because of the formation of individuals as liberal agents in the democratized era. Liberal agents who inadvertently participated in neoliberal governing in fragmented and paradoxical ways include leftist intellectuals who adapted to the liberalization of society (Žižek 2000). There is no "good" liberalism that stands alone apart from "bad" liberalism. If neoliberalism is a fake authority and unacceptable, then the same is true of liberalism itself.

THE PURSUIT OF WELL-BEING

Coda   There is no singular unity to which the name "liberalism" refers:
rather, there are as many liberalisms as there are procedures for
identifying contexts in which the governmental promotion of free
interaction is to be preferred. . . . In practice, however, while they
differ, sometimes vehemently, over points of detail, it is not difficult
to group the many different liberalisms into a number of distinctive
streams which divide and recombine as they meander through the
infested marshlands of modern history. By far the most influential
of these streams have passed over the fertile soils of enlightenment
rationalism and remain coloured by the historicist and developmental view that the greater part of humanity remained in considerable
need of improvement. It is here that we find the laissez-faire liberalism of the market; the new or social liberalism of the late nineteenth
century and its welfarist progeny; the various national liberalisms,
all of which favoured state intervention to control the effects of
market relations; and the imperial and anti-imperial liberalisms of
the colonial era.

BARRY HINDESS, "LIBERALISM: WHAT'S IN A NAME?"

The historical particularity of the Asian Debt Crisis in conjunction with
the Kim Dae Jung presidency propelled an intensification of the liberal
ethos and a neoliberal political economy in various levels and domains
in South Korean society, from government policies to NGO activities to
individual decision making. While the crisis had a disastrous impact on
people's lives due to loss of employment and income, the material impact and discourse of the crisis also facilitated the introduction of the
neoliberal welfare principles of employability, rehabilitation capacity, and
flexibility as the optimal way to induce unemployed people to join in the

recovery and rebuilding of national prosperity. The rationalization of neo-liberal measures as the most advantageous for social governing during the crisis was not effected solely by the Kim Dae Jung presidential office. It was also taken up and orchestrated by civil leaders and organizations that wanted to enhance democratic society and the quality of life. This involved making the state accountable to the dispossessed, as it had not been in the past, at the same time as making individuals self-reliant so that they could function as liberal citizens free of subjection to and dependence on the state. Thus, producing self-sufficient subjects was desired and practiced both by civilians who valued autonomy from the state as the primary measure of democracy and by state elites pushing neoliberal policies.

These (neo)liberal social engineers or crisis knowledge brokers employed particular governing technologies. These technologies include the slogan of governmental-nongovernmental (GO-NGO) partnerships, the invocation of "family breakdown," the resurrection of conservative gender norms and practices, and the promotion of "venture" and "creativity" as liberal pioneering values and survival options. By using these governing technologies, the South Korean crisis knowledge brokers were involved not only in the governing of the population as a whole, but in the production of governable subjects who were categorized as "deserving" or "undeserving" welfare subjects: "IMF homeless" or the "rootless" in regard to homelessness, and as "new intellectuals" or "good-for-nothings" in regard to youth underemployment.

Despite the multiple factors and agents of (neo)liberal welfare governing, the state was the focal point for disseminating and magnifying (neo)liberal welfare logic and practice through the implementation of a neoliberal welfare policy that penetrated citizens' everyday lives. The Kim Dae Jung administration's inauguration of a state welfare system was widely understood and supported as an inevitable measure to deal with the aftermath of the crisis. However, productive welfarism had much wider implications and consequences than just as a response to the crisis. In the evolvement of the South Korean capitalist state, productive welfarism, a neoliberal welfare state, replaced the developmental state. Kim Dae Jung and other political elites who saw democratization as the grounds for liberalizing markets meticulously prepared the postdevelopmental and neoliberal state by betting on "welfare." Welfare was a social domain where state intervention would be readily accepted and in which everyone would participate. It was a trope to overcome the "scars" and "damage" of class conflict and labor disputes of the era when labor was the major domain of political and social movements. In spite of the conciliatory gesture of the welfare state to transcend labor issues, "welfare" in productive welfarism was never disassociated from "labor." Unemployed people and homeless people were nurtured through temporary employment (that is, public works programs) and temporary shelters, if they were lucky enough to fit the category of "deserving." However, the unprecedentedly generous state benefits were not just for enhancing quality of life (that is, biopower) but for cultivating particular surplus labor populations to match the demand of new capitalist labor markets. In other words, welfare exists for wealth and wealth is the premise of welfare. This is where Foucault's govern-mentality and biopower meet Marx's exploitation of surplus populations. Studying welfare and social governing becomes a rich site for theoretical exploration. The inauguration of the neoliberal welfare state in the ab-sence of any other welfare state highlights the logic of capitalist evolve-ment with its seemingly abrupt shift from the state-planned economy of the developmental state to the free market economy of the neoliberal state.

It is important to stress that the aim of the capitalist state to maximize wealth did not change from the transition of the developmental state to the neoliberal welfare state. Productive welfarism was on the same con-tinuum as the developmental state in that the governing strategies were still seeking prosperity through the enhancement and exploitation of labor power.

This is the context in which I argue that a pro-state position is not a gauge of anti-neoliberalism. On the one hand, those who are anti–state power in a democracy fall into the trap of giving a hand to the free mar-ket by empowering the neoliberal ideology of freedom in general. On the other hand, if people advocate state power to keep the nonmarket domain from privatization, they fall into the dilemma of embracing state power for maximizing national wealth in a capitalist world, and assuming that nationalism can counter neoliberalism.

Therefore, positioning the state versus (civil) society or the state ver-sus the market is not a constructive way to distinguish neoliberal from non-neoliberal, not to mention capitalist from anticapitalist. All fall into (neo)liberal and capitalist pursuits because of the unquestioned urgency of promoting wealth or economic growth. Giving too much attention to the state (either as a negative force or as a productive force) risks reproducing a stagnant understanding of neoliberalism as something that only concerns macro forces, such as state machinery, international financial institutions such as the IMF and World Bank, or financial capitalists or elites.[1]

My purpose in studying the neoliberalization of the South Korean context is to explore the links between neoliberalism as a process of subjectification in daily practice and thinking and neoliberalism as a political-economic institutional regulation. For instance, if the fostering of workers is justified for their contribution to national prosperity (making it acceptable to measure the value of the homeless and the unemployed through employability), then welfare gives way to the pursuit of wealth and to judging the value of people and labor through the eyes of capital. The South Korean case speaks to other countries or groups that oppose neoliberalism without acknowledging the link to the liberal concept of the value of work in our daily lives. A paragraph in *The Nation*, in which the contributor Katrina vanden Heuvel reflects on Labor Day, grabbed my attention: "As the gap widens between the very rich and the working poor, Americans should support policies and ideas that make this economy work for *those who have helped create America's wealth* (vanden Heuvel 2006, emphasis added). Vanden Heuvel makes the point that workers are valuable and deserve better support because they are the backbone of national wealth. In other words, working-class value is unwittingly shared with capitalist value, despite their different positions. Whether the capital is needed for basic subsistence and security or for maximizing the capacity to possess and protect wealth, it is taken for granted as a precondition for all individuals' and societies' well-being. It is an irony that we have come to measure the value of labor through capital even though capitalist value (that is, the capital) is criticized for the exploitation of labor. Measuring labor through capital affirms and reproduces capitalist value (Yi Chin-kyông 2004, 2005: 61–76). This irony is vividly exemplified in a situation that shakes the established wealth-creating infrastructure, namely the unpredictable movements of capital — such as the bankruptcy of a national bank or giant conglomerates — that entail mass layoffs in South Korea. Such movements of capital may first cause social chaos and dramatic changes in individual lives, and then precipitate efforts from all parts of the society to recover from the disaster. This is done with the common goal of rebuilding national and individual prosperity with a sympathetic hand to deprived people, including the working poor, the laid-off, and the homeless.

Although it is true that capitalists and laborers have different economic resources, which affect their living conditions and quality of life, there is an aspect that we tend to easily dismiss, living in a capitalist world: the consensus that wealth and prosperity are the precondition for welfare and the romanticization of the worker's value because she or he produces national wealth. If we endorse making the individual, family, and national wealth the premise of welfare, or more concretely, if we do not find a problem in commodifying every domain in our lives (even for the sake of justice or equality), we become subsumed to and embody capitalist value and its profit making—capitalist value through commodification and accumulation become the foundation of a managing and governing individual and social life. There is no such thing as a good capitalism that legitimizes the pursuit of capital. Further, it is very tricky and deceiving to think that a good liberalism is able to and must counter capitalist movements. The very foundation of liberalism is discursively, politically, and economically engineered to conceal the multiple coordinations behind capitalist production: wage labor, primitive accumulation, the invisible hand, civil society, local autonomy, and individual freedom. The liberal thinking manifested in social governing through welfare (the governmentality of the welfare state), especially in neoliberal regimes, shows that it is problematic to pursue the hope of "good" liberalism. Social democratic and former dissident group activists did not simply give in to the neoliberal state regime but unwittingly joined the consolidating force with the best intentions to improve South Korean society after the crisis.

The point is to be aware of the location of neoliberalism's operation, or source of power, as not just in supranational financial institutes, such as the IMF, or in multinational corporations and state machinery—but in our individual bodies, in our own thoughts. This is not to disempower any movement against capitalism and macro-neoliberalism, but to reorient our conception of capitalism and neoliberalism. Foucault's understanding of biopower is helpful in understanding how capitalists and the capitalist state seek the maximization of wealth by caring for and cultivating a labor population at the minimum cost by making the individual bodies self-governable. But what we might have missed, or do not want to face, is that support for the governing logic is endorsed by people who appreciate the liberal democratic values operating in the daily practice of self-enhancing and self-governing—not just governors, but also workers, union leaders, and leftist reformers.

The salience of "well-being" commodities and discourse in South Korea since the crisis shows that neoliberal governing logic continues to be prevalent. For example, toward the end of 2003, a South Korean acquaintance urged her partner to quit drinking and smoking, "Honey, we are 'people who pursue well-being' (*welbing chok*). Please, take care of your body in the new year as a member of the people who pursue well-being." Well-being (*welbing*) implies the sophisticated management of a healthy and enjoyable lifestyle and signals fully ingrained middle-class values and status, a well-established concept in Western societies. The term became ubiquitous in South Korea in 2002, when the country purportedly began to recover from the crisis. In 2003, major newspapers reported that "well-being products" (*welbing sangp'um*) and activities, such as yoga, spa treatments, wine, organic food, and air purifiers, were bestsellers in the domestic market, and forecasted even greater levels of their consumption by 2004. Although it was certainly not the first time that South Korean people had become keenly concerned with matters of individual health and the pursuit of a better life, what was new was the general lack of disdain toward this intense, individualized focus on bourgeois taste and self-care, which was no longer considered self-centered, selfish, or extravagant. Rather, such concerns were deemed to be valid and essential.

Some might describe the well-being phenomenon as simply an aspect of middle-class culture that only affluent people enjoy and are implicated in. It is certainly true that many South Korean progressive and leftist intellectuals tend to target consumer culture and middle- and upper-class culture. However, the everyday lives of the general public, as reflected in the discourses on well-being and consumption of well-being products, could be and should be researched more critically in connection to the amplification of neoliberalism through governing welfare society. This is an area that would benefit from further study, because welfare is enunciated not only at the policy level but also in people's daily lives, in their liberal desire and right to enjoy the "good life."

CODA

NOTES

Preface

1. The introduction details the political and historical background of the Asian Debt Crisis. The South Korean government officially announced 2001 as the end of the crisis because that is when the nation had repaid its debt to foreign lenders. Despite this official "end" and the subsequent economic recovery (albeit only partial), the impact of the crisis on the working poor and on the dispossessed is ongoing.

2. My conceptualization of liberalism and neoliberalism is built on both Foucauldian literature (Foucault 1990, 1991) and Marxist understanding (Harvey 2005; Jessop 2002). See the introduction of this book.

3. This book uses *youth* interchangeably with *young adults* to refer to college and high school graduates just entering the job market. In the South Korean context, people in their late thirties who are not married are also considered youth. In addition, *un(der)employed* is often used to describe the unstable boundary between youth employment and unemployment.

4. As Arjun Appadurai (1996) notes, the global ethnoscape contains many multidimensional "scapes" (economy, technology, mass media, culture). The analysis of mass media and juxtaposition of crucial literature and social events are important to contextualize people's narratives and political economy.

5. In the Korean social context, "intellectual" usually refers to someone with a university education.

6. Although it is not uncommon for bureaucracy to be used interchangeably with the state, the former is an institutional apparatus of the latter (Hall 1984:19).

7. Regarding the limitations of the term *governance* and its distinction from *governmentality*, see Sigley 2006; Larner and Walters 2004.

8. It is important to note that studies illuminating the multilayered and intricate inner dynamics of state bureaucracy are rare, though growing, since Nader suggested "studying up" almost three decades ago (1974). Recent studies include Ferguson 1994, Gill 2000, Gupta 2001, and Hertzfeld 1992.

9. Examples of anthropological works on homelessness that include homeless people as central subjects include Lyon-Callo 2004, Gowan 2000, Fowler 1996, Passaro 1996, and Susser 1999.

10. They included the Organization for Women's Economic Independence (FREE-WAR, 1999–2001); Wild Flower (Tûl-kkot, a guerilla radical feminist campus group, 1996–1998); Stone Flower (Tol-kkot, a guerilla radical off-campus feminist group, 1997–1999); Among Us (Kkiriggiri, a political organization of Korean lesbian feminists formed in 1995, which became a counseling center for lesbians in 2004); Between Friends (Ch'in'gusai, a sociopolitical organization of Korean gay men begun in 1994); Come Together (a Yonsei University queer student organization begun in 1996); *Karaora Feminist Zine* (a guerilla feminist zine, 1997–2000); Group for College Women's Economic Survival (Yômôksal, 1997–1998); and the Koma Cultural Event Team (Koma Munhwa Kihoektan, 1997–2003).

11. *Arûbait'û* derives from the German *arbeit*, meaning "work." In Korea it became a conventional term for the tutoring of middle and high school students by college and graduate students. More generally, the word is often extended to include all part-time jobs for young people.

12. It was not a coincidence that I was motivated to extend beyond my original research population. I had attended college in Seoul in the late 1980s and early 1990s and was part of the so-called last generation of student activists—against the military dictatorship, U.S. military and economic imperialism, cold-war ideology, and the capitalist exploitation of cheap laborers and peasants. Wanting to keep alive the memory of colleagues and activists who were injured, jailed, traumatized, or dead, I was driven to action when I perceived the resurgence of conservative nationalism and the escalation of neoliberal economic and welfare policies during the crisis.

13. The primary think tank for unemployment issues was the Seoul City Committee for Unemployment Policy (SCCUP), which will be detailed in the ethnographic chapters of this book. SCCUP consisted of various experts, such as researchers from state-sponsored research institutes and universities as well as nongovernmental organization (NGO) leaders and renowned journalists. It is an example of promoting the partnership between government and NGOs or outsourcing as a neoliberal state strategy.

14. There were many other public works programs hiring young adults, such as the data digitalization project (chôngbohwa saôp), which used unemployed youth to transfer government paper documents onto computers.

15. Recognizing that the government had turned a blind eye to gender discrimination in the labor market, these feminists had developed a deep distrust of state institutions and city governments (see chapter 2 for more on layoffs of women workers made by the Korean Farmer Association Bank, or Nonghyôp Ûnhaeng).

16. I worked on the team for about nineteen months (January 1999 to July 2000), including paid work for a full year and unpaid voluntary work for the rest of the time. The work that I did during the negotiation period from September to December 1998 was unpaid.

17. For instance, the city administration saw team reports as something separate from city reports, and their publication as questionable. However, when a team

report on underemployed youth was seen as a useful tool for promoting city policy on young adults, funding for publishing it was immediately warranted (see chapter 4).

Introduction: The Emergence of the Neoliberal Welfare State

1. See Esping-Anderson 1990 and Flora and Heidenheimer 1987 regarding the classical liberal welfare regime.

2. Bob Jessop 1994 explains that post-Fordism is a capitalist mode that has both a tendency toward destabilizing labor markets and means of production and an ability to stabilize institutions, rules, and norms. If Fordism is exemplified by the assembly-line system and solidly regulated mass production, post-Fordism is illustrated by an unstable service and information industry.

3. Louis Althusser's concept of historical conjuncture as a revolutionary situation is insightful. While the situation invokes determinative cause, it presupposes ethnographic and historical trace of hegemonic forces. See Althusser 1969.

4. I further explain the "developmental state" later in the introduction.

5. The Asian Debt Crisis was most often called the "IMF crisis" in South Korea. *Oehwan wigi* literally means foreign-debt crisis, but South Korean people conventionally refer to it in relation to the IMF bailout of South Korea. *Aiemep'û sat'ae* (literally, IMF crisis) was the most popular label. South Koreans' term for the crisis reinforced popular thinking that the national emergency was caused by a foreign power interfering with South Korea's sovereignty.

6. Cho Soon-Kyung argues that the unemployment rate even before the crisis was almost 20 percent, because it did not count women and youth who wanted jobs but were not registered as unemployed (1999: 178). She calls this population the "disappointed unemployed" (*silmang sirôpcha*).

7. It is interesting to note that Joseph Stiglitz, the former chairperson of the World Bank, also criticized the role of the IFIs, in particular the IMF. See Polak 1994 regarding tension between the World Bank and the IMF.

8. The previous president, Kim Young Sam, was criticized and ridiculed by the South Korean masses for his inability to prevent the crisis, so the country was ready for a political hero.

9. Chôlla Province has a history of economic neglect and of indigenous communist guerilla activities starting with Japanese colonialism (1910–1945) through the U.S. occupation era (1945–1948) to the Korean War (1950–1953) (Cumings 1997). It has also been a site of fervent peasant movements against big Korean landlords (Abelmann 1996, 1997a; Eckert 1991). The highlight of Chôlla's significance in the history of the Korean democratization movement is the upheaval in Kwangju, the largest city in the province. There, Kwangju civilians (officially a few hundred, unofficially a few thousand) who countered a succession of draconian military regimes were accused of being communists and massacred by South Korean military troops led by Chun Doo Hwan and Roh Tae Woo in 1980 soon

143

after the assassination of Park Chung Hee, the first military coup leader. This uprising was hidden from the public through media censorship for a decade because Chun and Roh, two military commanders who led the Kwangju massacre, assumed the presidency one after the other. Further, the military violence was committed with the knowledge of the U.S.–Asia-Pacific military leadership, which has had authority to move South Korean troops since the Korean War (Shin and Hwang 2003). The uprising and massacre became a crucial aspect of the collective memory and fed the desire to end the military regime in 1987 as well as to raise critical voices against U.S. military hegemony in the Korean peninsula. Although there are several other provinces, tensions between Kyôngsang and Chôlla provinces are the most explicit and strongly embodied in the everyday lives of South Koreans.

10. Reunification policy and welfare policy were the two top successes of Kim Dae Jung's presidential politics (Pak Pyông-su 2001). According to studies of reunification policy (Kim-Paik 2002; S. Lee 2007; Park 2007), officials considered the South Korean attempt at reunification with North Korea to be pivotal for the survival of South Korea's economy in the global market, despite the expense (South Koreans were very critical of the cost of sending subsidies to North Korea during the crisis). I look forward to scholarly work that analyzes Kim Dae Jung's humanitarian policies, including reunification, in relation to their implications for capitalist state development.

11. I credit Sungjo Kim for the history of Kim Dae Jung's liberal ideas in his early years (personal communication, September 2007). See also Yu Ch'ôl-kyu 2004.

12. The donation campaign operated through the religious leaders was called the "national movement for overcoming unemployment" (NMOU, sirôpkûkpok kungmin udong) and advertised by Han'gyôre sinmun, a progressive newspaper. This volunteerism from civic groups with liberal ethics is unwittingly complicit with neoliberal social governing. See Hyatt 2001 for the relationship between volunteerism and neoliberal governmentality in the American context.

13. Nationalist ideologues, identified with the National Liberation (NL, Minjok-Haebang), saw the agony of Koreans affected by the division of North and South Korea as a wretched outcome of cold-war ideology. NL's goal was reunification. This differed from leftist ideologues, identified with the People's Democracy (PD, Minjung-Minju), who identified the root cause of oppression of the masses (minjung) as capitalist state development and class conflict, and aimed for workers' and peasants' revolution (Abelmann 1996, 1997a; Chun 2003; S. Kim 1997; Koo 2001; N. Lee 2007; Park 2002; Prey 2004; G. Shin 2002, 2006). Although this explanation is oversimplified, the democratization movement clearly consisted of two strategic directions—class emancipation and liberation from imperialism (that is, reunification). For a detailed history of the 1987 democratization, see Koo 1993, 2001; and N. Lee 2005, 2007. In brief, the triggers of the mass movements were the secret service's use of sexual torture and killing of student activists (for

example, Kwon Insook, Pak Chong-chôl) and riot police's use of tear gas, gun-shots, and repressive measures (for example, Yi Han-yôl).

14. Brown 2003 and Brown and Halley 2002 note the similar situation of the U.S. left, whose member chose to support liberal welfare democracy despite their aware-ness of its limits.

15. *(Neo)liberalism* or the *(neo)liberal*, meaning both liberal(ism) and neoliberal(ism), signals a basic premise of this book: liberalism and neoliberalism share a core epistemology. My argument that South Korean liberal social forces contributed to neoliberalization is built on this premise.

16. For China, see Anagnost 2006; Farquhar and Zhang 2005; Hoffman 2006; Lofel 2007; Pun 2005; Ong 2006; Wang Hui 2003; Yan 2003. For Eastern Europe and Russia, see Berdahl, Bunzl, and Lampland 2000; Burawoy and Verdery 1999; Gal and Kligman 2000a, 2000b; Haney 1999, 2000; Verdery 2003. Ann Anagnost (2004, 2006) succinctly shows the complicated positionalities of neoliberalism between socialist China and global markets through the commodification of cor-poreal quality and the illegal blood trade. Judith Farquhar and Qoicheng Zhang (2005) focus rather on the genealogy of "care of the self" in China. Lisa Hoffman (2006) understands neoliberalism in China as the wedding of post-Mao social-ism with neoliberal governmentality. She illuminates the relationship by show-ing how the young generation is effectively a combination of both Mao's nation-alistic discourse and neoliberal self-enterprising discourse. Consistent with her coauthored piece on neoliberalism in *Anthropology News* (Hoffman, DeHart, and Collier 2006), she demonstrates a localized neoliberalism. Aihwa Ong is a pioneer anthropologist who has explored conceptual notions such as modernities (1996), transnationalism (1997, with Nonini), citizenship (1999, 2003), and neoliberal-ism (2006, with Collier 2005). Because of her focus on Southeast Asia and East Asia, her theorization with a nuance of locality is very insightful. Her recent book *Neoliberalism as Exception* (2006) illuminates neoliberalism through excluded citi-zens, such as migrant workers. However, the book does not fully articulate how neoliberalism itself can be an exception to the nation-state without a preceding liberal regime. Ngai Pun (2003, 2005) and Hairong Yan (2003) show the uneven consequences of neoliberal labor regulation through migrant factory workers and domestic workers.

17. (Neo)liberal governmentality does not rely on any direct interventions or protec-tive actions (Barry, Osborne, and Rose 1996; Burchell, Gordon, and Miller 1991; Dean 1999; Foucault 2008; Lemke 2001). Rather, it is enacted by various institu-tions and social actors, but at a distance, and not necessarily through central gov-erning institutions. Thus, (neo)liberal governing can be characterized by the fol-lowing: the management of populations through quasi-welfare agencies (Gupta 2001); gendered construction of welfare subjectivity (Kingfisher 2002); an explo-sion of auditing and monitoring (Power 1994); the invention of accountancy and calculating selves (Miller and Hopwood 1994; Miller 1992); the policing of fami-

lies through motherhood (Donzelot 1979); the disciplining of domestic security through crisis discourse or risk mentality (O'Malley 1996, 1999); and the disciplining of "community" or "self-management" through freedom and autonomy (Rose 1990, 1999). These processes are further established through the expansion of experts and self-manageable units (that is, families, residential communities, NGOs, and nonprofit organizations) who consult on and monitor social issues.

18. In South Korea, biopower became prominent in government structure after the fall of the military state in 1987 and when Kim Dae Jung promulgated the first welfare state, productive welfarism. However, corporate structure had been employing the (neo)liberal technique of biopower through the expansion of benefits since the 1980s in order to reduce labor disputes (Koo 2001; Janelli 1993; Jang 2006).

19. Confucian ethics that emphasize filial piety help maintain the family-supported social security system. This network is also crucial to maintain and promote affluence (Son Beyong-Don 1997).

20. Roger Janelli (1993) and Choong Soon Kim (1992) vividly show the overwhelmingly wide range of chaebôl products and services in the everyday life of lay people in South Korea. The workers in chaebôl companies are subtly pressured to use products made by their companies in order to show loyalty. For example, workers are expected to use Hyundai cars if they work for any company under the umbrella of the Hyundai corporation.

21. Productive welfarism has both made contributions and had its limitations. Among South Korean policies relevant to education, health, national pensions, and public assistance, public assistance has been the least supported. In many advanced countries, public assistance programs are also minor because national pension and health systems are relatively sturdy and able to buttress basic social security. In contrast, South Korea had not been equipped with strong, centralized programs. Therefore, the minimal attention to public assistance programs turned out to be a critical pitfall because it led to an inability to cover basic subsistence in the time of a national economic crisis. Productive welfarism barely expanded public assistance programs during the crisis. Rather it promulgated urgent welfare issues, such as a homeless policy, as temporary welfare issues. Kim Dae Jung's productive welfarism deployed the homeless policy as a red herring; it foreshadowed an accountable and benevolent welfare state that took care of the most deprived group and thus garnered wholehearted support from the national population. But instead it was assigned to and remains a temporary or emergency social policy without the guarantee of a long-term institutionalized welfare plan. See chapter 3 for more on this subject.

22. It was also a new policy logic in South Korea to assume that people in poverty are unwilling to work. The general assumption had been that people wanted to work but had trouble surviving in the postwar developing economy where the competition for work was so harsh.

23. This doublespeak of neoliberal policy is reminiscent of U.S. policies such as No Child Left Behind and the Clean Air Act, which highlight social responsibility for retracting social provision. Thanks to Ann Anagnost for pointing this out.

24. Kaushik Sunder Rajan (2006) articulates finance capitalism through genome research and the pharmaceutical industry since the late 1990s in a way that is insightful and resonant with my focus on the emergence of South Korean "venture capital." Sunder Rajan shows that biotechnological development (that is, genome research) is overdetermined by capital's intervention, in particular the investment of speculative capitalists. Revisiting Marx's distinction between merchant capital and industrial capital, he explains that the former seeks profits from circulation through speculating commercial values, whereas the latter makes surplus value through producing and exchanging commodities. Sunder Rajan argues that commercial, merchant, and finance capital is dominant over industrial capital in the United States. Biotechnological business earns profits more by investment and increased stock market value than by selling pharmaceutical products (2006: 8–11).

25. *Paeksu* means "white hand" in Chinese. (The word is a Korean pronunciation of Chinese characters.) It is an idiom for people who don't have to work hard to make a living and so their hands are not stained or darkened. A Taiwanese acquaintance told me that *hûksu* ("black hand" in Mandarin) implies blue-collar or lower-working-class people. It seems that "hand" signifies "labor" in these East Asian societies, which share, at least partially, a writing culture based on Chinese characters, although there is no idiomatic usage of *hûksu* in South Korea, or *paeksu* in Taiwan. Some Korean *paeksu* are in contact with Japanese *freeta* or *freeter*, sharing their identity as jobless people living a creative lifestyle. Both Korean *paeksu* and Japanese *freeta* vacillate between the pride of being counterculture members and the shame of being perceived as economically incompetent (Muraki 2008; and personal communication with Jonathan Hall). See also Arai 2005.

1. Seoul Train Station Square, House of Freedom

1. It was designed in 1925 by C. K. Larandei, a German architect (Seoul, Jung-gu Culture and Tourism, "Seoul Station Building," http://tour.junggu.seoul.kr/english/culture/culture_view.php?idx=15). The fact that an architectural style reminiscent of the Renaissance symbolizes Japanese colonialism in Korea is a good example of how, in some East Asian nations, Western European colonization was mediated by Japanese colonialism, rather than experienced directly. In Korea, European or Western culture is a transposed and doubly colonized product.

2. The April Revolution of 1960 was a mass political uprising in which students and citizens overthrew the authoritarian Syngman Rhee government. It was the first mass demonstration against the state causing death (183 were killed, 6,259 were wounded) since the Korean War (Cumings 1997).

3. The April Demonstration Withdrawal was a large gathering of about 400,000

students and citizens on May 15, 1980, to demand the lifting of martial law declared by General Chun Doo Hwan when the first military dictator, Park Chung
Hee, was assassinated. Students and citizens withdrew the following morning
because of the military threat (N. Lee 2007). The Kwangju massacre was a state-
led massacre of civilians under Chun Doo Hwan's command in Kwangju and was
legitimized by the accusation that the civilians were communists. The massacre
was executed with the tacit approval of the U.S. Pacific military command, which
has controlled the South Korean military force since the Korean War (Shin and
Hwang 2003).

4. "Poor relief" usually refers to a limited state welfare system to deal with economic deprivation that relies heavily on charity, rather than on structured welfare
policies. The sign for the renamed Homeless Rehabilitation Center's clinic can be
seen in figure 5.

5. Examples include *Lodû mubi* (Road movie), directed by Kim In-sik; *Sûlpûn yuhok*
(Sad temptation), a TV drama, scripted by No Hi-kyông and produced by Yun
Hûng-sik (1999); *Kasi kogi* (Needle fish), a bestseller novel by Cho Ch'ang-in
(2001); and *Uri ga sarang han namja* (Men whom we loved), a novel by renowned
psychoanalyst Yi Na-mi (1999).

6. Ahn Yông-chun (1998) reports that there were even donations from the overseas
Korean community in the United States.

7. Although this section focuses on the spatial *transformation* of the square and
homelessness, the urban spatial *segregation* of the labor market is also a way to
link street vendors and homeless people. However, the street vendors just out of
college were understood as self-employed entrepreneurs in relation to welfare
policies promoting flexible labor during the crisis, rather than as cheap labor.

8. However, by 2000, SCCUP had also gradually become an advisory group rather
than a decision-making group.

9. The House of Freedom is a huge building and is open to all street people. I review
the system and background of the House of Freedom in detail in the last section
of this chapter.

10. There is a charity facility for long-term street people with severe physical or mental disabilities (Choi Kyông-hui 2001; Cho Sông-chin 2004; Sôn U-ch'ôl 2002).
There are reports on male day-laborers who oscillate between cheap lodgings in a
small bed-sitting room of less than 30 square feet (*jjokpang*) and street living, depending on affordability (Kim Sôn-hui 2001; Kim Su-hyun 2002); and on women
and children who have experienced domestic violence and who do not find long-
term shelters (Kim Kwang-rye 2001; Kim Su-hyun 2001; Seoul City Youth and
Women Unemployment Monitoring Team 1999a).

11. Although it is rare to find long-term qualitative research on homeless people (cf.
Wôn Chông-suk 2001), there has been a growing amount of short-term, survey-
based research on the homeless in master's theses. See Kim Yông-to 1995 and
Pak Ch'ang-yông 2002 for homelessness and housing issues; Choi Yun-sun 2002

and Sin Wôn-u 2003 for mental health for homeless people; Choi Chun-yông 2000 and Mun Chong-im 2002 for the role of institutionalized religions for the homeless issue; and Kang Mi-won 2000 for runaway youth.

12. "Perspectives on Homeless People," OASIS, December 11, 1998.

13. This is the context in which Chon Tae-Il, a textile worker, demanding an end to labor exploitation in P'yônghwa market, committed self-immolation on November 13, 1970 (Chun 2003). It is notable that the government posting (figure 6) describes the location of the House of Freedom as the former site of a commercial high-school building but does not mention the Pangnim factory, which was built for the factory workers.

14. Jason Read (2002) also notes the contingency (in his term, the aleatory foundation of capitalist accumulation) by reinterpreting Marx's theory of "primitive accumulation" as an ongoing process. See also Sunder Rajan 2006 for the connection between biopower and biocapital.

15. Another Italian Marxist, Maurizio Lazzarato (1996, 2004), uses the notion of "immaterial labor" to emphasize the growing significance of social relations as a part of labor value in post-Fordist contexts.

16. The closing of the House of Freedom in 2004 further elucidates neoliberalizing processes. The background of the closure involves residents' complaints regarding safety and falling real-estate value, plus the developer's legal victory over the city in taking over the building. The government recognized homeless people to be permanent welfare subjects in a 2003 ordinance entitling them to shelter, food, and basic health care. However, the state passed on the financial responsibility for homeless provision to the municipal government without budgetary support, which made implementation impossible.

2. "Family Breakdown," Invisible Homeless Women

1. Rayna Rapp (1992) urges us to make a distinction between families and households, as they are commonly conflated. While households are "the empirically measurable units" and "the entities in which people actually live," family is an analytical term for the composition of the nuclear family and the network of kin relations (51–53). My discussion of family builds upon Rapp's definition.

2. Chông Chi-uh, Haep'i endû (Happy end) (1999). Kyung-Hyun Kim, a South Korean film specialist, compares Haep'i endû to another, older South Korean film, Hanyô (Housemaid) (1960), in his book, The Remasculinization of Korean Cinema (2004).

3. See Nam Jung-hyun 1964: 141–168. I thank Theodore Hughes for bringing my attention to this connection.

4. It is not clear how he knew the sex of his unborn child. Although using ultrasound to determine an infant's sex is common in South Korea nowadays, the technology was not available in the 1960s. However, the doctor who performed the abortion could have revealed the sex of the child.

5. In the aftermath of 1987, when mass protests achieved electoral democracy, South

Korea experienced a growth of popular civil movements for women's rights, sexual identity, the environment, and economic justice. See Cho 2000a, 2000b.

6. Progressive women's organizations—such as the Korean Women's Hotline (Yôsông ûi Chônhwa), a hotline for domestic violence; the Korean Sexual Violence Relief Center (Sôngp'ongnyôk Sangdamso); and Korean Women Link (Yôsông Minuhoe)—became very active in the early 1990s. Feminism at this time contributed to recognizing women's individuality based on their sexual autonomy. This is distinct from the previous era's feminist focus on collectivity in association with antiauthoritarian and labor movements. See Moon 2002 and S. Kim 2004.

7. The middle class became included as a subject and object of social activism, partially because of white-collar workers' participation in 1987 social activism, and partially because the achievement of the status of middle class became the normative goal of blue-collar workers (Koo 2001; Suh 2003).

8. The Korean Social and Cultural Institute held a public discussion, "Crisis of Korean Middle Class and Family Breakdown—Causes and Solutions," in 1999. The city of Seoul also held a symposium on family breakdown during women's week in July 2000.

9. Seung-Kyung Kim and John Finch (2002) show that conservative assumptions about gender roles in the family are challenged by practices of middle- and working-class households.

10. See Yim Pôm (1998), "Ihon 90 nyôn ûi 2 pae" (Divorce doubled over the '90s); Kim U-sôk, Yi Hun-bôm, and Chông Che-won (1998), "Munôji nûn kajông" (The family is collapsing); and Yi Tae-hûi (1999), "Ajôssi ka anieyo, tonieyo: 15 sal ûi wonjokyoje ch'unggyôk" (He isn't an elder, he's just money: Shocking teen prostitution). This last article begins, "After running away, girls work part-time in a gas station or coffee shop, and later become prostitutes through Internet chat rooms, charging eighty dollars a night, but sometimes end up being robbed by adult male clients."

11. Regarding negative editorials on families of same-sex couples, see *Kyunghyang sinmun*, October 2, 2000; *Han'guk ilbo*, December 8, 1999. On divorce among elderly couples, see *Tonga ilbo*, October 5, 1999; *Tonga ilbo*, May 7, 1999. *Hwanghon ihon* literally refers to "divorce at golden sunset." *Hwanghon* (golden sunset) is a romantic, euphemistic way of referring to the elderly. It is a paradox to place "golden sunset" and "divorce" together, as divorce is not a respected action, especially within the context of the elderly.

12. In this particular example, the woman (Yi Si-hyông) ultimately won her case in 2000. However, in a similar case in 1998, a woman (Kim Ch'ang-cha) sued with the support of women's organizations, but she lost in the high court. See Yi Chae-ûn 2004.

13. *Tongsôngyônaeja* is also used to mean "homosexual" but the Korean term with "yôn" in the middle has a derogatory meaning. Although it is used less and less in public, some conservative groups and individuals intentionally use it vehemently,

as the Los Angeles Korean church did in its campaign in 1999 against a protection law for lesbians and gays.

14. It was the first time that progressive women's organizations publicly supported same-sex-loving people.

15. See note 11 for examples of newspaper editorials.

16. Charting the feminist social response in the era of postdemocratization is beyond the scope of this book. Risking oversimplification, I would argue that the feminist movement was not docile during the postdemocratization era; however, during the crisis, it prioritized its efforts to respond to the crisis and get institutional recognition from the presidential office. As a result, it was not successful in attacking gender discrimination at the ground level of the crisis-related restructuring process and homeless policies. Regarding the success of the institutionalization and mainstreaming of the women's movement in relation to the growth of civil society, see S. Kim 2004 and Moon 2002. Kim's piece succinctly shows the dilemma of women's NGOs, which received unprecedented support from the presidential office during the crisis.

17. Although Moon 2004 does not discuss the young male generation's conservatism during the crisis, her piece shows the history of South Korean nationalism and the Cold War military regimes as core elements of military institutionalization and culture in South Korea. See also Shin 2006 and Jager 2003.

18. Two women workers, Kim Hyang-ah and Kim Mi-suk, sued the bank for violation of labor law in 1999 but court decisions favored the employer. The women appealed through the highest courts in November 2002, but were not successful.

19. Yoon Eun-chông's documentary film in 1999 sponsored by Yôsông Minuhoe Koyong P'yôngdûng Ch'ujinbonbu (Women Link, Equal Employment Committee).

20. The chant was also contained in a pamphlet distributed at the rally.

21. The state sponsored a program to help female breadwinners (that is, middle-aged mothers) open small businesses (yôsông kajang ch'angôp). Yet to obtain financial support from the state, female breadwinners were required to provide collateral from the closest male adult in the family. See Poster and Salime 2002 for similar observations.

22. A reporter told the team that he would not pursue homeless women's issues because he did not want to deal with the city officials' offensive responses.

23. There was also the Flower Village (Kkot Maûl), a long-term shelter (for both genders) run by a religious community but funded by the city. The shelter served people who were seriously disabled and not expected to adjust to "normal" society (Chông Wôn-oh 1999).

24. I introduce two homeless women's narratives in chapter 3.

25. Literature on the welfare state tends to highlight either the maternalist or paternalist character of the society. Linda Gordon (1993) criticizes the dualistic categorization of a maternalist welfare regime versus a paternalist welfare regime.

Following Gordon, I contend that the two coexist and in fact mirror each other. Family breakdown discourses during the crisis in South Korea correspond to her contention that paternalist and maternalist discourses operate at the same time. In "Gender, State and Society," Gordon identifies three specific contexts of maternalist welfare regimes in U.S. history. The first context was a conviction that reformers should function in a motherly role toward the poor (particularly children and single mothers). In the second context, women believed that it was their work, experience, or destiny as mothers that made them uniquely able to lead the campaign for public social provision and made other women deserving of help. Lastly, a maternalist orientation was manifested by the women's interest in giving money directly to women, through mothers' aid programs, as opposed to proposals for family-allowance programs that give money to children through their fathers. Gordon proposes that only through contrasting maternalism to distinctly nonmaternalist but equally feminist political stances can we clarify the precise content of maternalism. Maternalist feminists argued that women needed protection because of their responsibility as mothers of future generations. This argument was sometimes biological, sometimes social, but always expressed a commitment to gender differentiation. It is difficult to understand this view outside its political context, which included another feminist orientation that was directly critical of this emphasis on male-female difference; equal-rights feminists feared that special protections for women would ultimately undermine women's advancement, and many emphasized the fundamental similarities of men and women.

26. Cf. Susser 1999. Ida Susser's piece analyzes family norms in relation to the homeless policy and the shelter system in New York City.

27. This categorization of family breakdown is still present in the most recent reports on homeless women (Kim Kwang-rye 2001; Kim Su-hyun 2001: 31, 45).

28. Salimtô Newsletter (fall 1999). The cover page features a picture of a homeless shelter hosting collective marriage ceremonies. The newsletter also reported anecdotes about each couple's successes.

29. Ann Anagnost's context for the use of affective labor is American middle-class families' adoptions of Chinese children (2000). Akiko Takeyama (2005, 2007) uses affective labor in a very different context in relation to the commodification of romance in a Japanese host bar.

30. Elsewhere I describe the discursive change of "father" from indifferent breadwinner to affectionate caregiver in South Korean literature (for example, Cho Ch'ang-in's Kasi kogi [Needle fish], 2001) and homeless rehabilitation programs. See J. Song 2003, chapter 3.

31. This issue is related to a South Korean feminist movement to eliminate the household-head system (hojuje). The household-head system recognizes only a patrilineal person as the head of a household, which gives legal authority to the children and patrilineal kin men over the wife when the breadwinning man is absent. In early 2005, this controversial system was legally removed as a result

of strenuous feminist effort. This historic feminist achievement and the inauguration of the Ministry of Women (changed in 2005 to the Ministry of Gender
Equality and the Family, and changed again in 2008 to the Ministry of Gender
Equality) both took place in the postcrisis era. It is notable, though, that the postcrisis feminist achievements in South Korea up to 2008 have been a matter of
debate between radical feminists (who do not think a close association between
women and family enhances women's liberation) and reformist feminists (who
make women's caretaker role in the family a priority). Young-Gyung Paik's study
of "low fertility and aging society" (chôchulsan koryônghwa) (2006) demonstrates
that liberal policies of policing gender and family through reprivatizing women's
labor remained in place even after the crisis.

32. This affective value of women's emotional labor is similar to the immaterial labor
that Maurizio Lazzarato discusses as a characteristic of post-Fordism. My contention with the Italian Marxists' expansion and reinterpretation of Marxism by
focusing on the blurred boundary between work and nonwork, material and non-
material, is that they dismiss the historic aspects of women's emotional labor. I
am interested in further developing the evolvement of this affective value in neoliberalism by looking at the relationship between the post-Fordist labor quality
that highlights communication and social relation skills and the gendered value
of affective labor in subsequent research.

33. The position of women's welfare counselor was created at the end of Kim Young
Sam's presidency (1993–1997), in concert with laws aimed at preventing domestic
violence and protecting its victims. However, local police officers did not enforce
the new laws. They persisted in their conventional attitudes toward domestic violence, maintaining that public officers should not intervene in a "family matter."
As a result, most police reports of domestic violence ended up giving more credi-
bility to the view of male patriarchs. See Ms. Pak's case in chapter 3.

34. This remark about the function of family corresponds to the point that Yi Tûk-
chae makes in his book, Kajokchuûi nûn yaman ida (Familism is barbarous) (2001);
he writes that "family is sacred but familism is alarming." I elaborate on this in
chapter 5.

3. Homeless Women's Needs

1. Regarding the relationship between gender and welfare history of the United
States, see Fraser 1989; Gordon 1990, 1994; and Skocpol 1992. On gender and
welfare state regimes from a comparative perspective, see O'Connor, Orloff, and
Shaver 1999; and Sainsbury 1999. There is an emerging body of feminist literature on gender and welfare beyond the contexts of Western Europe and North
America. For Eastern European nation-states, see Gal and Kligman 2000a, 2000b;
and Haney 1998, 1999. For East Asia, see Peng 2003, 2004.

2. There are anthropologists who research neoliberal welfare systems along with
gender. Catherine Kingfisher's edited volume Western Welfare in Decline is an ex-

ample. Building upon the gender analyses of national welfare systems in North America, Europe, Australia, and New Zealand by Nancy Fraser, Ann Shola Orloff, Julia O'Connor, and Diane Sainsbury, Kingfisher succinctly sums up women's increasing burden. Kingfisher notes, "Current welfare state restructuring . . . may in fact serve to undermine women's capacities to 'demand and utilize social rights' (Orloff 1993: 309) — despite the fact that many reforms are ostensibly designed to buttress women's capacities as 'individual'" (Kingfisher 2002: 11).

3. Joanne Passaro's study shows that similar gendered assumptions were applied differently in American homeless policy (Passaro 1996). Homeless women were considered to be more deserving of government support, based on the assumption that they would be more easily rehabilitated if they were taken off the street.

4. In the long tradition of political and urban anthropology that has drawn attention to subaltern issues such as the urban poor and the unstable condition of workers, the discussion of a "public anthropology" has recently emerged. Public anthropology does not advocate anthropology as something learned in academia, and then applied in nonacademic institutional contexts, such as state institutions or NGOs. Rather, it urges the continuous negotiation of the position of the anthropologist, and a corresponding refinement in anthropological methodologies in the very research context that challenges the division between the inside and outside of both academia and the discipline. Examples of general discussions on public anthropology include Lamphere 2004, and Lassiter, Cook, and Field 2005. Regarding organ trafficking, see Scheper-Hughes 2000, 2005. For controversial discussions on anthropologists' involvement in the process of destruction of the Yanomami, see Borofsky and Albert 2005. On poverty, see Farmer 2003; Good 2001; Goode and Maskovsky 2001; Hyatt 2001; Lyon-Callo 2004; Morgen 2002; and Morgen and Weigt 2001. On refugees, see Ong 2003. Vincent Lyon-Callo's activist stand on homeless research (2001, 2004) supports shelter staffs' progressive politics that have been constrained by bureaucratic rules.

5. I call the site "W" to protect Ms. Kim's privacy and to not compromise the safety of other homeless women who stay there.

6. This phrase is usually used to express cynicism.

7. Her comment on the IMF crisis confirms the newness of the homeless policy during the crisis.

8. I was surprised by her question but soon realized that I could pass as a homeless woman. There wasn't much difference in looks between her and me: neither of us was wearing makeup, and we both wore casual, worn-out, unfashionable clothes, and carried backpacks instead of handbags.

9. Ms. Pak said she wanted her children to go to school, but when children register at school, it is necessary for their father — as long as they are under their father's legal custody — to sign for entry. Their father could easily have found his children wherever they went. The head of the shelter where Ms. Pak stayed pointed out that the regulations of school registration prevented children who escape from violent fathers from receiving any kind of education, even in the form of auditing classes.

It was up to the principal in private schools to decide whether, in special cases, a child could audit classes. Most principals did not consider domestic violence cases. Most women with children in the homeless women's shelter went through similar difficulties educating their children. Thus, many women left their children with the fathers to enable them to continue going to school. This information allows us to think of possible reasons why homeless mothers would leave their children at home rather than to moralize their decision as Ms. Pang, the city official discussed in chapter 2, did.

10. She did not refer to her family of origin or her extended family.

11. On the lack of enforcement by local police of new domestic violence laws in the late 1990s, see note 33 in chapter 2.

12. Ms. Pak could not stay at shelters for victims of domestic violence because they did not provide any work opportunities or career development. In comparison to middle-class women who could find respite at shelters for domestic violence while they prepared legal action to receive divorce compensation, economically deprived women could not afford a two-month period of rest and seclusion because they had the burden of earning a living as well as recovering from domestic violence (Seoul City Youth and Women Unemployment Monitoring Team 1990a: 107–8).

13. Each letter stands for a large prayer house run by enterprising churches in South Korea.

14. I hesitated for a moment because it had been a long time since I had visited prayer houses.

15. One kidowôn apparently drove homeless people out in the winter of 1999. S kido-wôn has 700,000 members; the existence of such huge prayer houses reflects the growth of South Korean Christianity. Although both Protestant and Catholic churches grew rapidly in the last century in conjunction with the opening to "Western culture," Protestant churches are the most widespread by far. In 2000, half of the population of South Korea was Protestant and one quarter was Catholic (Buswell and Lee 2006).

16. Education sessions for social workers were regularly held by the City Women's Affairs Division. I got the impression that social workers did not welcome these meetings because they saw them as a city enforcement or surveillance of NGOs and nonprofit organizations.

17. A follow-up study of homeless women's shelters in 2001 confirmed the Unemployment Monitoring Team's 1999 assessment, although it does not clearly acknowledge the team's report (Kim Su-hyun 2001). This may be because the 2001 report was conducted by a city-affiliated research institute that followed the city officials by distancing itself from public works program workers' reports (see preface).

18. According to the Public Livelihood Protection Law, anyone between the ages of eighteen and sixty-five is assumed to have an income-earning ability unless they are mentally or physically disabled. In 2004, working poor referred to people with a monthly income of less than $370 (368,000 won) for a single household and $1,050 (1,056,000 won) for households with four members, which was the official

minimum monthly wage. In 2008 the minimum monthly income announced by the Ministry of Labor was $852 (852,020 won) for 226 hours.

19. Since 1987, the program has covered the fees of vocational high schools for children in all four categories.

20. For example, Ms. Pak's case shows that school registration for the children of women fleeing domestic violence is difficult because of the need for fathers to register their children.

21. The Roh Moo Hyun administration (2003–2008) has created temporary jobs in school counseling at several designated working poor local communities. The target group for counseling is students in the schools, but the role of the counselor is to educate teachers and parents and connect school with local organizations (Yi Hye-yông 2006). The program is well regarded, but it is unclear whether the current Lee Myung Bak administration (2008 to the present) will continue to fund it.

22. There is a government telephone referral service for women (called "1366"). However, all shelters for women, whatever their needs, have limited tenure (between two and nine months), except for Flower Village (Kkot Maûl), which is for physically or mentally disabled and abandoned people.

23. The origins of maternalist social policies in South Korea are assumed to be in the Japanese colonial influence. The protection of widows in postwar policies is common in many countries. According to Aya Ezawa, the Japanese imperial regime introduced a maternal protection law and a child protection law in 1910 (personal communication, July 19, 2001). This was almost contemporary to the maternal and child protection laws in Korea in 1911. It would be interesting to explore the history of social policies with a particular focus on maternalist policies, in Korea, Japan, and other East Asian countries. The history of social policies in Korea before the Korean War has rarely been studied. Ito Peng (2004) compares recent Japanese and Korean welfare policies; Joseph Wong (2004) compares the Taiwanese and Korean systems.

24. See note 25 in chapter 2 for a discussion of the feminist debate on "maternalist" versus "paternalist" states.

25. Similar incidents are reported in *Yesan edo sông i itta* (Gender issues in the budget), by Korean Women Link (2005).

26. In 1999, the total number of homeless women in shelters was about 125. In 2001 the number of sheltered homeless women was 86 in five homeless women's shelters (children included), and another 21 in family shelters. But fluctuations were high and one homeless women's shelter reported that 253 women had left in three years. In other words, there were probably many more sheltered homeless women than reported.

27. Reverend Kang is discussed later in this chapter and in chapter 5.

28. See Korea Urban Research Institute 1999 and Kim Su-hyun 2002. Also, Chu Chong-kuk (2003) reported that the urban absolute poverty rate dramatically increased from 2.8 percent in 1997 to 7.3 percent in 1999.

29. The subject of institutes for vagabonds is a huge topic, but an understudied one, partially because there is a lack of research on homelessness, but more because these institutes are part of the socially taboo subject of the mental health care system (Choi Yun-sun 2002; Cho Sông-chin 2004; Sin Wôn-u 2003; Sôn U-ch'ôl 2002). In addition, these institutes are privately run by either religious groups (for example, Flower Village) or Korean charity enterprises operating as a front for more illegal activities. There are a few state-run institutes, such as the TCSW, which is discussed later in this chapter.

30. She described an incident in which a homeless man beat his homeless girlfriend to death because she allegedly had an affair with another homeless man.

31. Akhil Gupta (2001) observed a similar mechanism in India, where the state controlled local welfare services for children by checking numbers. Local agents were pressed by governmental officials to maintain full capacity of the facilities. ¹⁵⁷

32. Although I knew the city of Seoul supported 4 women's shelters and 2 family shelters out of 125 shelters, it was hard to contact the "right" person to provide concrete information about homeless women and a critical perspective on the policies on homelessness.

33. This is another example of the effects on homeless policies of combining neoliberal strategy (partnerships between NGOs and GOs) with a long-standing regulative technique (top-down bureaucracy).

34. Yearly leases (chônse) are the convention for renting in South Korea. Monthly rent (wôlse) is also possible, but used to be very rare (Nelson 2000: 57). During the crisis years, landlords who were also short of regular income began to rent out their places using monthly payment contracts.

35. The practice of asserting "proper procedure" (chôlch'a) is, like "responsibility holder" (ch'aegim sojae), a bureaucratic trope that indexes the defensiveness of mid- and low-level officials in the city bureaucracy under a heavy workload: it is used to excuse rejection of orders from the high-level, to mask evasion of one's responsibility and procrastination, to accuse others, or to claim rights over a task.

36. Emi is a vernacular version of mother, such as mommy; pyông refers to disease in Korean.

37. According to senior staff for the women's shelter, "Governmental policy [regarding homelessness] is tailored to homeless men. When the city provides a subsidy for homeless people during the traditional holidays, that stuff is all for men, not a thing for women. And when we request some essential support from the Welfare Ministry, we often hear scornful words from the official in charge, like 'there are only a few homeless women, aren't there?'" (Sin Chông-sôn 2000).

38. My role in the team, to provide advocacy for the support of homeless women without challenging the city officials and experts who make them into objects of charity, is similar to Reverend Kang's efforts to fit into the neoliberal state rhetoric of rehabilitation.

39. Another interesting aspect of her narrative is that she reaffirmed the family as the primary organization to provide comfort even as she urged the social embrace of individuals who cannot or do not want to rely upon family (see chapter 5).

40. Hae-Joang Cho (1988) notes that Korean women did not necessarily sacrifice themselves in the Confucian maternalist ideology, but rather exerted authority by achieving the status of being a mother of sons in the patrilineal and patriarchal Korean Confucian society.

4. Youth as Neoliberal Subjects

1. See the introduction for a discussion of information technology (IT) envisioned as a future capitalist development in Korea in comparison with Tessa Morris-Suzuki's observations on 1980s Japan (1988).

2. A venture company in South Korea refers to a small office business based on IT. Examples include Internet business and a Web portal.

3. Kaushik Sunder Rajan's argument that finance capital is resurging merchant capital that was conquered by industrial capital during the period of industrial capitalism is convincing (2006). Jason Read's theorization of ongoing primitive accumulation through the finance capital sector is related to Sunder Rajan and useful for viewing history through the dynamic movement of capital (2002).

4. Many young professionals sought careers abroad during the Korean labor and industrial changes. For highly educated women, the primary reason was the lack of jobs and promotions due to gender discrimination at home. Further, young professionals in general who seek work abroad are examples of the liberal ethos and subjectivities that look for alternatives to the stifling neo-Confucian and militaristic environment of big corporations and the social pressures to succeed in that culture.

5. Regarding praise for South Korea's successful utilization of public works programs as a model for other Asian nations during the regional debt crisis, see Oh Sang-sôk 2000. There is no direct research on the impact of the data digitalization project (or IT investment project) on young adults' unemployment. However, the public works program in general was seen by the IMF and the World Bank as having contributed to a reduction in unemployment rates. The data digitalization project is ongoing and expected to produce some positive effects, especially considering its enormous budget (Sin Sang-yông 2004).

6. Even before the crisis, Dr. Oh had used a liberal perspective on youth, education, and gender issues to compete with the orthodox Marxist views that were the dominant ideology of political and social activism during the military dictatorship era.

7. Mr. Cho took the peculiar tone of an older brother scolding his "immature" (ch'ôlbuji) younger sisters. Not all male city officials displayed such a paternalistic and patriarchal attitude to team members, who were mostly young unmarried women. However, male city officials often switched from the professional com-

municative code to the one used between older men and younger women—father and daughter, or older brother and younger sister—regardless of their nonkin relations. On the inaccuracy of Mr. Cho's statement about "blood tax": it is possible that government workers' wages were reduced to create extra funds for the cost of implementing the unemployment policy (such as the public works program and vocational training or homeless policy), but the budget for the social policy, including the public works program, came from immense funds that were specifically designated for the unemployment welfare policy from the IBRD (the International Bank for Reconstruction and Development under the World Bank) and the IMF. The bulk of the funds made available from cutting government workers' wages were used for restructuring government in general. These funds were applied to the expense of auditing and evaluating governmental offices and personnel (for downsizing) by nongovernmental professional groups, as well as to the payment of unemployment insurance to government officials who chose to take voluntary layoffs (myŏnyet'oejik).

8. Chu Dôk-han, the organizer and a leading member of the National Good-For-Nothing Association, published two books that allude to his agenda of creating resources for paeksu (1998a, 1998b).

9. The Independent Festival was first held in 1998 and continued until 2000. The alternative and fringe groups of artists, who resisted dependence on the government, modeled the festival after the Edinburgh Fringe Festival and defined the festival's spirit as an "independent, civil, and minority volunteer art festival." The festival emerged in defiance to a governmental proposal to create a youth festival in 1998. However, after their presentation at the workshop hosted by the team, festival activists proposed that the city of Seoul create a public works program to support the festival, which was having financial difficulties.

10. Sunder Rajan (2006) shows biotechnology as a newly commodifying domain that is constantly played as a game in the future to "generate the present that enables the future," making underemployed youth into deserving welfare subjects by envisioning them as a new future human capital—"creative" and "self-sufficient" workers who would not just produce and sell new commodities (through "venture business") but also could be valued and invested by finance capital (that is, start-up seed money from investors and stock market value). As the Italian Marxists discuss about the production of the "possible" (Lazzarato 2004) and Foucauldian analysis of political economy of "hope" (Rose and Novas 2005), these gambling aspects—seeking new markets and immaterial commodities—manipulate the future as a straw man to set the present in motion.

Lisa Hoffman's observation of Chinese patriotic professionalism in the job search process parallels my research on Korean welfare subjectification of youth as "new intellectuals" (Hoffman 2006). Both deal with a neoliberal governmentality different from that in advanced liberal countries. Also, in both instances, young adults are imbued with the idea of self-reliance and the entrepreneurial spirit. However, there is a major difference: I do not find a clear sign of patriotism among the underemployed Korean youth in terms of their job-hunting decisions. This may be because the liberalization since the early 1990s distanced them from the collectivistic illiberal tradition inherited from both the military government and militant political activism (Moon 2005), especially through the crisis, which severely blocked their career development.

11. Some taxi drivers at the major train stations in Seoul illegally doubled their prices at night because they knew there was little other transportation available. My encounter with Mr. Yu presented an entirely different scenario.

12. Yonsei University has a reputation for being urban, liberal, and Westernized in contrast to other private universities founded by domestic donors, such as Korea University, which used to be stereotyped as being populated by students of rural origin and conservative attitudes. However, this distinction has become fairly moot in the last decade, during which most Korean universities have established images of themselves as international schools by recruiting foreign students and instructors who teach in English.

13. This might be related to Samsung's history of not allowing labor unions and instead offering high-quality worker benefits.

14. "To animyôn mo da" is a Korean maxim deriving from a Korean traditional game called yut. Competing between individuals or teams, Koreans play yut by throwing four wooden poles on the ground to mark points on a map. In this game, if one wooden pole is turned around, it is To, which marks the lowest point. If nothing is pulled back, it is called Mo, which marks the highest point. It signifies that nobody knows what will happen when making significant decisions in life because successful decisions depend on the slightest differences in luck.

15. Undated report from the Seoul Industry and Economic Bureau. This report was probably released before the opening event on June 30, 1999.

16. See Laura C. Nelson's *Measured Excess* (2000) for the development of urban planning in Seoul, especially south of the Han River.

17. The city administration's mobilization of young artists for venture industry and the team's featuring of alternative artist groups as deserving welfare subjects exemplify the tendency for art and culture to become a neoliberal capitalist marker in pursuit of "antipolitical" and "independent" human values. Anna Szemere (2000) observes a phenomenon of "antipolitics" in art's autonomy in the transformation of postsocialist Hungary, without making the explicit connection to neoliberalism.

18. The extra payment for two weeks of hard work was $150 for the whole team, which consisted of five members at the time.

19. A derogatory expression that is usually used by elders.

5. The Dilemma of Progressive Intellectuals

1. Regarding peasant-intellectual alliance, see Abelmann 1996.

2. According to Antonio Gramsci, "all men are intellectuals: but not all men have

in society the function of intellectuals" (1971). *Organic intellectuals* are intellectuals who change society through ideological apparatuses such as education and the media by articulating the feelings and experiences that the masses are unable to express for themselves.

3. This change had more of an impact on Korean leftists advocating class revolution (People's Democracy) than on leftists seeking reunification with North Korea (National Liberation) (Park 2002).

4. However, there was violent repression of student demonstrations in Yonsei University in 1996. Student activists still saw a reason to confront state aggression, but were unsuccessful in garnering wide support.

5. The first civilian president was Roh Tae Woo, ironically a military coup leader who had ordered the Kwangju massacre. He gave up his military status to become a presidential candidate.

6. *Moraesigye* is about people's traumatic experiences during the Kwangju massacre. *Yŏmyŏng ŭi nundongja* focuses on aboriginal communism in Korea, which originated in the anti–Japanese imperialism era and was persecuted under the U.S. military occupation regime. Korean aboriginal communism emerged as an antifeudal struggle in relation to the socioeconomic discrimination against nonelites in the neo-Confucian caste system, quite separate from the Marxist knowledge that arrived through China and the Soviet Union (Cumings 1997; Paik 1992). See Suh 1967, 1970, and 1981 for a detailed history of Korean communism. The drama also features the "comfort women" issue and the Cheju Uprising (South Korean communist struggles in Cheju island, at the south end of the Korean peninsula, from 1948 to 1954, including a massacre of civilians by the South Korean and U.S. army).

7. See also Choi Yun's *Hoesaek nunsaram* (Grey snowman) (1992).

8. Nancy Abelmann (1996) demonstrates the personal costs paid by dissenting intellectuals or peasant activists during the transition from the militant leftist movement in the 1980s to the civil society movements in the 1990s. See particularly her discussion of Yun, who was a leader in a dispute against a capitalist landowning company (that exploited peasants' labor and crops) and agreed to purchase the land from the capitalist company. Seung-Kyung Kim (1997) and Hagen Koo (2001) also describe how female labor activists accommodated their personal and familial needs during the transition.

9. From the official homepage of PSPD, http://blog.peoplepower21.org/English.

10. "Department store" style refers to NGOs which take up all kinds of advocacy work, including consumer rights, in the process losing their radical direction on certain issues (S. Kim 2004).

11. I am indebted to Jin Ho Jang's elaboration of finance capital in South Korea in this discussion of small shareholder activism.

12. Thanks to Soo-Jung Lee for introducing me to this book.

13. He claims that South Korean citizens are accustomed to being deceived by the mass media and by the state's fundraising campaigns (for example, the gold-

collection campaign), which he sees as a fraud designed to shift recovery costs to families. He also uses the term *sado-masochism* (*sadijŭm/majohijŭm*) to describe the relationship between the state administration and citizens.

14. He was an activist scholar who had a profound concern for the urban working poor, including day laborers. In this context, homeless issues became an extension of his interest in the urban working poor. In addition, he himself was struggling in a marginalized job market as a semi-independent researcher, lacking secure employment and influence.

15. This kind of comparison is not uncommon. However, because I attended college from the late 1980s to the early 1990s, I experienced the transition from confrontational activism (directed against capitalism and state fascism, including cold-war ideology and the military government) to conciliatory activism (directed against everyday fascism, including the 1980s student activist culture itself).

16. See chapter 2 of the present work and Song 2006, where I analyze the discourse of "family breakdown" in relation to neoliberal governmentality. See also Kim and Finch 2002.

17. The Compensation Proposition for victims of the Kwangju massacre (1980) was launched in 1998 after President Kim Dae Jung was inaugurated.

18. It is especially rare for parents to send their children to a mental hospital because of the social norm of family being the primary institution of physical and mental health.

Coda: The Pursuit of Well-Being

1. Readers might ask what political alternatives or "politics of the possible" for activist intellectuals I can offer. I am continually seeking a better way of tackling the current situation in South Korea without reducing it to the well-worn concepts of "revolution from below" or "proletariat of the world, unite!" I am very wary of the similarities between the psychology of the revolutionary propaganda of "hope" and the market production of the "possible" (Lazzarato 2004).

GLOSSARY OF SELECT KOREAN WORDS AND PHRASES

aedûl appa (애들아빠): the father of my children
aegi ômmadûl (애기 엄마들): mothers of children
aiemep'û *or* **aimep'û sat'ae** (아이엠에프 사태): IMF crisis, Asian Debt Crisis
aiemep'û silchik nosukcha (아이엠에프 실직 노숙자): IMF homeless, short-term
  street people
arûbait'û (아르바이트): part-time jobs
asurajang (아수라장): a hell of a battlefield

bench'yô ch'angôp (벤처 창업): to found a venture company
bench'yô kiôp (벤처 기업): venture companies
bench'yô ôpkye (벤처 산업, 벤처 업계): venture industry
bench'yô saôp (벤처 사업): venture business
bench'yô yôlp'ung (벤처 열풍): venture wind

chaebôl (재벌): big corporations or conglomerates
ch'aegim sojae (책임소재): process of identifying the "proper" person in charge
chaehwalûiji (재활의지): intention to rehabilitate (oneself)
chaeya seryôk (재야세력): dissident groups promoting democratization
chagi kwalli (자기관리): self-management
chagi kyebal (자기계발): self-cultivation
chahwal / chaehwal shimt'ô (자활/재활 쉼터): recovery/rehabilitation shelter
Ch'amyô Yôndae (참여연대): People's Solidarity for Participatory Democracy
  (PSPD)
ch'angjojôk (창조적): creative
ch'angôp chôngsin (창업정신): the entrepreneurial spirit for successful self-
  realization
ch'angûisông (창의성): creativity
chayulsông (자율성): autonomy
Chayu ûi Chip (자유의 집): House of Freedom
Che i ûi Kôn'guk Wiwônhoe (제 2의 건국위원회): Committee of the Second
  Foundation of the Nation
Cheju Sa Sam Hangjaeng (제주 4.3 항쟁): Cheju Uprising
ch'eyuk taehoe (체육대회): sport contests

ch'imae halmôni (치매할머니): old women with dementia

chisigin (지식인): intellectuals

chôch'ulsan koryônghwa (저출산 고령화): low fertility and aging society

Chogye (조계종): the largest Buddhist denomination in South Korea

ch'ôlbuji (철부지): an immature youngster

chôlch'a (절차): proper procedure

Chôlla-to (전라도): Chôlla Province

ch'ômdan int'ellijyôntû pilding (첨단인텔리젼트 빌딩): ultra-smart building

chôngbohwa saôp (정보화 사업): data digitalization project

Ch'ôngnyôn Yôsông Sirôp Taech'aek Monit'ôring T'im (청년여성실업대책모니터링팀): Youth and Women Unemployment Monitoring Team

chôngsang saenghwal e ûi chaehwal ûiji (정상생활에의 재활의지): intention to rehabilitate toward a normal life

Chôn'guk Paeksu Yônhap (전국백수연합): National Good-For-Nothing Association

Chônnam Taehakkyo (전남대학교): Chônnam University

chônse (전세): yearly leases

ch'ôryayebae (철야예배): all-night church services

Chosôn mulsan changnyô undong (조선물산장려운동): Korean production movement

Chosôn wangjo (조선왕조): Chosôn dynasty

chumin tûngnok chûng (주민등록증): resident registration cards

Chungang ilbo (중앙일보): "Central daily"; a South Korean daily newspaper

Ch'ungch'ông-to (충청도): Ch'ungch'ông Province

chungsanch'ûng / chung'gan kyegûp (중산층 또는 중간계급): middle class

emi pyông (에미병): "mommy's pain"

en chi o hakkwa (엔지오 학과): academic "NGO department"

Haep'i endû (해피 엔드): "Happy end" (film)

Han'guk ilbo (한국일보): "Korea daily"; a Korean daily newspaper

Han'guk kyôngje siumun (한국경제신문): "Korean economic newspaper"; a Korean daily newspaper

Han'gyôre sinmun (한겨레 신문): "United daily"; a Korean daily newspaper

Hanyang Taehakkyo (한양대학교): Hanyang University

hoesik (회식): meals paid for by employers

hojuje (호주제): household-head system

Hûimang ûi Chip (희망의 집): Houses of Hope

hwanghon ihon (황혼이혼): elderly divorce ("divorce at golden sunset")

Hwan'gyông Yônhap (환경연합): Korean Federation for Environmental Movement

hyôlse (혈세): blood tax

hyômogam (혐오감): uneasiness

Ilsi Sirip Punyô Pohoso (일시시립부녀보호소): Temporary City Shelter for Women (TCSW)

Inch'ôn (인천): a port city near Seoul

Indojuûi Silch'ôn Ûisa Hyôbûihoe (인도주의실천의사협의회): Humanitarian Practice Medical Doctors' Association

inkkwôn (인권): human right

kach'ul sonyô (가출소녀): runaway girls

kaesông (개성): individual character as an asset

kajok sahoe (가족사회): familial society

kajông haech'e / kajok haech'e (가정해체, 또는 가족해체): family breakdown

kidowôn (기도원): prayer houses

kimbap (김밥): seaweed rolls

kohangnyôk sirôpcha (고학력실업자): a highly educated unemployed person

kohangnyôk sirôp konggong kûllo saôp (고학력실업 공공근로 사업): public works programs for the highly educated unemployed

konggong kûllo saôp (공공근로사업): public works programs

Koyong Anjông Taech'aek-kwa (고용안정대책과): Labor Policy Division

kuch'ông (구청): the district office

kujojojông (구조조정): structural adjustment

kukch'ae posang undong (국채보상운동): repay debt movement

kuksu and udong (국수와 우동): noodles

kûllobal sidae (글로발 시대): the global era

kûlloûiyok (근로의욕): desire to work

kûm moûgi undong (금모으기 운동): gold-collection campaign

kun'gasanjômje p'yeji undong (군가산점제폐지 운동): the campaign for the removal of promotion credits for men for mandatory military service

Kwangjang (광장): "The square" (novel)

Kwangju (광주): A central city in the Chôlla Province and the site of a massive civilian massacre during a South Korean military coup

kyeyakchik (계약직): contract job

Kyônggi-to (경기도): Kyônggi Province

Kyônghyang sinmun (경향신문): "Trend daily"; a Korean daily newspaper

Kyônje Chôngûi Silch'ôn Yônhap (Kyôngsillyôn) (경제정의실천연합 [경실련]): Citizens' Coalition for Economic Justice (CCEJ)

Kyôngsang-to (경상도): Kyôngsang Province

kyôulnagi undong (겨울나기 운동): movement to survive winter

mihonmo sisôl (미혼모 시설): shelters for unmarried pregnant women

Minjok-Haebang (민족해방): National Liberation (NL)

minjuhwa undong (민주화 운동): democratization movement

minjung (민중): (subaltern) masses

Minjung-Minju (민중민주): People's Democracy (PD)

minjung sinhak (민중신학): liberation theology

minkwan hyômnyôk (민관협력): partnership between GOs and NGOs

moja poho sisôl (모자보호 시설): shelters for single mothers

165

Moraesigye (모래시계): "Sandglass" (TV drama)
mubôpchidae (무법지대): lawless
Munhwa Pangsong (문화방송): Munhwa Broadcasting Company (MBC)
myôngyet'oejik (명예퇴직): voluntary early retirement or layoffs

nodong undong (노동운동): labor movement
Nonghyôp Ûnhaeng (농협은행): Korean Farmer Association Bank
nosukcha (노숙자): homeless people
Nosukcha Chiwônsent'ô (노숙자 지원센터): Homeless Assistance Center
nosukcha k'adû (노숙자 카드): homeless identification card
Nosukcha Sangdamso (노숙자 상담소): Homeless Counseling Center
Nosukcha Taech'aek Hyôbûihoe (노숙자대책협의회): Seoul City Commission on Homeless Policy
Nosukcha Taech'aek-pan (노숙자 대책반): Homeless Policy Division
Nosukcha Tasisôgi Chiwônsent'ô (노숙자 다시서기 지원센터): Homeless Rehabilitation Center (HRC)

oehwan wigi (외환위기): Asian Debt Crisis (the crisis)
onô (오너): ownership

p'ach'ulso (파출소): local policy branch
paeksu (백수): good-for-nothings
p'agyônjik (파견직): subcontract work
pan-chaebôl (반재벌): antimonopoly
Pangnim pangjik kongjang (방림방직공장): Pangnim textile factory
Pangsong Yulli Wiwônhoe (방송윤리위원회): Broadcasting Ethics Committee
pan-tokchae (반독재): antidictatorship
Pogôn Pokchi-kuk (보건복지국): Health and Welfare Bureau
p'ojangmach'a (포장마차): mobile bars and restaurants
p'oktong ûi wihômsông (폭동의 위험성): potential for violent action
pôm kungmin kyôryôn undong (범국민결연운동): pan-national network movement
purangin (부랑인): the "rootless"; vagabond or long-term street people
purang yôsông (부랑여성): rootless women
pyôljjôngjik (별정직): regular government positions for specialists, who are hired outside of the hiring system and the government employment exam

saep'aratk'e chôlmûn aedûl (새파랗게 젊은 애들): "green youngsters like unripe radishes"
Sa-Il-Gu Hyôngmyông (사일구 혁명): April Revolution
sanae k'ôp'ûl (사내커플): spousal employees
Sanôp Chiwôn Chôngch'aek-kwa (산업지원정책과): Industrial Policy Division
Sanôp Kyôngje-kuk (산업경제국): Industry and Economy Bureau
segyehwa (세계화): globalization
sich'ông (시청): Seoul city offices

silmang sirôpcha (실망실업자): disappointed unemployed

simin sahoe undong (시민사회운동): civil society movements

simin ûi kwôlli (시민의 권리): citizen's right

sin chisigin (신지식인): new intellectuals

sin chisigin sang (신지식인상): new intellectual award

sirôp kûkpok kungmin undong ponbu (실업극복국민운동본부): national
movement to overcome unemployment (NMOU)

Sirôp Taech'aek-pan (실업대책반): Unemployment Policy Division

soaekchuju undong (소액주주운동): small shareholder activism

soju (소주): Korean sake

sômin (서민): working poor

sôngdo (성도): church memberships

sôngjôngch'i (성정치): sexuality politics

sông p'ongnyôk p'ihaeja shimt'ô (성폭력피해자 쉼터): shelters for victims of
domestic and sexual violence

Sôngp'ongnyôk Sangdamso (성폭력 상담소): Korean Sexual Violence Relief Center

Sôul-si Sirôp Taech'aek Wiwônhoe (서울시실업대책 위원회): Seoul City
Committee for Unemployment Policy (SCCUP)

Sôul-yôk Hoegun (서울역 회군): April Demonstration Withdrawal

Sôul-yôk kwangjang (서울역 광장): Seoul Train Station Square

Taech'u-ri (대추리): town in Kyônggi Province where U.S. military bases are to be
moved despite resistance by locals

temppura (뎀뿌라): fried vegetables and seafood

Tonga ilbo (동아일보): "East Asia daily"; a Korean daily newspaper

Tongnip Yesulje (독립예술제): Independent Festival, or Seoul Fringe Festival

tongsa (동사): death due to the cold

tong samuso (동사무소): ward office

tongsôngaeja (동성애자): same-sex lover

tongsôngae kajok (동성애가족): same-sex couple–based families

ton yoksim (돈욕심): zeal for money

welbing (웰빙): well-being

welbing chok (웰빙족): South Koreans who actively pursue well-being

welbing sangp'um (웰빙상품): well-being products

wôlse (월세): monthly rent

Yobohoyôsông T'im (요보호여성팀): Team for Women in Need, a section in the
Social Welfare Division

Yômyông ûi nundongja (여명의 눈동자): "Eyes of sunrise" (TV drama)

Yôngdûngp'o Sanôp Sônkyohoe (영등포 산업선교회): Yôngdûngpo Industrial
Mission

yôsông kajang ch'angôp (여성가장 창업): female breadwinners (middle-aged
mothers) who open small businesses

Yôsông Minuhoe (여성민우회): Korean Women Link

Yôsông Minuhoe Koyong P'yôngdûng Ch'ujinbonbu (여성민우회 고용평등 추진 본부): a progressive women's group monitoring gender equality in employment

yôsông nosukcha (여성노숙자): homeless women

Yôsông Nosukcha Shimt'ô Yôndae (여성노숙자 쉼터연대): Homeless Women's Shelter Network

Yôsông Pokchi Sangdamso (여성복지상담소): Women's Welfare-Counseling Center

Yôsông ûi Chônhwa (여성의 전화): Korean Women's Hotline

Yôyôn (여연): Korean Women's Associations United

yut (윷): a traditional game in Korea

168

BIBLIOGRAPHY

Abelmann, Nancy. 1996. *Echoes of the Past, Epics of Dissent: A South Korean Social Movement.* Berkeley: University of California Press.

———. 1997a. "Reorganizing and Recapturing Dissent in 1990s South Korea: The Case of Farmers." In *Between Resistance and Revolution: Cultural Politics and Social Protest,* ed. Richard Gabriel Fox and Orin Starn. New Brunswick, N.J.: Rutgers University Press.

———. 1997b. "Women's Class Mobility and Identities in South Korea: A Gendered, Transgenerational, Narrative Approach." *The Journal of Asian Studies* 56 (2): 398–420.

———. 2003. *Melodrama of Mobility: Women, Talk, and Class in Contemporary South Korea.* Honolulu: University of Hawai'i Press.

Ahn Ch'ang-hyôn. 1998. "Kim Mo-im changkwan nosukcha hyônjang 'chamhaeng' Sôsomun kûpsikso ch'aja Sôul-yôk sô yasik to nanuôjuô" (Minister Kim Mo-im "secretly visited" homeless people in Sôsomun Park and Seoul Train Station). *Han'gyôre sinmun,* June 3, social section, 22.

Ahn Yông-chun. 1998. "Konan sok ûi namjjok edo chaemidongp'o, 'choguk ûn hana'" ("There is only one home country" for Korean immigrants in the United States who send donations to South Korea in crisis). *Han'gyôre sinmun,* April 15, section 12.

Althusser, Louis. 1971. *Lenin and Philosophy and Other Essays.* Trans. Ben Brewster. New York: Monthly Review.

———. 1990 (1969). "Contradiction and Overdetermination." In *For Marx.* Trans. Ben Brewster, 89–128. New York: Verso.

Anagnost, Ann. 2000. "Scenes of Misrecognition: Maternal Citizenship in the Age of Transnational Adoption." *positions: east asia cultures critique* 8 (2): 389–421.

———. 2004. "The Corporeal Politics of Quality (Suzhi)." *Public Culture* 16 (2): 189–208.

———. 2006. "Strange Circulations: The Blood Economy in Rural China." *Economy and Society* 35 (4): 509–529.

Appadurai, Arjun. 1996. *Modernity at Large: Cultural Dimensions of Globalization.* Minneapolis: University of Minnesota Press.

Arai, Andrea G. 2005. "The Neo-Liberal Subject of Lack and Potential: Developing 'the Frontier within' and Creating a Reserve Army of Labor in 21st century Japan." *Rhizomes: Cultural Studies in Emerging Knowledge* (10). http://www.rhizomes .net/issue10/arai.htm.

Aslanbeigui, Nahid, and Gale Summerfield. 2000. "The Asian Crisis, Gender, and the International Financial Architecture." *Feminist Economics* 6 (3): 81–103.

Barry, Andrew, Thomas Osborne, and Nikolas Rose, eds. 1996. *Foucault and Political Reason: Liberalism, Neo-Liberalism, and Rationalities of Government.* Chicago: University of Chicago Press.

Berdahl, Daphne, Matti Bunzl, and Martha Lampland, eds. 2000. *Altering States: Ethnographies of Transition in Eastern Europe and the Former Soviet Union.* Ann Arbor: University of Michigan Press.

Borofsky, Robert, and Bruce Albert. 2005. *Yanomami: The Fierce Controversy and What We Might Learn from It.* Berkeley: University of California Press.

Brown, Wendy. 1995. *States of Injury: Power and Freedom in Late Modernity.* Princeton: Princeton University Press.

———. 2003. "Neo-Liberalism and the End of Liberal Democracy." *Theory and Event* 7 (1). http://muse.jhu.edu/journals/theory_and_event.

Brown, Wendy, and Janet Halley, eds. 2002. *Left Legalism/ Left Critique.* Durham: Duke University Press.

Brunhoff, Suzanne de. 1976. *The State, Capital, and Economic Policy.* Trans. Mike Sonenscher. London: Pluto Press.

Burawoy, Michael, and Katherine Verdery, eds. 1999. *Uncertain Transition: Ethnographies of Change in the Postsocialist World.* Lanham, Md.: Rowman and Littlefield.

Burchell, Graham. 1996. "Liberal Government and Techniques of the Self." In *Foucault and Political Reason: Liberalism, Neo-Liberalism, and Rationalities of Government,* ed. Andrew Barry, Thomas Osborne, and Nikolas S. Rose, 19–36. Chicago: The University of Chicago Press.

Burchell, Graham, Colin Gordon, and Peter Miller, eds. 1991. *The Foucault Effect: Studies in Governmentality.* London: Harvester Wheatsheaf.

Buswell, Robert E., and Timothy S. Lee, eds. 2006. *Christianity in Korea.* Honolulu: University of Hawai'i.

Butler, Judith. 1990. *Gender Trouble: Feminism and Subversion of Identity.* New York and London: Routledge.

Chang, Ha-Joon. 2002. *Kicking Away the Ladder: Development Strategy in Historical Perspective.* London: Anthem.

Chang, Ha-Joon, Chông Sûng-il, and Yi Chong-tae. 2005. *K'waedo nanma Han'guk kyôngje* (A trenchant analysis of the difficult Korean economy). Seoul: Puki.

Chang, Kyung-sup. 1997. "The Neo-Confucian Right and Family Politics in South Korea: The Nuclear Family as an Ideological Construct." *Economy and Society* 26 (1): 22–42.

———. 1999. "Compressed Modernity and its Discontents: South Korean Society in Transition." *Economy and Society* 28 (1): 30–55.

Chang, Phil-hwa. 1998. "Impact of Economic and Financial Crisis on Women in

South Korea." In *Asia-Pacific Economic Cooperation (APEC) Ministerial Meeting on Women.* Manila: Philippines.

Chin, Soo Hee. 1998. "Recent Trend of Women's Unemployment and Desirable Policy Measures." *Yonsei Journal of Women's Studies* 4: 13–35.

Cho, Hae-Joang. 1986. "Male Dominance and Mother Power: The Two Sides of Confucian Patriarchy in Korea." In *The Psycho-Cultural Dynamics of the Confucian Family: Past and Present,* ed. Walter H. Stote. Seoul: International Cultural Society.

———. 1988. *Han'guk ûi yôsông kwa namsông* (Korean women and men). Seoul: Munhak kwa chisôngsa.

Cho, Hee-Yeon. 2000a. "Democratic Transition and Changes in Korean NGOs." *Korea Journal*: 275–304.

———. 2000b. "The Structure of the South Korean Developmental Regime and Its Transformation—Statist Mobilization and Authoritarian Integration in the Anticommunist Regimentation." *Inter-Asia Cultural Studies* 1 (3): 408–426.

———. 2002. "Sacrifices Caused by State Violence Under Military Authoritarianism and the Dynamics of Settling the Past During the Democratic Transition." *Korea Journal* (Autumn): 163–193.

Cho Ch'ang-in. 2001. *Kasi kogi* (Needle fish). Seoul: Palgûn sesang.

Choi Chun-yông. 2000. "Siljik nosukcha munje haegyôl ûl wihan kyohoe ûi yôkkal: Yejang-Tonghap ch'ûk ûi kyôngu" (The role of churches and the issues of the IMF homeless: The case of Presbyterian Church of Korea). Master's thesis, Presbyterian College and Theological Seminary, Seoul.

Choi In-hoon. 1976 (1960). *Kwangjang* (The square). Seoul: Munhak kwa chisôngsa.

Choi Kyông-hui. 2001. "Purangin ûi uuljûng kwa chaakaenyôm kwa ûi kwan'gye yôn'gu: Purangin pokchisisôl saenghwalin ûl chungsim ûro" (A study of the relationship between long-term street people's depression and self-perception: A case based on residents in a charity facility for long-term street people). Master's thesis, Inha University, Inchôn, South Korea.

Choi Yun. 1992. *Hoesaek nunsaram* (Gray snowman). Seoul: Chosôn ilbo.

Choi Yun-sun. 2002. "Chôngsin chilhwan nosukin ûi chiyôksahoe chôngchak pangan e kwanhan yôn'gu" (A study of the settlement of homeless people with mental illness in local society). Master's thesis, Myoungji University, Seoul.

Chông Sông-jin. 2006. "Keinzûjuûi in'ga, 21 segi sahoejuûi in'ga" (Keynesianism or twenty-first-century socialism?). *Marûkûsûjuûi yôn'gu (Marxism 21)* 3 (1): 107–135.

Chông Tae-ung. 1998. "Hûndûlli nûn sahoe: Chungsanch'ûng ûi mollak" (Faltering society: Collapse of the middle class). *Han'guk kyôngje,* June 1. http://www.hankyung.com.

Chông Wôn-oh. 1999. *Han'guk ûi nosuk wôn'in e kwanhan yôn'gu* (Research on the origin of homelessness). Seoul: Seoul Development Institute.

Chông Yông-ho. 1992. "Chôngbohwa sahôe tamnon punsôk ûl t'ong han ideology yôngu" (Analysis of ideological discourse in an information society). Master's thesis, Yonsei University Sociology Department.

Cho Sông-chin. 2004. "Chôngsin yoyang mit purangin sisôl ipsoja ûi chôngsin chilhwan yubyôngryul punpo mit ûiryochuguhaengwui" (Tendency and treatment of mental illness for residents in retreat centers for mental health and charity facility for long-term homeless people). Ph.D. diss., Seoul National University.

Cho Soon-Kyung. 1998. "Minju chôk sijang kyôngje wa yugyo chôk kabujangje" (Democratic market economy and Confucian patriarchy). *Kyôngje wa sahoe (Journal of Economy and Society)* 38: 169–188.

———. 1999. *Yôsônghaego ûi silt'ae wa chôngch'aek kwaje* (Women's layoffs and suggestions for policy-making). Seoul: The Presidential Commission on Women's Affairs.

Chow, Rey. 1992. "Between Colonizers: Hong Kong's Postcolonial Self-Writing in the 1990's." *Diaspora: A Journal of Transnational Studies* 2 (2): 151–170.

Chu Chong-kuk. 2003. "Pin'gonnyul i ôihwan wûigi ijôn sujun hôibok mottae" (Poverty rate has not recovered to the pre–Asian Debt Crisis level). *Yônhap news*, January 7. http://news.naver.com.

Chu Dôk-han. 1998a. *K'aen maekchu rûl masi myô saenggak hae naen insaeng ûl chûlgi nûn pangbôp 170 kaji* (One hundred and seventy ways of enjoying life while drinking beer). Seoul: Saeroun saramdûl ch'ulp'ansa.

———. 1998b. *Paeksu do p'ûro raya saranamnûn da* (Paeksu can survive only by becoming professional). Seoul: Inhwa ch'ulp'ansa.

Chun, Bong Hyun (Simone). 2005. "Globalisation and the New Left Party in the Periphery: The Korean Democratic Labour Party (KDLP), 2000–2004." Ph.D. diss., University of California, Santa Barbara.

Chun, Soonok. 2003. *They are Not Machines: Korean Women Workers and Their Fight for Democratic Trade Unionism in the 1970s*. Alder Shot, UK: Ashgate.

Clarke, John. 2004. *Changing Welfare, Changing States: New Directions in Social Policy*. London: Sage.

Comaroff, Jean, and John Comaroff. 2000. "Millennial Capitalism: First Thoughts on a Second Coming." *Public Culture* 12 (2): 291–343.

Cumings, Bruce. 1997. *Korea's Place in the Sun: A Modern History*. New York: W. W. Norton.

———. 1999. "Webs with No Spiders, Spiders with No Webs?" In *The Developmental State*, ed. Meredith Woo-Cumings, 61–92. Ithaca: Cornell University Press.

Dean, Mitchell. 1999. *Governmentality: Power and Rule in Modern Society*. London: Sage Publications.

Deuchler, Martina. 1992. *The Confucian Transformation of Korea: A Study of Society and Ideology*. Cambridge: Harvard University Press.

Donzelot, Jacques. 1979. *The Policing of Families*. Trans. R. Hurley. New York: Pantheon Books.

Eckert, Carter J. 1991. *Offspring of Empire: The Koch'ang Kims and the Colonial Origins of Korean Capitalism, 1876–1945*. Seattle: University of Washington Press.

Eckert, Carter J., Ki-baik Lee, Young Ick Lew, Michael Robinson, and Edward W. Wagner. 1990. *Korea Old and New: A History*. Massachusetts: Harvard University Press.

172

Esping-Anderson, Gøsta. 1990. *The Three Worlds of Welfare Capitalism*. Princeton: Princeton University Press.

Farmer, Paul. 2003. *Pathologies of Power: Health, Human Rights, and the New War on the Poor*. Berkeley: University of California Press.

Farquhar, Judith, and Quicheng Zhang. 2005. "Biopolitical Beijing: Pleasure, Sovereignty, and Self-Cultivation in China's Capital." *Cultural Anthropology* 20 (3): 303–327.

Ferguson, James. 1994. *The Anti-Politics Machine: 'Development,' Depoliticization, and Bureaucratic Power in Lesotho*. Minneapolis: University of Minnesota Press.

Flora, Peter, and Arnold J. Heidenheimer, eds. 1987. *The Development of Welfare States in Europe and America*. New Brunswick: Transaction Books.

Foucault, Michel. 1977. "Intellectuals and Power." In *Language, Counter-Memory, Practice: Selected Essays and Interviews by Michel Foucault*, ed. Donald F. Bouchard. Trans. Sherry Simon, 205–217. Ithaca: Cornell University Press.

———. 1988. *Technologies of the Self: A Seminar with Michel Foucault*, ed. Luther H. Martin, Huck Gutman, and Patrick H. Hutton. Amherst: University of Massachusetts Press.

———. 1990. *History of Sexuality I: An Introduction*.Trans. Robert Hurley. New York: Vintage Books.

———. 1991. "Governmentality." In *The Foucault Effect: Studies in Governmentality*, ed. Graham Burchell, Colin Gordon, and Peter Miller. Trans. Colin Gordon, 87–104. Chicago: The University of Chicago.

———. 1995. *Discipline and Punish: The Birth of the Prison*. Trans. Alan Sheridan. New York: Pantheon Books.

———. 1997. *Ethics, Subjectivity and Truth*, ed. Paul Rabinow. Trans. Robert Hurley and others. New York: New Press.

———. 2003. *Society Must be Defended: Lectures at the College de France, 1975–76*. Trans. David Macey. New York: Picador.

———. 2008. *The Birth of Biopolitics*, ed. Michel Senellart. Trans. Graham Burchell. New York: Palgrave Macmillan.

Fowler, Edward. 1996. *San'ya Blues: Laboring Life in Contemporary Tokyo*. Ithaca: Cornell University Press.

Fraser, Nancy. 1989. *Unruly Practices: Power, Discourse, and Gender in Contemporary Social Theory*. Minneapolis: University of Minnesota Press.

———. 1990. "Struggle over Needs: Outline of a Socialist-Feminist Critical Theory of Late-Capitalist Political Culture." In *Women, the State, and Welfare*, ed. Linda Gordon, 199–225. Madison: The University of Wisconsin Press.

Gal, Susan, and Gail Kligman. 2000a. *The Politics of Gender: After Socialism*. Princeton: Princeton University Press.

———, eds. 2000b. *Reproducing Gender: Politics, Publics, and Everyday Life After Socialism*. Princeton: Princeton University Press.

Giddens, Anthony. 1998. *The Third Way: The Renewal of Social Democracy*. Malden, Mass.: Polity.

Gill, Lesley. 2000. *Teetering on the Rim: Global Restructuring, Daily Life, and the Armed Retreat of the Bolivian State*. New York: Columbia University Press.

Goldman, Michael. 2000. "The Birth of a Discipline: Producing Authoritative Green Knowledge, World Bank-style." Workshop on Transnational Ethnography, University of Illinois.

Goode, Judith. 2001. "Let's Get Our Act Together: How Racial Discourses Disrupt Neighborhood Activism." In *The New Poverty Studies: The Ethnography of Power, Politics, and Impoverished People in the United States*, ed. Goode and Jeff Maskovsky, 364–398. New York: New York University Press.

Goode, Judith, and Jeff Maskovsky, eds. 2001. *The New Poverty Studies: The Ethnography of Power, Politics, and Impoverished People in the United States*. New York: New York University Press.

Gordon, Colin. 1991. "Governmental Rationality: An Introduction." In *The Foucault Effect: Studies in Governmentality*, ed. Graham Burchell, Colin Gordon, and Peter Miller, 1–52. Chicago: The University of Chicago.

Gordon, Linda, ed. 1990. *Women, the State, and Welfare*. Madison: The University of Wisconsin Press.

———. 1993. "Gender, State and Society: A Debate with Theda Skocpol." *Contention* 2 (3): 139–156.

———. 1994. *Pitied But Not Entitled: Single Mothers and the History of Welfare, 1890–1935*. New York: Free Press.

Gowan, Teresa. 2000. "Excavating 'Globalization' in Street Level: Homeless Men Recycling Their Pasts." In *Global Ethnography*, ed. Michael Burroway et al., 74–105. Berkeley: University of California Press.

Gramsci, Antonio. 1971. *Selections from the Prison Notebooks*. Trans. Quintine Hoare and Geoffrey N. Smith. New York: International Publishers.

Guala, Francesco. 2006. "Critical Notice." *Economics and Philosophy* 22: 429–439.

Gupta, Akhil. 2001. "Governing Population: The Integrated Child Development Services Program in India." In *State of Imagination: Ethnographic Explorations of the Postcolonial State*, ed. Thomas Blom Hansen and Finn Stepputat, 65–96. Durham and London: Duke University Press.

Haboush, JaHyun Kim. 1991. "The Confucianization of Korean Society." In *The East Asian Region: Confucian Heritage and Its Modern Adaptation*, ed. Gilbert Rozman, 84–110. Princeton: Princeton University Press.

Haggard, Stephan, Daniel Pinkston, and Jungkun Seo. 1999. "Reforming Korea Inc.: The Politics of Structural Adjustment under Kim Dae Jung." *Asian Perspective* 23 (3): 201–235.

Hall, Stuart. 1984. "The State in Question." In *The Idea of the Modern State*, ed. Gregor McLennan, David Held, and Stuart Hall, 1–28. Milton Keynes, UK: Open University Press.

Hall, Stuart, David Held, Don Hubert, and Kenneth Thompson, eds. 1996. *Modernity: An Introduction to Modern Societies*. Cambridge: Blackwell Publishers.

Han, Jongwoo, and L. H. M. Ling. 1998. "Authoritarianism in the Hypermasculinized State: Hybridity, Patriarchy, and Capitalism in Korea." *International Studies Quarterly* 42: 53–78.

Haney, Lynne. 1998. "Engendering the Welfare State: A Review Article." *Comparative Study of Society and History*: 749–767.

———. 1999. "'But We are Still Mothers': Gender, the State, and the Construction of Need in Postsocialist Hungary." In *Uncertain Transition: Ethnographies of Change in the Postsocialist World*, ed. Michael Burawoy and Katherine Verdery, 151–187. Lanham, Md.: Lowman and Littlefield.

———. 2000. "Global Discourses of Need: Mythologizing and Pathologizing Welfare in Hungary." In *Global Ethnography: Forces, Connections, and Imaginations in a Postmodern World*, ed. Michael Burawoy et al., 48–73. Berkeley: University of California Press.

Harvey, David. 2005. *A Brief History of Neoliberalism*. Oxford: Oxford University Press.

Hertzfeld, Michael. 1992. *The Social Production of Indifference: Exploring the Symbolic Roots of Western Bureaucracy*. Chicago: University of Chicago Press.

Hindess, Barry. 1993. "Liberalism, Socialism and Democracy: Variations on a Governmental Theme." *Economy and Society* 22 (3): 300–313.

———. 2004. "Liberalism: What's in a Name?" In *Global Governmentality: Governing International Spaces*, ed. Wendy Larner and William Walters, 23–39. London: Routledge.

Hoffman, Lisa. 2006. "Autonomous Choices and Patriotic Professionalism: On Governmentality in Late-Socialist China." *Economy and Society* 35 (4): 550–570.

Hoffman, Lisa, Monica DeHart, and Stephen J. Collier. 2006. "Notes on the Anthropology of Neoliberalism." *Anthropology News* September 2006: 9–10.

Homeless Rehabilitation Center. 1998. *Nosuk ŭi wonin kwa yangsang* (The origin and situation of homelessness). Annual report. Seoul: The Homeless Rehabilitation Center.

———. 2000. *Nosukiu shimt'ŏ iyongja ŭi chahwal siltae* (The rehabilitation progress of clients using homeless shelters). Annual report. Seoul: The Homeless Rehabilitation Center.

Hort, Sven E. O., and Stein Kuhnle. 2000. "The Coming of East and South-East Asian Welfare States." *Journal of European Social Policy* 10 (2): 162–184.

Hughes, Theodore. 2002. "Reconstructing the 'Revolution' and the Specter of Coloniality: Ch'oe In-Hun's *The Square* and *Voice of the Governor-General*." A paper presented at the speakers' series "Korea Workshop 2002–2003," University of Illinois, Urbana-Champaign.

Hyatt, Susan Brin. 2001. "From Citizen to Volunteer: Neoliberal Governance and the Erasure of Poverty." In *The New Poverty Studies: The Ethnography of Power, Politics, and Impoverished People in the United States*, ed. Judith Goode and Jeff Maskovsky, 201–235. New York: New York University Press.

Jager, Sheila Miyoshi. 2003. *Narratives of Nation-Building in Korea: A Genealogy of Patriotism*. Armonk, N.Y.: M.E. Sharpe.

Janelli, Roger L., with Dawnhee Yim. 1993. *Making Capitalism: The Social and Cultural Construction of a South Korean Conglomerate*. Stanford: Stanford University Press.

Janelli, Roger L., and Dawnhee Yim Janelli. 1982. *Ancestor Worship and Korean Society*. Stanford: Stanford University Press.

Jang, Jin-ho Steven. 2006. "Approaching Neoliberalism as Financial Hegemony: Its History and Dynamics in South Korea." A paper presented at "The States and Spaces of Neoliberalism," the seventh transnational sociology workshop, Department of Sociology, University of Illinois, Urbana-Champaign, April 15, 2006.

Jessop, Bob. 1994. The Transition to Post-Fordism and the Schumpeterian Workfare State." In *Towards a Post-Fordist Welfare State?* ed. Roger Burrows and Brian Loader, 13–37. London: Routledge.

———. 2002. *The Future of the Capitalist State*. Cambridge: Polity.

Johnson, Chalmers A. 1982. *MITI and the Japanese Miracle: The Growth of Industrial Policy, 1925–1975*. Stanford: Stanford University Press.

Kang Mi-won. 2000. "Kachul nosuk ch'ôngsonyôn ûi kachul kwa yangmul namyong simhwa" (Runaways and drug abuse by the adolescent homeless). Master's thesis, Sogang University, Seoul.

Kang Se-jun and Kim Kyông-ho. 2004. "Sôulyôk 100 nyun mane sae tanjang" (The renovation of Seoul Train Station over one hundred years). *Han'gyôre sinmun*, January 3, special section 6.

Kawashima, Ken C. 2005. "Capital's Dice-Box Shaking: The Contingent Commodifications of Labor Power." *Rethinking Marxism* 17 (4): 609–626.

———. 2009. *The Proletarian Gamble: Korean Workers in Interwar Japan*. Durham: Duke University Press.

Kim, Byung-kook. 2000. "The Politics of Crisis and a Crisis of Politics: The Presidency of Kim Dae-Jung." In *Korea Briefing 1997–1999*, ed. Kong Dan Oh, 35–74. New York: M. E. Sharpe.

Kim, Choong Soon. 1992. *The Culture of Korean Industry: An Ethnography of Poongsan Corporation*. Tucson: University of Arizona Press.

Kim, Dae Jung. 1996. *Mass-Participatory Economy: Korea's Road to World Economic Power*. Cambridge: Center for International Affairs, Harvard University.

———. 1998. *Kungnan kûkpok ûi kil: Kim Dae Jung Taet'ongnyông ch'uiim 6-kaewôl yônsôlmun* (Ways of overcoming the national crisis). Seoul: Taet'ongnyông pisôsil.

Kim, Eun-Hee, Han-Hee Hahm, and Taek-Lim Yoon, eds. 1999. *Munhwa e palmok chap'in Han'guk kyôngje* (Cultural analyses of the Korean economic crisis). Seoul: Hyônmin sisût'em.

Kim, Eun Mee. 1997. *Big Business, Strong State: Collusion and Conflict in South Korean Development, 1960–1990*. Albany: State University of New York Press.

———. 1999. "Crisis of the Developmental State in South Korea." *Asian Perspective* 23 (2): 35–55.

Kim, Kyung-Hyun. 2004. *The Remasculinization of Korean Cinema*. Durham: Duke University Press.

Kim, Samuel, ed. 2000. *Korea's Globalization*. Cambridge: Cambridge University Press.

Kim, Seung-Kyung. 1997. *Class Struggle or Family Struggle?: The Lives of Women Factory Workers in South Korea*. Cambridge: Cambridge University Press.

———. 2004 "Consolidating Women's Rights in South Korea: The Role of Women's Movements in the Democratization." *Korea Observer* 35 (3): 463–483.

Kim, Seung-Kyung, and John Finch. 2002. "Living with Rhetoric, Living Against Rhetoric: Korean Families and the IMF Economic Crisis." *Korean Studies* 26 (1): 120–139.

Kim, Sunhyuk. 2000. "The Politics of Reform in South Korea: The First Year of the Kim Dae Jung Government, 1998–1999." *Asian Perspective* 24 (1): 163–185.

Kim Hyo-kûn. 1999. *Sin chisikin* (The new intellectuals). Seoul: Daily Economics.

Kim Hyun Mee. 2000. "Han'guk ûi kûndaesông kwa yôsông ûi nodongkwôn" (Modernity and women's labor rights in South Korea). *Yôsônghak nonjip* (Journal of Korean women's studies) 16 (1): 37–64.

Kim Kwang-rye. 2001. "Yôsông nosukcha siltae e kwanhan yôn'gu: Sôul-tûkpyôlsi rûl chungsim ûiro" (A study of homeless women: The case of Seoul). Master's thesis, University of Seoul.

Kim Kyông-dong. 1999. "Han'guk ûi chungsanchûng wigi wa kajok haech'ae: kû wônin kwa taechaek mosaek" (Korean middle-class crisis and family break-down: Causes and solutions). Paper presented at the Han'guk Sahoe Munhwa Yôn'guwôn che 27 ch'a konggae t'oronhoe (Korean Society and Culture Research Institute twenty-seventh public symposium), Seoul, May 13.

Kim-Paik, Youngnan. 2002. "Reconciling the Nation and Representing Motherhood: The Deployment of Gender During the Korean Separated Family Reunions." A paper presented at the Korea Workshop, 2002–2003, University of Illinois, Urbana-Champaign, October 2002.

Kim Sôn-hui. 2001. "Jjokpang kôjuja ûi sahoejok chiji wa chagi hyonûnggam kan ûi kwan'gye yôn'gu" (A study of the relationship between social support for day-laborers living in day-rental housing and the perception of self-efficacy). Master's thesis, Catholic University of Korea, Seoul.

Kim Su-hyun. 2001. *Sôul-si homnisû yôsông silt'ae wa taech'aek* (Homeless women in Seoul). Seoul: Seoul Development Institute.

———. 2002. *Sôul-si chungjanggi nosukcha chôngch'aek yôn'gu* (A study on long-term homeless assistance policy in Seoul). Seoul: Seoul Development Institute.

Kim Su-hyun, Sin Kyông-hui, Pak Ûn-ch'ôl, Ch'oi Nam-gil, Cho Myông-nae, Hong In-ok, and Kim Ûn-hui. 2001. *Nojômsang kwalli pangan chungjanggi taech'aek mosaek* (Middle-long-term plan for the management of street vendors). Seoul: Seoul Development Institute.

Kim U-sôk, Yi Hun-bôm, and Chông Che-won. 1998. "Munôji nûn kajông" (The family is collapsing). *Chungang ilbo*, August 18, cover section 1–2.

Kim Yông-to. 1995. "Mujutaekcha ûi chugô saenghwal poho rûl wihan pôpchôk kochal" (A legal study of livelihood protection for homeless people). Master's thesis. Wonkwang University, Iksan, South Korea.

177

Kingfisher, Catherine. 2002. *Western Welfare in Decline: Globalization and Women's Poverty*. Philadelphia: University of Pennsylvania Press.

Kittay, Eva Feder. 1999. *Love's Labor: Essays on Women, Equality, and Dependency*. New York: Routledge.

Kong Chi-yông. 1997. *Human Decency*. In *Wayfarer: New Fiction by Korean Women*, ed. and trans. Bruce Fulton and Ju-Chan Fulton. Seattle: Women in Translation.

Koo, Hagen, ed. 1993. *State and Society in Contemporary Korea*. Ithaca: Cornell University Press.

———. 2001. *Korean Workers: The Culture and Politics of Class Formation*. Ithaca: Cornell University Press.

Korea Urban Research Institute. 1999. *Nosukcha chaehwal ûl wihan kakkye ûi kwaje* (Suggestions for the rehabilitation of homeless people and the responsibility of multiple sectors). Seoul: Korea Urban Research Institute.

Korean Women Link (Han'guk Yôsông Minuhoe). 2005. *Yesan e do sông i itta: sông inji chôk kwanjjôm esô parabon chibang chach'idanch'e yôsôngjôngch'aek kwa yesan punsôk* (Gender issues in the budget: Analysis of policy and budget for women in municipal governance from a feminist perspective). Seoul: Korean Women Link.

Koven, Seth, and Sonya Michel, eds. 1993. *Mothers of a New World: Maternalist Politics and the Origins of Welfare States*. New York: Routledge.

Kwon, Huck-ju. 1999. *The Welfare State in Korea: The Politics of Legitimation*. New York: St. Martin's.

———. 2003. "Advocacy Coalitions and the Politics of Welfare in Korea After the Economic Crisis." *Policy and Politics* 31 (1): 69–83.

Kwon, Insook. 2000. "Militarism in My Heart: Women's Militarized Consciousness and Culture in South Korea." Ph.D. diss., Clark University, Worcester, Mass.

Kwôn Hyôk-ch'ôl. 1998. "Wae sajin jjiknûnga . . . pit kapadalla/Ko Kôn sijang Sôul-yôk nosukcha wa mannam sô môssûkhaejyô" (Why do you take pictures of us? . . . Pay our debts! / Mayor Ko Kôn became embarrassed in a meeting with homeless people in the Seoul Train Station). *Han'gyôre sinmun*, September 22, local section, 24.

Lamphere, Louise. 2004. "The Convergence of Applied, Practicing, and Public Anthropology in the 21st century." *Human Organization* 63 (4): 431–443.

Larner, Wendy, and William Walters, eds. 2004. *Global Governmentality: Governing International Spaces*. London: Routledge.

Lassiter, Luke Eric, Samuel R. Cook, and Les Field. 2005. "Collaborative Ethnography and Public Anthropology." *Current Anthropology* 46 (1): 83–106.

Lazzarato, Maurizio. 1996. "Immaterial Labor." In *Radical Thought in Italy: A Potential Politics*, ed. Paolo Virno and Michael Hardt, 133–146. Minneapolis: University of Minnesota Press.

———. 2004. "From Capital-Labour to Capital-Life." *Ephemera: Theory of the Multitude, Theory and Politics in Organization* 4 (3):187–208.

Lee, Namhee. 2005. "Representing the Worker: The Worker-Intellectual Alliance of the 1980s in South Korea." *The Journal of Asian Studies* 64 (4): 911–937.

—————. 2007. *The Making of Minjung: Democracy and the Politics of Representation in South Korea*. Ithaca: Cornell University Press.

Lee, Soo-Jung. 2007. "Making and Unmaking the Korean National Division: Separated Families in the Cold War and Post-Cold War Eras." Ph.D. diss., University of Illinois, Urbana-Champaign.

Lemke, Thomas. 2001. "'The Birth of Bio-Politics': Michel Foucault's Lecture at the College de France on Neo-Liberal Governmentality." *Economy and Society* 30 (2): 190–207.

—————. 2002. "Foucault, Governmentality, and Critique." *Rethinking Marxism* 14 (3): 49–64.

Li, Tania M. 2007. *The Will to Improve: Governmentality, Development, and the Practice of Politics*. Durham: Duke University Press.

Lie, John. 1998. *Han Unbound: The Political Economy of South Korea*. Stanford: Stanford University Press.

Lofel, Lisa. 1999. *Other Modernities: Gendered Yearnings in China After Socialism*. Berkeley: University of California Press.

—————. 2007. *Desiring China: Experiments in Neoliberalism, Sexuality, and Public Culture*. Durham: Duke University Press.

Lyon-Callo, Vincent. 2001. "Homelessness, Employment, and Structural Violence: Exploring Constraints on Collective Mobilizations against Systemic Inequality." In *The New Poverty Studies: The Ethnography of Power, Politics, and Impoverished People in the United States*, ed. Judith Goode and Jeff Maskovsky, 293–318. New York: New York University Press.

—————. 2004. *Inequality, Poverty, and Neoliberal Governance: Activist Ethnography in the Homeless Sheltering Industry*. Peterbrough, Canada: Broadview.

Marx, Karl. 1990 (1976). *Capital: A Critique of Political Economy, Volume I*. Trans. Ben Fowkes. New York: Penguin.

—————. 2004 (1963). *The Eighteenth Brumaire of Louis Bonaparte*. Trans. C. P. Dutt. New York: International Publishers.

Maurer, Bill. 2002. "Redecorating the International Economy: Keynes, Grant, and the Queering of Bretton Woods." In *Queer Globalizations: Citizenship and the Afterlife of Colonialism*, ed. Arnaldo Cruz-Malavé and Martin F. Manalansan, 100–133. New York: New York University Press.

Mehta, Uday Singh. 1992. *The Anxiety of Freedom: Imagination and Individuality in Locke's Political Thought*. Ithaca: Cornell University Press.

—————. 1999. *Liberalism and Empire: A Study in Nineteenth-Century British Liberal Thought*. Chicago: University of Chicago Press.

Miller, Peter. 1992. "Accounting and Objectivity: The Invention of Calculating Selves and Calculable Spaces." *Annals of Scholarship: An International Quarterly in the Humanities and Social Sciences* 9 (1–2): 61–86.

Miller, Peter, and Anthony G. Hopwood, eds. 1994. *Accounting as Social and Institutional Practice*. Cambridge: Cambridge University Press.

Mink, Gwendolyn. 1995. *The Wages of Motherhood: Inequality in the Welfare State, 1917–1942*. Ithaca: Cornell University Press.

Mitchell, Katharyne. 2004. *Crossing the Neoliberal Line: Pacific Rim Migration and the Metropolis*. Philadelphia: Temple University Press.

Mitchell, Timothy. 2002. *Rule of Experts: Egypt, Techno-Politics, Modernity*. Berkeley: University of California Press.

Moon, Seungsook. 2002. "Carving Out Space: Civil Society and the Women's Movement in South Korea." *The Journal of Asian Studies* 61 (2): 473–500.

———. 2004. "Trouble with Conscription, Entertaining Soldiers: Popular Culture and the Politics of Militarized Masculinity in South Korea." *Men and Masculinities* 8 (1):64–92.

———. 2005. *Militarized Modernity and Gendered Citizenship in South Korea*. Durham: Duke University Press.

Morgen, Sandra. 2002. *Into Our Own Hands: The Women's Health Movement in the United States, 1969–1990*. New Brunswick, N.J.: Rutgers University Press.

Morgen, Sandra, and Jill Weigt. 2001. "Poor Women, Fair Work, and Welfare-to-Work That Works." In *The New Poverty Studies: The Ethnography of Power, Politics, and Impoverished People in the United States*, ed. Judith Goode and Jeff Maskovsky, 152–178. New York: New York University Press.

Morris-Suzuki, Tessa. 1988. *Beyond Computopia: Information, Automation and Democracy in Japan*. London: Kegan Paul.

Mun Chong-im. 2002. "Nosukcha chahwal ŭl wihan Won-Pulgyo ŭi chiwon pangan e kwanhan yôn'gu" (A study of Won-Buddhism's support for the rehabilitation of homeless people). Master's thesis, Hansung University, Seoul.

Muraki, Noriko. 2008. "Citizen Professionals: College Women, Care Work, and the Transformation of Middle-Class Subjectivity in Post-Bubble Japan." Ph.D. diss., University of Illinois, Urbana-Champaign.

Muraki, Noriko, with Nancy Abelmann. 2003. "An Ambitious Counter-Interpretive Tale: Class and American Late Capitalism." [A review essay on Sherry B. Ortner's *New Jersey Dreaming: Capital, Culture, and the Class of '58*]. *Anthropological Quarterly* 76 (4): 749–760.

Nader, Laura. 1974 (1969). "Up the Anthropologist: Perspectives Gained From Studying Up." In *Reinventing Anthropology*, ed. Dell H. Hymes, 284–311. New York: Vintage Books.

Nam Jung-hyun. 1996 (1964). "Puju chônsangsô" (Letter to father). In *Nam Jung-hyun / Ch'ôn Sûng-se Punji / Hwanggu ûi pimyông oe* (Collection of Nam Jung-hyun and Ch'ôn Sûng-se), 141–168. Seoul: Dong-a Ch'ulpansa.

Nam Ki-chôl. 2000. "Nosuk kigan e ttarûn simni sahoejok oesang i poho sisôl toeso e michinûn yônghyang" (The influence of socio-psychological injury on those leaving homeless facilities in relation to the duration of their street living). Ph.D. diss., Seoul National University.

Nelson, Laura C. 2000. *Measured Excess: Gender, Status, and Consumer Nationalism in South Korea*. New York: Columbia University Press.

———. 2006. "South Korean Consumer Nationalism: Women, Children, Credit, and Other Perils." In *The Ambivalent Consumer: Questioning Consumption in East Asia and the West*, ed. Sheldon Garon and Patricia L. Maclachlan, 188–208. Ithaca: Cornell University Press.

O'Connor, Julia, Ann Shola Orloff, and Shelia Shaver, eds. 1999. *States, Markets, Families: Gender, Liberalism, and Social Policy in Australia, Canada, Great Britain, and the United States*. Cambridge: Cambridge University Press.

Ogle, George E. 1990. *South Korea: Dissent within the Economic Miracle*. London: Zed.

Oh Sang-sôk. 2000. "Konggong kûllo saôp strôpnyul churyôt ta" (Public works program reduced unemployment). *Han'gyôreh sinmun*, June 9, social section 17.

O'Malley, Pat. 1996. "Risk and Responsibility." In *Foucault and Political Reason: Liberalism, Neo-liberalism and Rationalities of Government*, ed. Andrew Barry, Thomas Osborne, and Nikolas S. Rose, 189–208. Chicago: The University of Chicago Press.

———. 1999. "Governmentality and the Risk Society." *Economy and Society* 28 (1): 138–148.

Ong, Aihwa. 1996. "Anthropology, China, and Modernities: The Geopolitics of Cultural Knowledge." In *Future of Anthropological Knowledge*, 60–92. London: Routledge.

———. 1999. *Flexible Citizenship: The Cultural Logics of Transnationality*. Durham: Duke University Press.

———. 2003. *Buddha is Hiding: Refugees, Citizenship, the New America*. Berkeley: University of California Press.

———. 2006. *Neoliberalism as Exception: Mutations in Citizenship and Sovereignty*. Durham: Duke University Press.

Ong, Aihwa, and Donald Nonini, eds. 1997. *Ungrounded Empires: The Cultural Politics of Modern Chinese Transnationalism*. New York: Routledge.

Ong, Aihwa, and Stephen J. Collier, eds. 2005. *Global Assemblages: Technology, Politics, and Ethics as Anthropological Problems*. Malden, Mass.: Blackwell.

Orloff, Ann Shola. 1993. "Gender and the Social Rights of Citizenship." *American Sociological Review* 58 (3): 303–328.

Paik, Nak-chung. 1992. "An interview with Bruce Cumings: From the Korean War to a Unified Korea." *Korea Journal*: 5–25.

Paik, Young-Gyung. 2006. "Mirae rûl wihyôp hanûn hyônjae: sigansông ûl t'ong hae pon chaesaengsan ûi chôngch'ihak" (The present threatening the future: Politics of reproduction through temporality). *Yôsông Iron (Theoria)* 14 (summer): 36–55.

Pak Ch'ang-yông. 2002. "Nosukin ûi anjông toen chugô konggan ûrosô kongdong-che e kwanhan yôn'gu: Kajok nosukin chungsim ûro" (A study of the community as a stable dwelling space for homeless people: Based on homeless families). Master's thesis, Chung-Ang University, Seoul.

Pak Kûn-ae. 1998. "Nosukcha chaehwal topki ponkyôkhwa" (Initiating assistance for the rehabilitation of homeless people). *Han'gyôre sinmun*, September 18, local section, 20.

181

Pak Kyông-tae. 2008. *Sosuja wa Han'guksahoe* (Minority and Korean society). Seoul: Humanitas Press.

Pak Pyông-su. 2001. "T'ongil 'u' kyoyuk/hwan'gyông 'ka'" (Reunification scores 'good'; education/environment does 'worst'). *Han'gyôre 21*, June 7, special issue 362. http://h21.hani.co.kr.

Pak Yong-hyôn. 1999. "Aiemep'û ka tturô non chugûm ûi tônôl" (The tunnel of death that the IMF crisis created). *Han'gyôre 21*, March 18, 249.

Park, Hyon Ok. 2007. "From National to Market Utopia: Spectacles of Unification and Neoliberal Democracy." Critical Korean Studies Workshop, October 26, 2007, Centre for the Study of Korea, Munk Centre, University of Toronto.

Park, Mi. 2002. "Ideology and Lived Experience: A Case Study of Revolutionary Movements in South Korea, 1980–1995." A paper presented at "Making Social Movements: The British Marxist Historians and the Study of Social Movements," Edge Hill College of Higher Education, Lancashire, UK, March 1, 2002.

Park, So Jin, and Nancy Abelmann. 2004. "Class and Cosmopolitan Striving: Mother's Management of English Education in South Korea." *Anthropological Quarterly* 77 (4): 645–672.

Park, Sook Ja. 1998. "Women's Unemployment in Economic Crisis: The Problems and Solutions." *Yonsei Journal of Women's Studies* 4: 36–64.

Passaro, Joanne. 1996. *The Unequal Homeless: Men on the Streets, Women in Their Place.* New York: Routledge.

Peck, Jamie. 2001. *Workfare States.* New York: Guilford.

Peck, Jamie, and Nik Theodore. 2001. "Exporting Workfare/Importing Welfare-to-Work: Exploring the Politics of Third Way Policy Transfer." *Political Geography* 20: 427–460.

Peng, Ito. 2003. "Gender, Demography, and Welfare State Restructuring in Japan." In *New Social Policy Agendas for Europe and Asia: Challenges, Experience, and Lessons*, ed. Katherine Marshall and Oliver Butzbach, 215–234. Washington: World Bank.

———. 2004. "Postindustrial Pressures, Political Regime Shifts, and Social Policy Reform in Japan and South Korea." *Journal of East Asian Studies* 4 (3): 389–425.

Perelman, Michael. 2000. *The Invention of Capitalism: Classical Political Economy and the Secret History of Primitive Accumulation.* Durham: Duke University Press.

Polak, Jacques J. 1994. *The World Bank and the IMF: A Changing Relationship.* Washington D.C.: The Brookings Institution.

Poster, Winifred, and Zakia Salime. 2002. "Micro-credit and the Limits of Transnational Feminism: USAID Activities in the United States and Morocco." In *Women's Activism and Globalization: Linking Local Struggles and Transnational Politics*, ed. Nancy A. Naples and Manisha Desai, 189–219. New York: Routledge.

Power, Michael. 1994. *The Audit Explosion.* London: White Dove.

Presidential Secretary Planning Committee to Improve the Quality of Life. 1999. *DJ welfarism: Saech'onnyôn ûl hyang han saengsan chôk pokchi ûi kil* (Kim Dae Jung's welfare principles: The ways of productive welfarism toward a new millennium). Seoul: T'oesôltang.

Prey, Rob. 2004. "Visions of Democracy: The Communication and Transformation of Revolutionary Ideologies in South Korea." *Global Media Journal* 3(4). http://lass .calumet.purdue.edu/cca/gmj/index.htm.

Pun, Ngai. 2003. "Subsumption or Consumption? The Phantom of Consumer Revolution in 'Globalizing' China." *Cultural Anthropology* 18 (4): 469–492.

———. 2005. *Made in China: Women Factory Workers in a Global Workplace*. Durham: Duke University Press.

Pyun Hwa Soon. 2000. "Kajokhaech'e ûi siltae mit taech'aek" (Situations and possible policies regarding family breakdown). Paper presented at the "Han'guk kajok kinûng ûi kyôlson kwa taech'aek pangan mosaek" (Symposium for the solution to the dysfunctional Korean family), South Korean Women's Development Institute, Seoul City, July 3.

Rapp, Rayna. 1992. "Family and Class in Contemporary America: Notes Toward an Understanding of Ideology." In *Rethinking the Family: Some Feminist Questions*, ed. Barrie Thorne and Marilyn Yalom, 49–69. Boston: Northeastern University Press.

Read, Jason. 2002. "Primitive Accumulation: The Aleatory Foundation of Capitalism." *Rethinking Marxism* 14 (2): 24–49.

Rose, Nikolas. 1990. *Governing the Soul: The Shaping of the Private Self*. London: Routledge.

———. 1996. *Inventing Our Selves: Psychology, Power, and Personhood*. Cambridge: Cambridge University Press.

———. 1999. *Powers of Freedom: Reframing Political Thought*. Cambridge: Cambridge University Press.

Rose, Nikolas, and Carlos Novas. 2005. "Biological Citizenship." In *Global Assemblages: Technology, Politics, and Ethics as Anthropological Problems*, ed. Aihwa Ong and Stephen J. Collier, 439–463. Malden, Mass.: Blackwell.

Sainsbury, Diane, ed. 1999. *Gender and Welfare State Regimes*. Oxford: Oxford University.

Salimt'ô Newsletter. 1999. Fall issue.

Scheper-Hughes, Nancy. 2000. "The Global Traffic in Human Organs." *Current Anthropology* 41 (2): 191–211, 222–4.

———. 2005. "The Last Commodity: Post-Human Ethics and the Global Traffic in 'Fresh' Organs." In *Global Assemblages: Technology, Politics, and Ethics as Anthropological Problems*, ed. Aihwa Ong and Stephen J. Collier, 145–167. Malden, Mass.: Blackwell.

Sedgwick, Eve Kosofsky. 1990. *Epistemology of the Closet*. Berkeley: University of California Press.

Seo, Tongjin. 1996. *Nuga sông chôngch'ihak ûl turyôwô harya?* (Who is afraid of sexuality politics?). Seoul: Munyemadang.

———. 2005. "Chagigyebal ûi ûiji, chayu ûi ûiji: chagigyebal tamlon ûl t'onghae pon Han'guk chabonjuûi chônhwan kwa chuch'ehyôngsông" (The will to self-empowerment, the will to freedom: The understanding of the transition of Korean capitalism and the transformation of subjectivity through the self-empowerment discourses). Ph.D. diss., Yonsei University, Seoul.

183

Seoul City Youth and Women Unemployment Monitoring Team (under Seoul City Subcommittee on Youth and Women's Unemployment). 1999a. *Yôsông nosukcha shimt'ô monit'oring pogosô* (First quarterly report: Needs of the homeless women's shelter). Seoul: SCCUP.

———. 1999b. *Ch'ôngnyôn chagu moim monit'ôring pogosô* (Second quarterly report: Unemployed young adults). Seoul: SCCUP.

Shin, Gi-Wook. 2002. "Marxism, Anti-Americanism, and Democracy in South Korea: An Examination of Nationalist Intellectual Discourse." In *New Asian Marxisms*, ed. Tani E. Barlow, 359–384. Durham: Duke University Press.

———. 2006. *Ethnic Nationalism in Korea: Genealogy, Politics, and Legacy*. Stanford: Stanford University Press.

Shin, Gi-Wook, and Kyung Moon Hwang. 2003. *Contentious Kwangju: The May 18 Uprising in Korea's Past and Present*. Lanham, Md.: Rowman and Littlefield.

Shin, Gi-Wook, and Kyung-Sup Chang. 2000. "Social Crisis in Korea." In *Korea Briefing 1997–1999*, ed. Kong Dan Oh, 75–100. New York: M. E. Sharpe.

Shin, Kwang-Yeong. 2000. "The Discourse of Crisis and the Crisis of Discourse." *Inter-Asia Cultural Studies* 1 (3): 427–442.

———. 2002. "Economic Crisis and Social Welfare Reform in South Korea." In *Cornell University Korean Studies Workshop*, 1–14.

———. 2004. *Han'guk ûi kyegûp kwa pulpyôngdûng* (South Korean class and inequality). Seoul: Ûlyumunhwasa.

Shin, Kwang-Yeong, Cho Ton-mun, and Yi Sông-kyun. 2003. *Kyôngje wigi wa han'gugin ûi pokchiûisik* (The economic crisis and welfare consciousness of Koreans). Seoul: Chipmundang.

Sigley, Gary. 2006. "Chinese Governmentalities: Government, Governance, and Socialist Market Economy." *Economy and Society* 35 (4): 487–508.

Sin Chông-sôn. 2000. "Yôsông nosukcha shuil kosi ôpne" (There is no place to stay for homeless women). *Hangyôre sinmun*, March 23, social section 17.

Sin Sang-yông. 2004. *Sôul si chôngbohwa saôp t'adangsông kômto e kwanhan yôn'gu* (A framework for reviewing the feasibility of IT investment projects in the Seoul metropolitan government). Seoul: Seoul Development Institute.

Sin Wôn-u. 2003. "Nosukin ûi simni sahoejok t'ûksông kwa nosuk kyônghôm i nosuk chônu ûi ûmju munje e michinûn yônghyang" (Socio-psychological attributes of homeless people and the influence of homeless experience on drinking problems before and after homeless life). Ph.D. diss., Seoul National University.

Skocpol, Theda. 1992. *Protecting Soldiers and Mothers: The Political Origins Of Social Policy in the United States*. Cambridge, Mass.: Belknap Press of Harvard University Press.

Smith, Anna Marie. 2007. *Welfare Reform and Sexual Regulation*. New York: Cambridge University Press.

Smith, Ruth L. 1990. "Order and Disorder: The Naturalization of Poverty." *Cultural Critique* 14: 205–229.

Snyder, Richard. 1999. "After Neoliberalism: The Politics of Re-regulation in Mexico." *World Politics* 51: 173–204.

Sôh Chông-kwôn. 1999. "Nosukcha taech'aek chaehwal chungsim ûro" (Direction of homeless policy changed to rehabiliation). *Segye ilbo*, September 14, Seoul section, 20.

Son Beyong-Don. 1997. "Kajok kan sodûkijôn ûi kyôljôngyoin" (Determining elements of interfamily inheritance and repayment). Ph.D. diss., Seoul National University.

Song, Ho Keun. 2003. "The Birth of a Welfare State in Korea: The Unfinished Symphony of Democratization and Globalization." *Journal of East Asian Studies* 3 (3): 405–432.

Song, Jesook. 2003. "Shifting Technologies: Neo-liberalization of the Welfare State in South Korea, 1997–2001." Ph.D. diss., University of Illinois, Urbana-Champaign.

————. 2006. "Family Breakdown and Invisible Homeless Women: Neo-Liberal Governance During the Asian Debt Crisis in South Korea, 1997–2001." *positions: east asia cultures critique* 14 (1): 37–65.

Song Ch'ang-sôk. 1999. "Pom . . . nosukcha ka tasi onda" (Spring . . . homeless people come out to the street again). *Han'gyôreh* 21, April 1, issue 251. http://www.hani.co.kr.

Sonn Ho-ch'ôl. 1999. *Sinjayujuûi ûi han'guk chôngch'i* (South Korean politics in the era of neoliberalism). Seoul: Purûn sup.

Sôn Tae-in. 1999. "Changkwan nosukcha ûi simya taehwa" (Evening chat between the minister and homeless people). *Tonga ilbo*, July 22, social section, 21.

Sôn U-ch'ôl. 2002. "Haengnyô chôngsin changaein ûi sahoejok chijimang e kwanhan yôn'gu" (A study of the social networks of long-term homeless people with mental disability). Master's thesis, Pusan National University, Pusan, South Korea.

Spivak, Gayatri. 1988. "Can the Subaltern Speak?" In *Marxism and the Interpretation of Culture*, ed. Cary Nelson and Lawrence Grossberg, 271–313. Urbana: University of Illinois.

Stacey, Judith. 2000. "Families Against 'the Family': The Transatlantic Passage of the Politics of Family Values." *Radical Philosophy* 89 (May/June): 2–7.

Stevens, Carolyn. 1997. *On the Margins of Japanese Society*. London: Routledge.

Stiglitz, Joseph. 2000. "What I Learned at the World Economic Crisis: The Insider." *The New Republic*. http://www2.gsb.columbia.edu/faculty/jstiglitz/download/opeds/What_I_Learned_at_the_World_Economic_Crisis.htm.

————. 2002. *Globalization and its Discontents*. New York: W. W. Norton.

Strathern, Marilyn, ed. 2000. *Audit Cultures: Anthropological Studies in Accountability, Ethics and the Academy*. London: Routledge.

Suh, Dae-Sook. 1967. *The Korean Communist Movement, 1918–1948*. Princeton: Princeton University Press.

———. 1970. *Documents of Korean Communism, 1918–1948*. Princeton: Princeton University Press.

———. 1981. *Korean Communism, 1945–1980: A Reference Guide to the Political System*. Honolulu: University of Hawai'i Press.

Suh, Doowon. 2003. "Korean White-Collar Unions' Journey to Labor Solidarity: The Historic Path From Enterprise to Industrial Unionism." *Research in the Sociology of Work* 11: 153–180.

Sunder Rajan, Kaushik. 2006. *Biocapital: The Constitution of Postgenomic Life*. Durham: Duke University Press.

Susser, Ida. 1999. "Creating Family Forms: The Exclusion of Men and Teenage Boys From Families in the New York City Shelter System, 1987–1991." In *Theorizing the City: The New Urban Anthropology Reader*, ed. Setha M. Low, 67–82. New Brunswick, N.J.: Rutgers University Press.

Szemere, Anna. 2000. "'We've Kicked the Habit': (Anti)politics of Art's Autonomy and Transition in Hungary." In *Altering States: Ethnographies of Transition in Eastern Europe and the Former Soviet Union*, ed. Daphne Berdahl, Matti Bunzl, and Martha Lampland, 158–180. Ann Arbor: University of Michigan Press.

Takeyama, Akiko. 2005. "Commodified Romance in a Tokyo Host Club." In *Genders, Transgenders and Sexualities in Japan*, ed. Mark McLelland and Romit Dasgupta, 200–215. New York: Routledge.

———. 2007. "Commodified Romance: Gender, Sexual, and Class Politics in a Tokyo Host Club." Ph.D. diss., University of Illinois, Urbana-Champaign.

Tang, Kwong-leung. 2000. "The Authoritarian Developmental State and Social Welfare in Korea." In *Social Welfare Development in East Asia*, ed. Kwong-leung Tang, 89–112. Hampshire, UK: Palgrave.

Trifiletti, Rossana. 1999. "Southern European Welfare Regimes and the Worsening Position of Women." *Journal of European Social Policy* 9 (1): 49–64.

United Nations Development Program (UNDP). 1999. *Human Development Report*. New York: Oxford University Press.

vanden Heuvel, Katrina. 2006. "Lessons for Labor Day." *Nation*, September 1, 2006. http://www.thenation.com.

Verdery, Katherine. 2003. *The Vanishing Hectare: Property and Value in Postsocialist Transylvania*. Ithaca: Cornell University Press.

Virno, Paolo. 2004. *A Grammar of the Multitude*. Trans. Isabella Bertoletti, James Cascaito, and Andrea Casson. London: Semiotext(e).

Visweswaran, Kamala. 1994. *Fictions of Feminist Ethnography*. Minneapolis: University of Minnesota.

Wade, Robert. 1998. "From 'Miracle' to 'Cronyism': Explaining the Great Asian Slump." *Cambridge Journal of Economics* 22, 693–706.

Wang Hui. 2003. *China's New Order: Society, Politics, and Economy in Transition*. Ed. and trans. Theodore Huters. Boston: Harvard University Press.

Warner, Michael, ed. 1993. *Fear of a Queer Planet: Queer Politics and Social Theory*. Minneapolis: University of Minnesota Press.

Weston, Kath. 1991. *Families We Choose: Lesbians, Gays, Kinship*. New York: Columbia University Press.

Wôn Chông-suk. 2001. "Nosukcha ûi sam ui kyônghôm: Sisôl nosukcha rûl chung-sim ûro" (The life experience of homeless people: A case of institutionalized homeless people). Ph.D. diss., Kyung Hee University, Seoul.

Wong, Joseph. 2004. *Healthy Democracies: Welfare Politics in Taiwan and South Korea*. Ithaca: Cornell University Press.

Woo-Cumings, Meredith. 1999. *The Developmental State*. Ithaca: Cornell University Press.

World Bank. 2000. "East Asia: Recovery Exhibits Greater Breadth and Depth, but Remains Uneven." http://www.worldbank.org/eapsocial/index.html.

Yan, Hairong. 2003. "Neoliberal Governmentality and Neohumanism: Organizing Suzhi/Value Flow Through Labor Recruitment Network." *Cultural Anthropology* 18 (4): 493–523.

Yi Chae-ûn. 2004. "Hwanghon ihon 'sûngso' kû hu" (After 'success' of silver divorce). *OhMyNews*, October 20, Womentimes section. http://www.ohmynews.com.

Yi Ch'ang-kon. 1998. "Chôsodûk siljikcha wôl 32 manwôn kkaji chiwôn" (Low-income unemployed people can receive subsidy up to 320 dollars). *Han'gyôre siumun*, April 17, social section, 20.

Yi Chin-kyông. 2004. *Chabon ûl nômôsôn chabon* (The capital surpassing the capital). Seoul: Kûrinbi.

———. 2005. *Mi-rae ûi maksûjuûi* (Marxism yet arrived). Seoul: Kûrinbi.

Yi Hye-yông. 2006. *Kyoyuk pokchi t'uja usôn chiyôk chiwôn saôp hwalsônghwa rûl wihan kajông, hakkyo, chiyôksahoe yôn'gye hyômnôk kanghwa pangan yôn'gu* (Research for strengthening cooperation among family, school, and local society for mobilizing support for the project of prioritized investment for education welfare). Seoul: Korean Education Development Institute.

Yi Mi-kyông. 1999. *Sinjayujuûi chôk 'pan'gyôk' ha esô haekkajok kwa 'kajok ûi wigi* (Nuclear family and "family crisis" under neoliberalist "attack"). Seoul: Kong-gam Publication.

Yim In-sook. 1999. "Shirôp kwa kajokpuranjôngsông" (Unemployment and family instability). Paper presented at Women's Studies Conference, Seoul, May 10.

Yim Pôm. 1998. "Ihon 90 nyôn ûi 2 pae" (Divorce doubled over the '90s). *Han'gyôre sinmun*, November 6, cover section 2.

Yi Na-mi. 1999. *Uri ka sarang han namja* (Men whom we loved). Seoul: Haenaem.

Yi Tae-hûi. 1999. "Ajôssi ka anieyo, tonieyo: 15 sal ûi wonjokyoje ch'unggyôk" (He isn't an elder, he's just money: Shocking teen prostitution). *Han'gyôre sinmun*, November 18, social section 19.

Yi Tûk-chae. 2001. *Kajokchuûi nûn yaman ida* (Familism is barbarous). Seoul: Sonamu.

Yoon, Bang-Soon. 1998. "Korean Women in the Global Economy: Industrialization and Gender Politics in South Korea." *Yonsei Journal of Women's Studies* 4: 140–180.

Yoon, Taek-Lim. 1999. "Kyôngje wigi wa kajok" (Economic crisis and family). In *Mumhwa e palmok chap'in Han'guk kyôngje* (Cultural analyses of Korean economic crisis), ed. E. H. Kim, H. H. Hahm, and T. L. Yoon, 187–228. Seoul: Hyônmin sisût'em.

Yu Ch'ôl-kyu. 2004. *Park Chung Hee model kwa sinjayujuûi sai esô* (In between Park Chung Hee style and neoliberalism). Seoul: Hamkke ingnûn ch'aek.

Žižek, Slavoj. 2000. *The Fragile Absolute, or Why is the Christian Legacy Worth Fighting For?* London: Verso.

Video Materials

Chông Chi-uh, dir. 1999. *Haep'i endû* (Happy end). South Korea. Produced by Myung Films.

Kim In-sik, dir. 2002. *Lodû mubi* (Road movie). Produced by Saidôs FNH.

Munhwa Broadcasting Company. 1991. *Yômyông ûi nundongja* (Eyes of sunrise). TV drama written by Song Chi-na, produced by Kim Chong-hak.

Seoul Broadcasting System. 1995. *Moraesigye* (Sandglass). TV drama written by Song Chi-na, produced by Kim Chong-hak.

———. 1999. *Sûlp'ûn yuhok* (Sad temptation). TV Special drama written by No Hi-kyông, produced by Yun Hûng-sik. Aired December 26.

———. 2004. *Bali esô saenggin il* (What happened in Bali). TV Special series drama written by Kim Ki-ho, produced by Choi Mun-sôk. Aired January to March.

Yoon Eun-chông, dir. 1999. *P'yônghwa ran ôptta* (There is no peace). Produced by Yôsông Minuhoe Koyongpyôngdûng ch'ujinbonbu.

INDEX

Abelman, Nancy, 117, 161n8
activists, xiii–xiv, xviii–xxii, 22, 123–
25; in democratization movement,
117–22, 161nn3–6, 162n15; dissident
groups (chaeya seryôk), 8–9, 64–65;
homeless shelter management by,
90–92; intellectuals (chisigin), xi, xxi,
35, 141n5, 160n2; labor movement,
40, 44, 48, 120; leftist movements, 9,
119, 144n13, 161nn3–6; narratives of,
127–34; neoliberal roles of, 35–37,
46, 50, 75, 90–93, 127–34, 139–40,
149n16; normative families promoted by, 64–66, 70–71, 93, 126–27,
158n39; political goals of, xiv, 2, 13,
132–34; state violence experienced
by, 120–22, 132–33, 161n8, 161nn4–
6; women's movement, 51, 54, 56–
57, 64–66, 149–50nn5–6, 151n14,
151n16. See also civil groups; labor
unions
affective labor, 63, 152nn29–30, 152n32
Althusser, Louis, 117–18, 143n3
Anagost, Ann, 145n16, 147n23, 152n29
Anglican Church of Korea, 30, 91
anti–excessive consumption movement
(kwasobi ch'ubang undong), 16
Appadurai, Arjun, 141n4
appropriate citizenship, 43. See also deserving citizens
April Demonstration Withdrawal (Sôul-
yôk Hoegun), 26, 147n3

April Revolution of 1960 (Sa-Il-Gu
Hyôngmyông), 26, 34, 147n2
Asian Debt Crisis (ôehwan wigi), ix–xi, 1–
3, 7, 134–35, 141n1, 143n5; economic
liberalization resulting from, 5–6;
structural adjustment (kujojojông)
requirements, xvii, 15, 17; unemployment rate during, xiv, 4, 15, 143n6
autonomy (chayulsông), 100

bad neoliberalism, 122–26
bailout of November 21, 1997. See Asian
Debt Crisis
Bali esô saenggin il (What happened in
Bali), 31
big conglomerates (chaebôl): IMF restructuring of, 15, 17, 112–13; laid-
off workers of, 35; neo-Confucian
environment of, 158n4; small shareholder activism campaign, 123–26;
state support of, 3–5, 16–17; welfare
roles of, 14–17, 146n20
binary personhood, 75
biopolitics, 45, 48
biopower, 12–14, 45, 99, 130, 139–40,
146n18, 149nn14–15
biotechnology, 159n10
Blair, Tony, 17–18
blood tax (hyôlse), 105, 158n7
British Enclosure movement, 125
Broadcasting Ethics Committee (Pang-
son Yulli Wiwônhoe), 53

in family breakdown discourses, 50–54; gendered frameworks of, 49–50, 54–57; heteronormativity of, xiii–xv, 52–53, 142n10; IMF homeless, ix, 20, 29–30, 39–48, 57–58, 148n4; middle class (*chungsanch'ûng, chung'gan kyegûp*), 21–22, 102; needs-talk determinations of, 73–75; new intellectuals, xviii, 20–23, 102–5, 135; self-governing subjects, 3, 11–12, 14, 48, 95–102, 117–18, 145n17, 159n10; un(der)employed youth, x–xii, 97–102, 109–10, 159n10; working poor (*sômin*), 21, 83–84, 102, 155n18; worthiness qualifications of, x–xii, 2, 23, 57–58

deserving homeless (*aiemep'û silchik nosukcha*). *See* IMF homeless

deserving youth. *See* new intellectuals; un(der)employed youth

developmental state, 3–4, 16–18, 44–45

dissident groups (*chaeya seryôk*), 8–9, 64–65. *See also* activists

divorce, 51, 150n11

domestic violence, 60, 64–66, 78–81, 150n12, 152n33, 155n12, 157n30

early retirement (*myôngyet'oejik*), xvii, 159n7

education: of homeless children, 154n9, 156n20; in information technology skills, 20–21; of new intellectuals, 17, 100, 103; state support for, 83, 156n19

elections of 1998, x, xvii

embedded liberals, 122–23

employment insurance, 81–82

entrepreneurship of the self (*ch'angôp chôngsin*), 97–102

experts, xi, xxi, 22; in emergency task forces, 36–37; on family rehabilitation, 70–71, 131; mass media workers, xiii; political goals of, xiv;

underemployed persons with higher education, xviii. *See also* activists; intellectuals (*chisigin*)

Ezawa, Aya, 156n23

familial society (*kajok sahoe*), 126–27

families, xiii–xv; affective labor in, 63, 152n29, 152n32; defined, 149n1; domestic violence in, 60, 64–66, 78–81, 150n12, 152n33, 155n12, 157n30; gendered divisions of labor in, xvi–xvii, xix, 2, 23, 49, 61–63, 142n15, 152nn29–30; in homeless shelters, 78–80, 87, 90, 92, 154n9; in neoliberal social engineering, 49–50, 82; paternalistic social order of, 14–15, 62–63, 146n19, 152n31; same-sex couples, 52, 150n11, 151n14; traditional maternalism in, 94

family breakdown (*kajông haech'e, kajok haech'e*) discourses, ix, 2, 22–23, 54, 82, 135, 150nn8–10; in family rehabilitation programs, 70–71, 131; homophobia in, 52–53, 150n11, 150–51nn13–14; immoral mothers and wives in, 50–53, 59–63; normative families promoted in, 52–53, 64–66, 70–71, 93–94, 130–31, 158n39; as root of homelessness, 61–63, 152nn26–28; silver divorce (*hwanghon ihon*) in, 51, 150n11; Yi's critique of, 126–27. *See also* homeless women

Farmer Association Bank, 54–57, 151n18

Farquhar, Judith, 145n16

female rootless (*purang yôsông*), 58–61, 78, 89, 92. *See also* homeless women

feminism, xv, 51, 54–57, 64–66, 149–50nn5–6, 152n31; in postdemocratic era, 151n14, 151n16

finance capitalism, 18, 147n24

Finch, John, 150n9

193

195

(NGOs): homeless support groups of, 30; (neo)liberal role of, 12; public-private partnerships (minkwan hyŏmnyŏk) of, 2, 8–10, 13, 91, 130, 157nn32–35

normative families, xiii–xv, 52–53, 63; activist promotion of, 64–66, 70–71, 93–94, 126–27, 130–31, 158n39; heteronormativity in, 61–62, 152n34; unmarried women and, 57

OASIS newsletter, 41
Oh, Dr., 104, 106–8, 158nn5–6
Ong, Aihwa, 145n16
organic intellectuals, 160n2
outsourcing, 30
Overall Plan for Startup Company Promotion, 113
ownership (onŏ), 100

Pae, Mr., 115–16, 160n19
Pak Chong-chŏl, 119
Pang, Ms., 59–60, 89–90
Pangnim textile factory, 43–45
pan-national network movement (pŏm kungmin kyŏryŏn undong), 64
Park Chung Hee, 2, 143n9; April Demonstration Withdrawal and, 26, 147n3; chaebŏls supported by, 16–17, 44
participant observation, 107
part-time jobs (arûbait'û), xiv–xv, 142n11
Passaro, Joanne, 154n3
paternalist welfare regimes, 84, 151n25
Peck, Jamie, 13
People's Democracy (PD) (Minjung-Minju), 144n13, 161n3
People's Solidarity for Participatory Democracy (PSPD) (Ch'amyŏ Yŏndae), 9, 123–26
Perelman, Michael, 13
poor relief programs, 30, 148n4
popular culture, 22–23

post-Fordist production, 2, 10–11, 143n2; biopower of, 12–14, 45, 99, 146n18; finance capitalism of, 18, 147n24; productive welfarism of, 18; women's affective labor in, 63, 152nn29–30, 152n32
power, 1, 12–14
prayer houses (kidowŏn), 79, 155nn13–15
Presidential Commission for Women's Affairs (PCWA), xvi, 101–2
Presidential Secretary Planning Committee to Improve the Quality of Life, 128
productive welfarism, 7, 134, 136, 146–47nn21–23; biopower of, 12–14, 45, 99, 130, 139–40, 146n18, 149nn14–15; British model of, 127; entrepreneurship of the self under, 95–102; labor controlled under, 17–19, 21–22, 137–38, 144n10; moral maternalist stance of, 60–63, 94, 151n25, 156n23; policies on women of, 81–84; self-governing subjects of, 3, 11–12, 14, 48, 95–102, 117–18, 135, 145n17, 159n10. See also deserving citizens; homelessness paradigms; unemployment paradigms
Protestant Church, 91
public anthropology, 154n4
public assistance program, 81–84
Public Livelihood Protection Law, 155n18
public works programs: data digitalization project (chŏngbohwa saŏp), 20–21, 98, 102–3, 158n5; employment contracts of, xx; for IMF homeless, 21, 43, 98; job-training programs, 83–84, 156n21; for new intellectuals, 102–5; proposals solicited for, 108; in shelters, xxi, 87–88; wages of, 88; for well-educated workers (kohaknyŏk sirŏp konggong kŭllo saŏp), ix, xviii, 21, 142n14

tenure limits of, 156n22; for victims of domestic violence, 78–81, 155n12; for women, xxi, 59–60, 68, 76–81, 90–91, 148n8, 151n23, 156n22

silver divorce (*hwanghon ihon*), 51, 150n11

Sim Chôl-ho, 31

small businesses of women (*yôsông kajang ch'angôp*), 151n21

small office or home operations (SOHO), 105

small shareholder activism (*soaekchuju undong*), 123–26

Smith, Adam, 13

social engineers, xiii–xiv, xviii–xxii, 22, 118, 136. *See also* activists; experts; government officials; un(der)employed youth

social governing, xii–xiii, xix–xx, 1–2; gendered frameworks of, 49–50, 94; moral consensus in, 61–62; self-governing subjects of, 3, 11–12, 14, 48, 95–102, 117–18, 135, 145n17, 159n10. *See also* deserving citizens; productive welfarism

social safety net, 132–34

Song Chi-na, 120

spatial text, x, 22; House of Freedom as, 25, 43–48; Seoul Train Station Square as, 25–34

spousal employees (*sanae k'ôp'ûl*), 54–57

Steinbeck, John, 63

Stiglitz, Joesph, 143n7

street vendors, 26, 28, 33–34, 147n6

student movement. *See* activists; democratization movement

Subcommittee on Youth and Women's Unemployment, 104, 106

Suh, Doowon, 9–10

Sunder Rajan, Kaushik, 147n24, 149n14, 158n3, 159n10

Sungjo Kim, 144n11

Susser, Ida, 152n26

Swallow House, 86–88

Symposium for the solution to the dysfunctional Korean family (Han'guk kajok kinûng ûi kyôlson kwa taech'aek pangan mosaek), 70–71

Syngman Rhee, 34

Takeyama, Akiko, 152n29

taxi drivers, 110–12, 160n11

Team for Women in Need of Social Welfare Division (Yobohoyôsông T'im), 59

team members of Youth and Women Unemployment Monitoring Team, 97, 108–9, 158n7

Teheran Road, 113–14

Telephone of Hope (Hûimang ûi Chôn-hwa), 31

Telephone of Love (Sarang ûi Chôn-hwa), 31

Telephone of Women (Yôsông ûi Chôn-hwa), 31

Temporary City Shelter for Women (TCSW) (Ilsi Sirip Punyô Pohoso), 59–60, 81, 88–90

Thatcher, Margaret, 127

Tripartite Committee, 7, 13, 40

Uh, Dr., 127–29, 162n14

un(der)employed youth, ix, xviii, 12, 19, 22–24, 141n3; entrepreneurship of the self among, 97–102; information technology skills of, 20–21, 96–97, 103, 158n1; media coverage of, xiii; new intellectuals (*sin chisigin*), 102–5; part-time work (*arûbait'û*) by, xiv–xv, 142n11; public works programs for, 20–21; venture business development by, 110–16; worthiness of, x–xii, 98, 109–10, 159n10; Youth and Women Unemployment Monitoring Team's work with, 105–10; youth-culture venture, 112–16, 160n17

undeserving subjects, 26, 75; good-

199

150n12, 152n33, 155n12; duties of marriage of, 52; employment options of, xvi–xvii, xix, 101, 142n15; feminist movement, 51, 54, 56–57, 149–50nn5–6; Korean Farmer Association Bank "voluntary" layoffs of, 54–57, 151n18; legal eligibility of, 63–64, 151n21; SCCUP's work with, xix, 57–58, 81, 84–86; self-representation of, 101–2; sex work options for, 60, 84; single and unmarried, 57, 60, 83–84; state social policies for, 81–84; unemployment of, xv–xviii, 4, 54–57; workplace exploitation of, 44, 48, 55, 149n13. See also gendered frameworks; homeless women

Women Link Equal Employment Committee (Yôsông minuhoe koyongp'yôngdûng ch'ujinbonbu), 56, 151n19

Women's Affairs Division, 81, 105, 155n16

Women's Welfare-Counseling Center (WWCC) (Yôsông Pokchi Sangdamso), 66–70

Won, Director, 86–88

Woo-Cumings, Meredith, 16–17

Worker's Strike (Nodongja Taet'ujaeng) of 1987, 120

workfare, 7, 17–18, 127. See also productive welfarism

working poor (sômin), 21, 83–84, 102, 155n18

workmen's compensation, 74

work with un(der)employed youth by Youth and Women Unemployment Monitoring Team, 105–10

World Bank, 5, 143n7, 158n5

World Cup of 2002, 33–34

World Trade Organization (WTO), 134

worthiness. See deserving citizens

W Station, 76–77, 154n5

Yan, Hairong, 145n16

Yang, Mr., 41–42, 58–59, 89–90

Yi Han-yôl, 119, 132

Yi Tûk-chae, 126–27, 152n34, 161n13

Yômyông ûi nundongja (Eyes of sunrise), 120, 161n6

Yoon Eun-chông, 151n19

youth, 107, 109, 141n3; entrepreneurship of the self of, 97–102; good-for-nothings (paeksu), xii, 20, 97, 105–6, 108, 147n25, 159n8; information technology skills of, 19–21, 96–97, 103, 158n1; new intellectuals (sin chisigin), 102–5; self-governing aspirations of, 95–97, 159n10; sexuality politics (sôngjôngch'i) movement and, xiii–xv, 142n10; venture business development by, 110–16; youth-culture venture, 112–16, 160n17. See also un(der)employed youth

Youth and Women Unemployment Monitoring Team (Ch'ôngnyôn Yôsông Sirôp Taech'aek Monit'ôring T'im), xviii–xxii, 141n4, 142nn16–17; homeless women programs of, 80–81, 155nn16–17; laid-off women supported by, 55–57; new intellectual campaign of, 104; team members of, 97, 108–9, 158n7; un(der)employed youth programs of, 105–10; women's shelter studies of, 81, 155n17; youth-culture venture, 112–16, 160n17

youth-culture venture (town project), 112–16, 160n17

Yu, Mr., 110–12

yut, 160n14

Zhang, Quicheng, 145n16

201

JESOOK SONG is an associate professor of
East Asian studies at the University of Toronto.

Library of Congress Cataloging-in-Publication Data
Song, Jesook, 1969–
South Koreans in the debt crisis : the creation of a
neoliberal welfare society / Jesook Song.
p. cm. — (Asia-pacific : culture, politics, and society)
Includes bibliographical references and index.
ISBN 978-0-8223-4464-3 (cloth : alk. paper)
ISBN 978-0-8223-4481-0 (pbk. : alk. paper)
1. Korea (South) — Economic conditions —1988–
2. Financial crises — Korea (South) 3. Welfare
state — Korea (South) 4. Public welfare — Korea
(South) 5. Neoliberalism — Korea (South) 6. Korea
(South) — Economic policy —1988– I. Title.
II. Series: Asia-Pacific.
HC467.96.S66 2009
330.95195 — dc22   2009008990